MW00982151

Robyn Burrows, nee Barton, was born and raised in the northern New South Wales town of Bourke and completed her schooling at Presbyterian Ladies' College in Pymble, Sydney. About ten years ago she began researching the history of the Gold Coast hinterland region, where she has lived for many years with her husband, three sons, two cats and a blue cattle dog. She has published two local history books and two historical novels, and is an accomplished artist, specialising in pen and ink drawings, some of which appear in this book.

Alan Barton was born in the south-western Queensland township of Cunnamulla in 1923. He spent his early childhood in the far western region of New South Wales, firstly on several stations owned by the legendary cattle king, Sir Sidney Kidman — for whom Alan's father acted as manager — and later on a property in the Wanaaring district which was selected jointly by Alan's father and uncle under a land ballot scheme. Except for a stint in the RAAF during World War II, Alan spent most of his life in Bourke, where he was well known as a local historian. Sadly, Alan passed away in 1996 shortly before the publication of *Henry Lawson: A Stranger on the Darling*, which he co-wrote with his daughter Robyn.

HENRY LAWSON

A STRANGER ON THE DARLING

ROBYN BURROWS AND ALAN BARTON

ILLUSTRATED BY ROBYN BURROWS

Angus&Robertson
An imprint of HarperCollins*Publishers*

This project has been assisted
by the Commonwealth Government
through the Australia Council,
its art funding and advisory body.

Angus&Robertson
An imprint of HarperCollins *Publishers*, Australia
First published in Australia in 1996
by HarperCollins *Publishers* Pty Limited
ACN 009 913 517
A member of the HarperCollins *Publishers* (Australia) Pty Limited Group

Copyright © Robyn Burrows and Estate of Alan Barton 1996
Copyright © Illustrations Robyn Burrows 1996

This book is copyright.
Apart from any fair dealing for the purposes of private study, research,
criticism or review, as permitted under the Copyright Act, no part may
be reproduced by any process without written permission.
Inquiries should be addressed to the publishers.

HarperCollins*Publishers*
25 Ryde Road, Pymble, Sydney NSW 2073, Australia
31 View Road, Glenfield, Auckland 10, New Zealand
77–85 Fulham Palace Road, London W6 8JB, United Kingdom
Hazelton Lanes, 55 Avenue Road, Suite 2900, Toronto, Ontario, M5R 3L2
and 1995 Markham Road, Scarborough, Ontario, M1B 5M8, Canada
10 East 53rd Street, New York NY 10032, United States of America

National Library of Australia Cataloguing-in-Publication data:

Burrows, Robyn, 1953–.
    Henry Lawson: a stranger on the Darling.
    Bibliography.
    Includes index.
    ISBN 0207 18969 2.
    1. Lawson, Henry, 1867–1922 — Biography. 2. Authors, Australian — Biography.
    3. Poets, Australian — Biography.
    I. Barton, Alan, 1923–1996. II. Title.
A828.209

Printed in Australia by Griffin Paperbacks, Adelaide

9 8 7 6 5 4 3 2 1
99 98 97 96

Men of Bourke, the world is moving, and you're moving with it, too,
And you live a little faster than your fathers used to do;
But although the bush was lonely, and the life was rather slow,
Don't forget the vanished seasons on the Darling long ago.

— 'A Stranger on the Darling'
Henry Lawson
Bourke, 1892

For my father, Alan Barton
... his dream
... our collaboration
... a tribute to his life and interests

Also for our forebears, Wakefield and Jessie Barton, who settled in the Wanaaring district west of Bourke around 1873. Of their family of fourteen, only six survived to adulthood and they were the first generations of Barton children to be raised on the Paroo River — Edmund, Blanche Rosalie, Alan Wickstead, Adelaide Mary, Elsie Pearl and Eldred Wakefield.

Alan Barton standing beside a large saltbush plant
on the site of the former Gumbalie Hotel
on the Warrego River, 1994.

CONTENTS

Chronology of Events *viii*

Acknowledgements *x*

Introduction *1*

1   THE CITY AND THE BUSH *11*
2   A STRANGER ON THE DARLING *16*
3   METROPOLIS OF THE GREAT SCRUBS *26*
4   ALL UNYUN MEN *43*
5   THE POET ON THE CENTRAL *67*
6   LAWSON MEETS JAMES GORDON *98*
7   THE UNION BURIES ITS DEAD *105*
8   THE TREK TO TOORALE *113*
9   OF ROUSEABOUTS AND SHEARING SHEDS *130*
10   WANDERING ABOUT THE WARREGO *157*
11   A SINGER OF WIDE SPACES *172*
12   THE HEART OF THE SWAG *202*
13   HUNGERFORD *213*
14   WHEN THE ARMY PRAYS FOR WATTY *231*
15   SEND ROUND THE HAT *259*
16   BACK TO THE CITY *296*
17   AFTERWARDS *309*

Epilogue *334*

Bibliography *336*

Index *338*

Index of first lines of verse *343*

Index of verse titles *344*

Index of prose titles *345*

Endnotes *346*

Maps *349*

CHRONOLOGY OF EVENTS, SEPTEMBER 1892–JUNE 1893

21 September 1892	Lawson arrives in Bourke by train; stays at the Great Western hotel in Richard Street; writes a letter to his Aunt Emma in Sydney.
27 September 1892	Writes a second letter to Aunt Emma.
28 September 1892	'Our Members Present and Future' published in the *Western Herald*.
1 October 1892	'A Stranger on the Darling' published in the *Western Herald*.
5 October 1892	'The Poet on the Central' published in the *Western Herald*.
15 October 1892	'The Poet by Telegraph' published in the *Western Herald*.
22 October 1892	'What Huey Didn't Do' and 'Have You Heard' published in the *Western Herald*.
29 October 1892	'Old Labour and the Echo' and 'The Lissington Verdict' published in the *Western Herald*.
November 1892	Meets James Gordon and obtains work as a house painter for John Hawley.
5 November 1892	'In a Dry Season', detailing Lawson's trip to Bourke, published in the *Bulletin*.
20 November 1892	Drover Hallahan drowns at North Bourke. Two days later, Lawson attends the drover's funeral, giving rise to the sketch 'The Union Buries Its Dead'.
23 November 1892	Lawson joins General Labourers' Union in Bourke.
24 November 1892	Letter to Arthur Parker tells of his intention to leave Bourke that day for an unnamed down-river shearing shed.
17 December 1892	'When Your Pants Begin to Go' published in the *Bulletin*.

25 December 1892	Lawson spends Christmas day in Bourke with his union friends.
26 December 1892	Second letter to Arthur Parker, informing him of his return to Bourke after spending a month away.
27 December 1892	Short note to Arthur Parker. Lawson leaves about this date for Hungerford on the New South Wales–Queensland border.
1 January 1893	Lawson and Gordon spend New Year at Fords Bridge on the Warrego River.
16 January 1893	Letter to Aunt Emma written after Lawson's arrival at Hungerford.
February 1893	'Saint Peter' published.
4 February 1893	'Crawlalong' published in the *Bulletin*.
6 February 1893	Letter to Aunt Emma written on Lawson's return to Bourke.
16 April 1893	'A Bush Funeral' (later 'The Union Buries Its Dead') published in the *Truth*.
13 May 1893	'When the Army Prays for Watty' published in the *Bulletin*.
27 May 1893	'Stragglers' published in the *Bulletin*.
3 June 1893	'Rats' and 'Two Sundowners' published in the *Bulletin*.
June 1893	Wrote 'All Unyun Men' in Bourke.
17 June 1893	'The Shearing of the Cook's Dog' published in the *Worker*.
June 1893	Lawson returns to Sydney at an unknown date.

ACKNOWLEDGEMENTS

It goes without saying that many people have helped both directly and indirectly with the creation of this book. The authors would like to thank the following:

Researchers Carmel McInerny and Debby Cramer for extracting old newspaper articles from the Mitchell and National Libraries.

The Henry Lawson Memorial and Literary Society for permission to reprint the article on Jim Gordon written by Harry Pearce in *The Lawsonian*, No. 219 September 1979.

Nola Daly of Lennox Head, granddaughter of Jim Gordon, for permission to reprint Gordon's reminiscences, and poems from *Call of the Bush* and *Under Wide Skies*.

Michael O'Shea of the AWU–FIME Amalgamated Union for the copy of AWU ticket and sketch of Tommy White.

Mitchell Library, Sydney for the copy of Lawson's 1892 photo.

The remainder of the photographs are the property of the estate of Alan Barton. All other sketches are by Robyn Burrows.

References taken from the *Sydney Morning Herald*, *Aussie*, *Sydney Bulletin*, *Windsor and Richmond Gazette* and *The Worker* newspapers have been acknowledged in the notes.

All efforts to find descendants of John Hawley, Billy Wood, Ernest De Guinney, Harry Smith and Edwin Brady have eluded us. However, these men have, at all times, been acknowledged as the authors of their appropriate works.

We would also like to thank Paul Roe and Diane Tyson for their encouragement and help with publicity.

INTRODUCTION

Henry Lawson: A Stranger on the Darling deals mainly with the nine months that Lawson spent in Bourke and the surrounding district during 1892–93.

My family has a special connection to this area. For almost as long as anyone in Bourke can remember, there have been Bartons living in the town or district. There were six brothers in the first Barton family, all tall men, over six foot. Their parents, Edmund and Sophia, had arrived in Adelaide in 1839, destined to live out their lives as poor potato farmers in the Brownhill Creek area.

Russell, the eldest brother, was the first to arrive in Bourke in 1864, overlanding ten thousand sheep to stock local properties. Later he purchased Mooculta Station, and held a financial interest in Willara and Brindingabba runs, along with his brother Wickstead. He was also involved in the copper mines in Cobar and Nymagee and later became one of the local members of Parliament for the Bourke electorate. In later years he owned a large tract of land in Five Dock, Sydney, where he built his home, 'Russell Lea'. This area is now known as the suburb of Russell Lea, and local roads such as Mooculta, Russell, Janet, Undine and McCulloch were named in connection with Russell's family.

The remaining five Barton brothers eventually settled in Bourke or the surrounding district during the latter part of the 1800s with their wives and families. Initially they were involved in local family businesses, which, besides the pastoral holdings, included a butcher shop, mobile wool-scouring plant, stock dealing and copper mining. Versatility was the name of the game in the bush.

Eventually the men diversified their interests. Pearce became well-known in the Gongolgan and Brewarrina districts. Edmund later took up the position of pastoral inspector for the local Land Department, and Grainger was manager of the Petrolia Boring Company, which was involved in sinking artesian bores about the local district. Wickstead moved his family to Nymagee, where he was probably an overseer for Russell's copper mine interests.

1

My great-great-grandfather, Wakefield Barton, was the fourth son in the family. He came to Bourke about 1871 with his wife Jessie and their three surviving children. After trying his hand in the family's butchering business in Mitchell Street, he took his small brood 'on the track', to Willara Station on the Paroo River, near Hungerford on the New South Wales – Queensland border. Later they moved to Wanaaring, where he purchased and operated the Paroo Inn. Or rather, Jessie ran the pub and added to their growing family while Wakefield travelled the countryside with his wool-scouring plant.

Life was tough in the bush. All told, Jessie gave birth to fourteen babies, but the rate of child mortality was high and Jessie lost several children in infancy. Death certificates cite causes such as 'teething' and 'accidental death', the latter referring to her six-year-old son who was crushed under a collapsing water cart. Two young daughters, aged sixteen months and four months, died within a day of each other from whooping cough. The rigours of childbirth, combined with an arduous life in the bush and more than her fair share of grief, took their toll and Jessie died at the age of forty-five from kidney failure.

By the turn of the century, Wakefield was the only brother remaining in Bourke, and many of his descendants still live in the town or on properties in the nearby Wanaaring and Hungerford districts.

It is probably this longstanding association with Bourke that led to my father's passion for local history, and over the years he researched many aspects of early life in the district: river navigation, general history, artesian bores, local families. You name it, he was interested in anything concerning Bourke, and willingly passed on his knowledge and research material to other writers. I regularly saw his name in the acknowledgement sections of subsequent publications.

About ten years ago he became interested in Henry Lawson's scantily documented visit to the area in 1892–93 and his research took a new path, and took over his life. It was during my 1994 visit to Bourke, researching for a novel I planned to write, that he showed me his Lawson research material, a huge folder full, telling me excitedly of a collection of previously undiscovered poems that had been found.

I suggested the possibility of a book. 'Let's put your name on the front cover, instead of inside,' I suggested. Back on the Gold Coast, I rang my agent in Sydney. Did she think there would be any interest from a publisher in the material? 'Go for it,' she replied. We did. Dad's notes arrived courtesy of Australia Post. With my two index fingers I started typing. The book you now hold before you is the result.

Sadly my father died while the final editing process of *Henry Lawson: A Stranger on the Darling* was in progress. This book was his dream, his goal, and it remains a testament to his life and his passion: the history of his beloved Bourke.

In many ways Henry Lawson's months in Bourke were a separate part of the poet's life, distanced from his city experiences not only by hundreds of miles but by a different kind of existence, and the story set out in this book must be taken in context with Lawson's life as a whole, certainly the events leading up to his arrival in the town in September.

By 1892 Henry Lawson was twenty-five years of age and reasonably well established in his skills as a versifier. Poems such as 'Faces in the Street', 'Andy's Gone With Cattle', 'The Teams' and 'The Roaring Days' had already endeared him to the reading public, and much of his published work was granted the distinction of accompanying illustrations by the most well-known artists of the time.

Several newspapers were eager to publish Lawson's work, most notably the Sydney *Bulletin*. Jointly owned by J. F. Archibald (who was also the editor) and William Macleod, the newspaper was the most significant literary journal of the time. Its success due to its combination of news, politics and economics written mainly by Australians and aimed at Australian audiences. Not only did it provide an outlet for the work of many up-and-coming young writers, such as Lawson, the *Bulletin* was also known for its encouragement of black and white art, giving prominence to cartoonists and illustrators such as Norman Lindsay, Will Dyson, Frank Mahony and Percy Leason.

A. G. Stephens later became the controller of the *Bulletin's* publishing division, and also editor of the newspaper's full-page literary section, known as the 'Red Page'. He helped many Australian writers, such as Mary Gilmore, Miles Franklin and Steele Rudd into print in book form. In later years he and Lawson had a falling out, and Stephens was often critical of Lawson's writing and opinion on Australian life, particularly his views on the bush.

Another main publisher of Lawson's work was the Brisbane *Worker*. Established as a Labour journal in 1890, its founding editor was William Lane, propounder of the 'Utopian' movement that eventually established a settlement in Paraguay, South America. Lane used the *Worker* to push his own revolutionary and Labour-orientated ideas, and he was happy to accept Lawson's radical, and sometimes almost-libellous, verse for publication.

Prompted by a constant and chronic lack of finances, Lawson often succumbed to the demands of editors, churning out propaganda verse. He suggested his own dislike of such penmanship when he wrote, 'So you're writing for a paper? Well, it's nothing very new to be writing yards of drivel for a tidy little screw', in 'The Cambaroora Star', which was published in December 1891.

By early 1892, the signs of an economic depression were upon Australia and jobs were scarce. Between January and May of that year, Lawson wrote eight anti-establishment poems for John Norton, the editor of *Truth*. This newspaper was owned by William Nicholas Willis, a political aspirant who promoted himself in his own publication. The caustic verse included 'The House of Fossils', 'More Echoes from the Old Museum', and 'Wales the First'. They were published under the pseudonym 'Cervus Wright', Lawson's own cryptic warning to those politicians he pilloried.

Though Henry Lawson and Andrew Barton Paterson were both enjoying popularity with their verse in the *Bulletin*, their views on bush poetry and the responsibility of writers to interpret bush conditions truthfully erupted into a very public debate in mid–1892. While Paterson's poems romanticised the bush, Lawson painted the outback as he saw it, or imagined it to be, dismal and lacking promise. Paterson, who will always be remembered for his ballads 'The Man From Snowy River' and 'Clancy of the Overflow', was a member of the Sydney legal fraternity and was writing anonymously under the pseudonym of 'Banjo'. Lawson was one of the few people who knew his real identity.

Whether the 'duel of verse' was contrived as a novel form of publicity for Lawson's and Paterson's writing, or whether it had deeper undertones, is uncertain. However the readers of the *Bulletin* were certainly treated to a succession of controversial poems during the next few months. Lawson opened the debate with 'Borderland', which was published on 9 July 1892. It was later re-titled 'Up the Country' when it was republished in Lawson's 1896 edition of *In the Days When the World Was Wide and Other Verses*. He began his verse with these few laconic comments:

> *I am back from up the country — very sorry that I went*
> *Seeking out the Southern poets' land whereon to pitch*
> *my tent;*
> *I have lost a lot of idols, which were broken on the*
> *track,*
> *Burnt a lot of fancy verses, and I'm glad that I am*
> *back.*
> *Farther out may be the pleasant scenes of which our*
> *poets boast,*
> *But I think the country's rather more inviting round*
> *the coast.*
> *Anyway, I'll stay at present at a boarding house in*
> *town,*
> *Drinking beer and lemon squashes, taking baths and*
> *cooling down.*

Lawson's descriptions were crude and greatly embellished with scenes of 'roasted bullock drivers', 'luny bullocks' and a 'sun-dried shepherd'. It is doubtful if, at that time, he had been further west than Bathurst and he had no real concept, except what he had been told by others, of the real outback.

While the idea for the 'duel of verse' may have been conceived as a joke, the barbs soon flew. Two weeks later, Paterson retaliated with 'In

Defence of the Bush'. It was an attack that seemed to be directed, in the main, at Lawson, rather than his poem.

> *So you're back from up the country, Mister Lawson,*
>   *where you went,*
> *And you're cursing all the business in a bitter*
>   *discontent;*
> *Well, we grieve to disappoint you, and it makes us sad*
>   *to hear*
> *That it wasn't cool and shady — and there wasn't*
>   *plenty beer,*
> *And the loony bullock snorted when you first came*
>   *into view;*
> *Well, you know it's not so often that he sees a swell*
>   *like you . . .*

The poem continued in a similar contemptuous tone, with the 'Banjo' pointing out to 'Mister Lawson' that the bush varied with the seasons and if Lawson were to make the same journey in a few months, he would find the countryside much changed. The words 'Mr Lawson' were later altered to 'Mister Townsman' when the poem was included in the first edition of *The Man From Snowy River and Other Verses*.

While Paterson had the anonymity of a pseudonym with his retort, Lawson laid himself bare to the criticism that followed. The controversy in verse continued for several months, with various other poets and writers such as John le Gay Brereton, Edward Dyson, A. G. Stephens and Joseph Furphy joining in.

With 'In Answer to Banjo and Otherwise', Lawson replied to Paterson's previous poem in a similar vein of caustic wit. He suggested that Banjo, in his bush wanderings, had 'travelled like a gent', and was content to experience the advantages of city life while writing in glowing terms of the wonders of the bush. The poem was later retitled 'The City Bushman'. Lawson then followed this poem with another on 10 September, the 'Grog-an'-Grumble Steeplechase', which was a parody of Banjo's 'Open Steeplechase'. Other poets and parodists continued the duel for a time, while Lawson and Paterson took a back seat to the proceedings.

Paterson retaliated with 'An Answer to Various Bards' on October 1. Again, the poem was an attack on Lawson, referring to him as 'the sad and soulful poet with a graveyard of his own' and including thinly veiled references to Lawson's sometimes excessive drinking habits with the references to 'beer', 'pubs' and 'bars'.

By the time Paterson's last poem was published, Lawson was in the far western New South Wales town of Bourke. His passage there had been financed by J. F. Archibald of the *Bulletin*, and, in his own words, Lawson confirmed: 'Towards the end of '92 I got £5 and a railway ticket from the *Bulletin* and went to Bourke. Painted, picked up in a shearing shed and swagged it for six months . . . '[1]

Primed by the union leaders, Lawson spent his first few weeks in the town writing almost-libellous verse for the local newspaper, the *Western Herald and Darling River Advocate*. The poems elicited several retaliatory replies from a rival paper, the *Central Australian and Bourke Telegraph*. For many years, researchers investigating the poems believed that no copies of the *Western Herald* had survived, and that the poems would never be recovered. It was not until 1992 that Lawson's verses were discovered, exactly one hundred years after their initial publication.

The chance discovery of the poems is, in itself, an interesting story. In 1992 a group of local residents decided to hold a festival, designed to help local tourism and promote Bourke within the far western region. Mateship was decided upon as the ongoing theme of the festival and it was voted that each year one personality would be selected to represent the concept of mateship. That first year, Henry Lawson was nominated, celebrating the centenary of the poet's arrival in that town.

Paul Roe was the chairman of the committee. While on a trip to Sydney, researching the life of Lawson at the Mitchell Library, he noticed a microfilmed copy of a letter Lawson had written to his Aunt Emma in 1892, detailing the fact that he, Lawson, was 'doing a little work, *sub rosa*, for the *Western Herald*' and the labour leaders had given him 'some points for a local political poem', indicating that there would be a 'sensation' when the paper came out the following day.'

Returning to Bourke, and with the help of local *Western Herald* journalist Kris Meares, Paul checked the reels of microfilmed newspaper which were housed in the local library. Expecting to find one poem, they were amazed by their subsequent discovery. In total, Lawson wrote seven, perhaps eight, poems for the *Western Herald and Darling River Advocate* during the following month. The title of this publication is taken from the second of these poems, 'A Stranger on the Darling'. These eight poems are included in a later chapter of this book, the first time in over a century that they have been presented as a collection.

While writing his 'Bourke' poems, Lawson obtained temporary employment as a house painter. He later worked as a rouseabout at Toorale woolshed before trekking many miles overland, eventually reaching the village of Hungerford on the New South Wales –Queensland border. There, for the first time, Lawson saw the outback as it really was. 'You can have no idea of the horrors of the country out here,' he wrote to his Aunt Emma in Sydney. 'Men tramp and beg and live like dogs.' Gone were any idealistic images he may previously have held. His writings now possessed a distinct theme of remoteness and aridity, though often carrying a casualness about them which served only to reinforce the 'casualness' of the bush.

Henry Lawson: A Stranger on the Darling traces Lawson's wanderings about Bourke and 'on the track', and recounts the men he became friendly with. It was from these men that he later created the characters for many of his short stories and verse, although he dissuades us from too close an association by writing: 'I do not identify myself . . . or my friends with any character in my work . . . Names, locality, and distance and direction are often altered for convenience of rhyme . . . '

Despite his denials, it is easy to identify Lawson's writing with the experiences he had throughout his life, and he finally admitted this when he wrote 'most of my hard-up experiences are in my published books, disguised but not exaggerated', in 'Pursuing Literature in Australia', which was published in 1899.

Lawson recorded little of his time spent in Bourke and biographers have long puzzled over the chronology of his wanderings about the region. Thankfully some events that occurred during those months were enlarged upon in later times by others, such as Billy Wood, Jim Gordon, Edwin Brady and John Hawley. Using these reminiscences, many written over thirty years later, *Henry Lawson: A Stranger on the Darling* is a reconstruction of how the authors imagine Lawson spent his time in Bourke and beyond during 1892–93.

Long after Lawson had left the Bourke district, he was producing verse and stories based on his western experiences. Although the majority of these were published during 1893, after his return to Sydney, he continued to write about the bush for years, as demonstrated by his 1905 poem, 'The Heart of the Swag'. Jim Gordon, Lawson's 1892–93 trekking partner, later enlarged upon this idiosyncrasy when he wrote: 'What he saw today, he seldom wrote of to-night, but in six months time, or a year or two years, that was his method.' Another classic example of this was when Lawson wrote his well-known poem 'Bourke', almost ten years after he had left the town. This popular work aligned Lawson closely with the far west and clearly showed his affection for the bush people and the unions.

Lawson's later life has been well documented over the years: his marriage, voyage to London, judicial divorce, suicide attempts, all coupled with an ever-present drinking problem. Perhaps he was proclaiming his own attitude to life when he wrote in 'The Wander-light' in 1902: 'I'm at home and at ease on a track that I know not, And restless on a track that I know'.

Lawson indeed was a restless, enigmatic character. After reading numerous biographies of the poet, then the stories and verse itself, one is left feeling some empathy with him, and a vague sense of having known the man, though for most of us that is an impossibility. W. E. FitzHenry once wrote in amazement that we '. . . who after all knew him so little, should be so profoundly stirred'.

Robyn Burrows
1996

CHAPTER 1

The City and the Bush

When your money is low, and your luck has gone
  down,
There's no place so lone as the streets of a town;
There's nothing but worry, and dread and unrest,
So we'll over the ranges and into the West.[2]

The year was 1892. Henry Lawson — painter, poet and fervent Labour supporter — was finding it almost impossible to sustain a living in Sydney from his writing, and the few pounds he earned were quickly spent in the nearby bars of Lower George Street. He divided his time between the home of his Aunt Emma (his mother's elder sister) at Dawes Point, when he was broke, and cheap lodgings in the centre of the city when he had a pound or two to spare.

It was about this time that Lawson met fellow-journalist and poet Edwin J. Brady. Brady was the editor of the *Workman*, a Labour-influenced newspaper run under the sponsorship of the Sydney Trades and Labour Council. An energetic and inventive person who enjoyed observing the activities of the Sydney waterfront, Brady eventually began writing ballads of the sea and became, like Lawson, a contributor to J. F. Archibald's *Bulletin*. Later he became Secretary of the Australian Socialists' League.

Lawson and Brady met after Brady 'lifted' one of Lawson's poems, 'The Cambaroora Star', from the Brisbane *Boomerang* and reprinted it in the *Workman* without Lawson's permission and, persumably, without payment to the poet. Surprisingly this led to a great friendship between the two men. Brady later recalled the meeting:

> I occupied a small, untidy cubicle adjacent to a more untidy composing den in the nether part of an arcade which opened on to George-street, Brickfield Hill. The editorial salary was £3 per week . . . but who thought of salaries in those glorious days! 'The Cause' was the consideration.
>
> The sub-editor was an old hand named Scissors, well-known in newspaper circles; and the chief-of-staff a person named Paste, who has stuck to the business since time immemorial. With the help of these two I had lifted a recent thing of Henry's called 'The Cambaroora Star' without author's or publisher's permission, and reprinted it bodily in the WORKMAN. I was sitting in shirt sleeves one sunny morning meditating over a new Fabian essay of Bernard Shaw's, which I intended to steal, when a lean, tall young man entered the cubicle, a lonesome-looking person about two years older than myself. He examined me with reflective brown eyes, and enquired with a curious lisp if I was the editor. After I had proudly acknowledged the fact he informed me that he had come to thank me for the honour I had paid him in stealing 'The Cambaroora Star' for the official organ of Labour. [3]

The two men went downstairs to a nearby pub and a friendship was formed over 'long sleevers of colonial [beer] for threepence . . . broken ship's biscuits and small squares of cheese'. They talked of politics and poetry and the Cause, and 'Australia that starves its poets and erects statues to their memories'. According to Brady, a 'friendship of a lifetime had been appropriately cemented. Thereafter we met frequently, according to the customs and conveniences of our day.'

Until this time, Lawson had been no further west than Bathurst. His writings on the bush had been based solely on his childhood experiences around Mudgee and Gulgong and he had only an artist's impression of the real outback. 'Banjo' Paterson may have depicted the bush as '. . . the vision splendid of the sunlit plains extended, and at night the wondrous glory of the everlasting stars' [4] but Lawson suspected, from his early days spent around the western district goldfields, that the bush meant hardship and loneliness. He wanted to write about the real outback, about the heartbreak and poverty he knew he would find there.

J. F. Archibald, chief editor and proprietor of the Sydney *Bulletin*, believed in Lawson's writing ability. He also knew that Lawson was not an imaginative writer and his work to date, if not autobiographical in nature, closely followed his life experiences. Lawson wrote of what he saw with little embellishment, and Archibald knew that Lawson needed new 'copy' for his work. Realising that Lawson was on the path to becoming a confirmed alcoholic, Archibald decided that a change of scenery might be in the poet's best interest. Using Brady as an intermediary, he decided to remove Lawson from the city into the more challenging environment of the outback of the colony.

Edwin Brady, in an article published in the *Bulletin* on 22 January 1925, takes credit for the next course of events in Lawson's life.

> Some months later I was living in a ground-floor room of an umbrella-repair shop in Regent-street, Redfern, writing hard, mostly for John Norton and Archibald, and postponing the turkey and champagne for future occasions. I do not know where Henry was living, but he arrived at my caravanserai of an early morning in one of his blackest moods . . . We walked down to the old BULLETIN office in Pitt-street, and went upstairs to the editor's office. Archibald, keeping his hand on the copy he was revising, screwed partly round in his chair, and regarded us with what I thought was an uncivil eye. Henry found occasion to go downstairs about something.

Still keeping his hand on the MSS. before him, Archibald suddenly wheeled right round and asked me to sit down. Then this kindly, black-bearded, fatherly arbiter of a hundred Australian literary ambitions demanded: 'What's the matter with Lawson?'

I sparred for wind. 'He's all right,' I began.

'No,' said 'J.F.', 'he is *not* all right: he is coming here in the morning with tobacco-juice running down his jaw, smelling of stale beer, and he has begun to write about "The Rocks". The next thing he will be known as "the Poet of the Rocks", and —'

'Look!' I cried, seized by an inspiration. 'I think if Lawson got away to the bush he would be all right.'

Archibald turned back in his chair and regarded the MSS. thoughtfully. 'Why doesn't he go back to the bush?' he demanded over his shoulder.

'No money,' I ventured.

'Well,' he said, 'you go to him and speak to him. If Macleod or I speaks to him he will think there's something behind it.'

The town of Bourke was an obvious choice for Archibald's proposed temporary banishment of Lawson. Besides being easily reached by rail, Bourke at that time was a town representative of the friction between the Amalgamated Shearers' Union and the Pastoralists' Union in respect of shearing rates and conditions of employment. The result was a veritable hotbed of active unionism, and Archibald wanted Lawson to be on the scene to report back to the *Bulletin*.

Also Bourke at that time was a recruiting centre for prospective members of the New Australia Co-operative Settlement Association which intended, under William Lane's supervision, to take a ship-load of dissidents to a 'Utopian' settlement to be founded in Paraguay in South America.

Brady did as Archibald requested. What happened during the next eight or nine months has been seen by some historians as the most important part of Lawson's career. As a result of the conversation between Edwin Brady and J. F. Archibald, Brady ultimately wrote in 1925:

So I went downstairs, picked up Henry, took him over to the First and Last [hotel], walked around smellfull Circular Quay and put it to him. And as a result Henry Lawson, duly financed by THE BULLETIN, went away to Bourke; and Australia got 'Steelman and Mitchell,' 'When the Union Buries Its Dead,' 'Lake Eliza' and much of the imperishable matter contained in 'While the Billy Boils.' It was a good morning's work, and although Archibald and Lawson are otherwhere, none of us have any occasion to be ashamed of it, I think.[5]

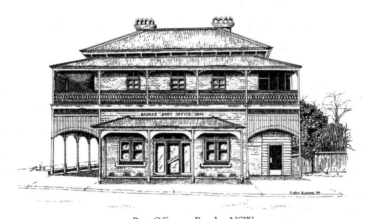

Post Office — Bourke, NSW

CHAPTER 2

A Stranger
on the Darling

*It was somewhere in September and the sun was going
   down,
When I came in search of 'copy', to a Darling-River
   town;*[6]

Archibald provided Lawson with a rail ticket to Bourke – one way –
and the sum of five pounds to assist with expenses for the first few
weeks. The rail pass was valued at four pounds and it was evident that
whether Lawson was successful or not in his western venture he was
obliged to pay his return fare to Sydney.

   It was probably about 20 September 1892 when Henry Lawson
boarded the Western Mail at Redfern Station, which was then the
terminus for the city rail line, and headed for Bourke. Amongst his
meagre possessions he carried a collection of books belonging to his
friend Arthur Parker, and a set of paintbrushes. Archibald, perhaps
fearing a last-minute boycott of his well-laid plan, sent a few of the
Bulletin people to the station to wave him on his way. Commenting on

Lawson's departure from Sydney, A. G. Stephens, the editor of the *Bulletin*'s publishing division, recorded some years later: 'Here was this unfortunate towny, deaf and shy and brooding, sent with a railway ticket and a few spare shillings to carry his swag through the unknown where he knew nobody . . . '

Progressively the train ascended into the Blue Mountains, then descended to the Lithgow valley via the now-famous zig-zag railway line. Katoomba. Medlow Bath. Mount Victoria. Mountain railway stations. Valleys dropped dizzily away from the rail line into dark shadows. Wisps of fog. Though it was September, the night air was cold. Between snatches of sleep, we picture Lawson watching the black shapes of the night as the carriages moved on and past.

The train then progressed onward through the western slopes. Wallerawang: did Lawson feel a tinge of homesickness as he watched the passengers alight for the branch rail line to Mudgee? 'In a Dry Season' describes Lawson's trip. It was published in the *Bulletin* on November 5 of that year.

Slop sac suits, red faces, and old-fashioned, flat-brimmed hats, with wire round the brims, begin to drop into the train on the other side of Bathurst; and here and there a hat with three inches of crape [*sic*]round the crown, which perhaps signifies death in the family at some remote date, and perhaps doesn't. Sometimes, I believe, it only means grease under the band. I notice that when a bushman puts crape round his hat he generally leaves it there till the hat wears out, or another friend dies. In the latter case, he buys a new piece of crape. This outward sign of bereavement usually has a jolly face beneath it. Death is about the only cheerful thing in the bush.

Millthorpe. Orange. Stuart Town. Swinging lamps sent shadows darting along almost-deserted platforms. Hollow, night-time voices called 'all aboard'.

After Dubbo the air warmed, but was not yet hot. It was daylight now and Lawson eagerly released the catches and pushed up the window. He inhaled the wonderful mystical fragrance of the bush.

Cinders flew from the engine as the steady chuffing of the train drew him further into the real outback. He scribbled rapidly in a notebook, transferring images, smells and sounds into words.

The railway towns consist of a public house and a general store, with a square tank and a school-house on piles in the nearer distance. The tank stands at the end of the school and is not many times smaller than the building itself. It is safe to call the pub 'The Railway Hotel', and the store 'The Railway Stores', with an 's'. A couple of patient, ungroomed hacks are probably standing outside the pub, while their masters are inside having a drink — several drinks. Also, it's safe to draw a sundowner sitting listlessly on a bench on the verandah, reading the *Bulletin*.

The Railway Stores seem to exist only in the shadow of the pub, and it is impossible to conceive either as being independent of the other. There is sometimes a small, oblong weather-board building — unpainted, and generally leaning in one of the eight possible directions, and perhaps with a twist in another — which, from its half-obliterated sign, seems to have started as a rival to the Railway Stores; but the shutters are up and the place empty.

The only town I saw that differed much from the above consisted of a box-bark humpy with a clay chimney, and a woman standing at the door throwing out the wash-up water.

By way of variety, the artist might make a water-colour sketch of a fettler's tent on the line, with a billy hanging over the fire in front, and three fettlers standing round filling their pipes . . .

We crossed the Macquarie — a narrow, muddy gutter with a dog swimming across, and three goats interested.

A little further on we saw the first sundowner. He carried a Royal Alfred,* and had a billy in one hand and a stick in the other. He was dressed in a tail-coat turned yellow, a print shirt, and a pair of moleskin trousers, with big, square calico patches on the knees; and his old straw hat was covered with calico. Suddenly he slipped his swag, dropped his billy, and ran forward, boldly flourishing the stick. I thought that he was mad, and was about to attack the train, but he wasn't; he was only killing a snake.

* *Royal Alfred*: type of swag

The train rattled across the countryside and was finally out onto the western plains. It slowed and eventually stopped at each small township along the way. Narromine. Trangie. Nevertire.

Somebody told me that the country was very dry on the other side of Nevertire. It is. I wouldn't like to sit down on it anywhere. The least horrible spot in the bush, in a dry season, is where the bush isn't — where it has been cleared away and a green crop is trying to grow. They talk of settling people on the land! Better settle *in* it. I'd rather settle on the water; at least, until some gigantic system of irrigation is perfected in the West.

The land flattened out and the trees were sparse, sometimes only existing as a ragged line on the horizon. Nyngan. Girilambone. Coolibah. Byrock. At Byrock Lawson saw 'a splendid-looking black tracker in a masher uniform and a pair of Wellington boots.' There was also a group of shearers who, although shabbily dressed, carried an air of independence about them.

About Byrock we met the bush liar in all his glory. He was dressed like — like a bush larrikin. His name was Jim. He had been to a ball where some blank had 'touched' his blanky overcoat. The overcoat had a cheque for ten 'quid' in the pocket. He didn't seem to feel the loss much. 'Wot's ten quid?' He'd been everywhere, including the Gulf country. He still had three or four sheds to go to. He had telegrams in his pockets from half a dozen squatters and supers offering him pens on any terms. He didn't give a blank whether he took them or no. He thought at first he had the telegrams on him but found he had left them in the pocket of the overcoat aforesaid. He had learned butchering in a day. He was a bit of a scrapper himself and talked a lot about the ring. At the last station where he shore he gave the super the father of a hiding. The super was a big chap, about six-foot-three, and had knocked out Paddy Somebody in one round. He worked with a man who shore four hundred sheep in nine hours. Here a quiet-looking bushman in a corner of the carriage grew restless, and presently he opened his mouth and took the liar down in about three minutes.

During the late afternoon of 21 September, Lawson's train left the scrubland some thirteen miles (twenty kilometres) from Bourke and passed over the treeless flood plain of the Darling River basin. In Lawson's own words from the poem 'Sweeney', which was published in the *Bulletin* on 16 December 1893, 'it was somewhere in September, and the sun was going down, when I came in search of 'copy', to a Darling-River town'.

Finally the township of Bourke came into view, firstly the stock trucking yards a little out of town, alongside which could be seen the skeletal beginnings of the Bourke Meat Preserving Company's buildings which were under construction. Late afternoon sunlight reflected on galvanised-iron roofs. Lawson remembered: 'At 5.30 we saw a long line of camels moving out across the sunset. There's something snaky about camels. They remind me of turtles and goannas. Somebody said, "Here's Bourke."'

He stepped from his carriage to the sounds of the now-stationary locomotive releasing its excess steam and the rattling of horse-drawn carriages assembling outside the station. The most pressing matter was to find accommodation. After walking a short distance of about two blocks he came to the Great Western Hotel in Richard Street, which was then classified as a union-patronised pub. The licensee was John Lennon, a strong supporter of the newly-formed Labour League. Here Lawson acquired board and lodgings before going for a stroll around town, hoping to catch a glimpse of the Darling River.

In settling down in his new lodgings, Lawson wrote to the person who was closest to him, his aunt, Mrs Emma Brooks of North Sydney. The short letter confirms the date of his arrival in Bourke.

Great Western Hotel
Bourke.
Sept. 21 – '92

Dear Aunt,
Struck Bourke this afternoon at 5 and am staying as above. Will of
course have no news until tomorrow. The bush between here and
Bathurst is horrible. I was right, and Banjo wrong. Country very
dry and dull, but I am agreeably disappointed with Bourke. It is a
much nicer town than I thought it would be. I got a lot of very good
points for copy on the way up. Think I'll be able to hang out all
right. Board and lodgings £1 per week, and very good. Might take a
job here if I see a chance. Had several interviews with Bushmen on
the way up. Most of them hate the bush. Had a great argument
with a shearer about the number of sheep a man can shear in a day.
I know nothing whatever about the business, but he did not know
that. I have already found out that Bushmen are the biggest liars
that ever the Lord created. Took notes all the way up. I will take
time to write to you at length this week. I took a stroll out to find
the Darling but have not found it yet. There is a sheet of the
Bulletin with my answer to Banjo here. Hope you will pull through.
Keep up your heart.

Yours the same,
Henry Lawson

In seeking out the Darling River after booking in at his hotel, Lawson appears neither to have wandered very far, nor sought directions from any of the locals. Actually just three blocks away, down Richard Street, he could easily have viewed this river that he later registered in rhyme, as it meandered its way some nine hundred miles southwards to its confluence with the Murray.

In his letter, Lawson highlighted the point that he 'was right and Banjo wrong'. This was a reference to the recent debate in rhyme, on the merits of bush life versus those of urban life, between himself and 'Banjo' Paterson in the *Bulletin*, shortly before his departure from Sydney. And he must surely have chuckled to himself when he saw a 'sheet of the *Bulletin*' with his 'answer to Banjo' pinned in a prominent place in the hotel. This was probably 'In Answer to Banjo and Otherwise', which had been published over a month earlier.

Lawson's use of the word 'Bushman' is significant. He grew to have a great admiration for the men of the west and often referred to them with a capital 'B', at times almost seeming to raise them to hero status.

Lawson's presence in Bourke appears to have been somewhat of a closely guarded secret and only a few trustworthy souls knew his real identity. However his appearance in town was undoubtedly preceded by a telegram from Sydney to the local union officials, informing them of his imminent arrival. His reference in Aunt Emma's letter – 'Will of course have no news until tomorrow' – suggests that plans had already been made, prior to his departure from Sydney, and that he anticipated a meeting with the union men the following day.

Some time during the next week Lawson had his portrait taken by Mr Charles Wilson, photographer of Mitchell Street, Bourke. Wilson's studio was situated in the Towers Drug building, next to Doctor Sides' surgery. Fortunately the photograph, like some of Lawson's letters, has survived to this present day. It reveals a youthful Lawson with dark, deep-set eyes, a thin face and a small moustache which in time he grew to larger proportions. In later years this moustache became one of his most distinctive physical features, concealing a somewhat unusual-shaped (and, some say, effeminate-looking) mouth. He wore this moustache with little trimming for the rest of his life.

The second letter from Lawson to his aunt was written a week after the first, while he was still a guest at the Great Western Hotel.

Great Western Hotel,
Bourke.
27 September 1892.

Dear Aunt,

The paper you sent came to hand all right, though rather late. I saw it in the rack about two days after it arrived. You needn't mind sending any papers, as all the city papers come here sooner than you could send them. Thanks all the same. The private barmaids sent me to bed boozed last night, but they won't do it again, — no. They are a pair of ex-actresses and cunning as the devil. I'm an awful fool.

This is a queer place. The ladies shout. A big jolly-looking woman — who, by-the-way, is the landlady of a bush pub — marched into the bar this morning, and asked me to have a drink. This is a fact; so help me, Moses! She came in a waggonette.

I am doing a little work, sub rosa, for the Western Herald. Will send a copy tomorrow. The editor sent for the Labour leaders to give me some points for a local political poem. The chaps have seen the proof and are delighted. Will make about £1 1s. this week. The editor wanted to give me a notice, but I preferred to keep dark for a while. There'll be a sensation when his paper comes out tomorrow. His brother is a very rich and very good-natured squatter near here. I gave him a show as a probable member of Parliament. Also the landlord where I'm staying. The Labour men say that nothing hits like rhyme.

I'll get a billet on the station next week if something better don't turn up. I'm worried to think that you must be in an awful fix, but I think there will be better days for both of us soon.

I can get painting to do in town next week, but I won't do any good here. Every body shouts. I must take to the bush as soon as I can. I am working up stuff for the Bulletin but — between you and me — I don't mean to sacrifice myself altogether. More next week. Burn this.

Your affectionate nephew,
Henry Lawson

The last words of the letter — 'burn this', were a directive to his aunt. Thankfully she didn't, and the letter survived to add to our store of information.

As well as 'working up some stuff for the *Bulletin*', Lawson mentions working *sub rosa*, meaning 'privately' or 'confidentially' — probably under a pseudonym — for the *Western Herald*, which was one of the two local Bourke newspapers. The paper was owned by Edward Davis Millen and edited by Phil Chapman, who possibly held some financial interest in the paper as well. For some reason, either Lawson or the newspaper wanted to keep the authorship of the work a secret. Perhaps, as the *Bulletin* had funded his trip to Bourke and provided some expense money, Lawson may have had some agreement, whether written or verbal, with the *Bulletin* concerning publication of his work.

The union men had primed Lawson on parochial matters and a local political poem, with which the unionists were 'delighted', was to be printed in the newspaper on 28 September, the following day. Lawson predicted that there would 'be a sensation' when the paper came out, indicating that the poem was probably of an inflammatory nature. The 'very rich and very good-natured squatter' he referred to would undoubtedly have been W. K. Millen, the brother of the owner (and not the editor) of the newspaper, and who owned a property at nearby Brewarrina.

On his wanderings about the town, Lawson must eventually have stumbled upon the river. He wrote of it in 'The Song of the Darling River', which was published in the *Bulletin* on 25 March 1899, and later in *Verses Popular and Humorous*.

THE SONG OF THE DARLING RIVER
The skies are brass and the plains are bare,
Death and ruin are everywhere —
And all that is left of the last year's flood
Is a sickly stream on the grey-black mud;
The salt-springs bubble and quagmires quiver,
And — this is the dirge of the Darling River:

'I rise in the drought from the Queensland rain,
I fill my branches again and again;
I hold my billabongs back in vain,
For my life and my peoples the South Seas drain;
And the land grows old and the people never
Will see the worth of the Darling River.

'I drown dry gullies and lave bare hills,
I turn drought-ruts into rippling rills —
I form fair island and glades all green
Till every bend is a sylvan scene.
I have watered the barren land ten leagues wide!
But in vain I have tried, ah! in vain I have tried
To show the sign of the Great All Giver,
The word to a people: Oh! lock your river.

'I want no blistering barge aground,
But racing steamers the seasons round;
I want fair homes on my lonely ways,
A people's love and a people's praise —
And rosy children to dive and swim —
And fair girls' feet in my rippling brim;
And cool, green forests, and gardens ever —'
Oh, this is the hymn of the Darling River.

The sky is brass, and the scrub-lands glare,
Death and ruin are everywhere;
Thrown high to bleach, or deep in the mud
The bones lie buried by last year's flood.
And the Demons dance from the Never Never
To laugh at the rise of the Darling River.

CHAPTER 3

Metropolis of the Great Scrubs

BOURKE
[written in 1902 and published in *When I Was King and Other Verses* in 1905]

I've followed all my tracks and ways, from old bark
    school to Leicester Square,
I've been right back to boyhood's days, and found no
    light or pleasure there.
But every dream and every track — and there were
    many that I knew —
They all lead on, or they lead back, to Bourke in
    Ninety-one, and two.

No sign that green grass ever grew in scrubs that
    blazed beneath the sun;
The plains were dust in Ninety-two, that baked to
    bricks in Ninety-one.
On glaring iron roofs of Bourke, the scorching,
    blinding sandstorms blew,

And there was nothing beautiful in Ninety-one and
    Ninety-two.

Save grit and generosity of hearts that broke and healed
    again —
The hottest drought that ever blazed could never parch
    the hearts of men;
And they were men in spite of all, and they were
    straight, and they were true;
The hat went round at trouble's call, in Ninety-one
    and Ninety-two.

They drank, when all is said and done, they gambled,
    and their speech was rough —
You'd only need to say of one — "He was my mate!'
    that was enough.
To hint a bushman was not white, nor to his Union
    straight and true,
'Twould mean a long and bloody fight in Ninety-one
    and Ninety-two.

The yard behind the Shearers' Arms was reckoned best
    of battlegrounds,
And there in peace and quietness they fought their ten
    or fifteen rounds;
And then they washed the blood away, and then shook
    hands, as strong men do —
And washed away the bitterness — in Ninety-one and
    Ninety-two.

The Army* on the grand old creek was mighty in those
    days gone by,
For they had sisters who could shriek, and brothers
    who could testify;

And by the muddy waterholes, they tackled sin till all
    was blue —
They took our bobs and damned our souls in Ninety-
    one and Ninety-two.

By shanty bars and shearing sheds, they took their toll
    and did their work —
But now and then they lost their heads, and raved of
    hotter hells than Bourke:
The only message from the dead that ever came
    distinctly through —
Was — "Send my overcoat to Hell' — it came to
    Bourke in Ninety-two.

I know they drank, and fought, and died — some
    fighting fiends on blazing tracks —
I don't remember that they lied, or crawled behind
    each other's backs:
I don't remember that they loafed, or left a mate to
    battle through —
Ah! men knew how to stick to men in Ninety-one and
    Ninety-two.

They're scattered wide and scattered far — by fan-like
    tracks, north, east, and west —
The cruel New Australian star drew off the bravest
    and the best.
The Cape and Klondyke claim their bones, the streets
    of London damned a few,
And jingo-cursed Australia mourns for Ninety-one
    and Ninety-two.

For ever westward in the land, Australians hear —
    and will not heed —

The murmur of the boardroom, and the sure and
stealthy steps of greed —
Bourke was a fortress on the track! and garrisons were
grim and true
To hold the spoilers from Out Back, in Ninety-one
and Ninety-two.

I hear it in the ridges lone, and in the dread drought-
stricken wild —
I hear at times a woman's moan — the whimper of a
hungry child:
And — let the cynics say the word: 'a godless gang, a
drunken crew' —
But these were things I never heard in Ninety-one and
Ninety-two.

They say that things have changed out there, and
western towns have altered quite:
They don't know how to drink and swear, they've half
forgotten how to fight;
They've almost lost the strength to trust, the faith in
mateship to be true —
The heart that grew in drought and dust in Ninety-one
and Ninety-two.

We've learned to laugh the bitter laugh since then —
we've travelled, you and I;
The sneaking little paragraph, the dirty trick, the
whispered lie
Are known to us — the little men — whose souls are
rotten through and through —
We called them scabs and crawlers then, in Ninety-
one and Ninety-two.

And could I roll the summers back, or bring the dead
  time on again,
Or from the grave or world-wide track, call back to
  Bourke the vanished men,
With mind content I'd go to sleep, and leave those
  mates to judge me true,
And leave my name to Bourke to keep — the Bourke
  of Ninety-one** and two.

* Salvation Army
** Lawson was never in Bourke during 1891 — his use of poetic licence was for
reasons of rhyme.

'Bourke, the metropolis of the Great Scrubs, on the banks of the
Darling River, about 500 miles from Sydney' [7], is the main pastoral
centre for the far north-west. The area was first explored by Charles
Sturt in 1829, and in 1836 Thomas Mitchell erected a stockade near
the river, which he named Fort Bourke after the then Governor of New
South Wales, Sir Richard Bourke.

The town, which was laid out in its present form in 1862, sprawled
eastwards from the river. The streets were wide and intersected at right
angles; a levee bank, built to keep out occasional unwelcome flood
water, surrounded the town.

At the time of Lawson's arrival, the economy was thriving and the
three thousand residents were well served by approximately two
hundred businesses, which included nineteen hotels, three solicitors and
five doctors. There were several large bond stores, such as K. C.
McKenzie's, E. Rich & Co. and Permewan Wright Ltd. These businesses
often received intercolonial cargoes, which came under the jurisdiction
of the three customs agents attached to the local customs office.

As well as the usual baker and confectioner, auctioneer and
commission agent, draper, saddler, council chambers, butcher,
newsagency, blacksmith and tobacconist, the town boasted specialty
stores such as a jewellers, a billiard room and Clark's fish and oyster
shop. Mr Upton was the barber and fresh vegetables were supplied by
two market gardens operated by industrious Chinese. A boiling-

down works, soap factory and sawmill completed the scene.

There were three churches, and the town's finances were administered by the CBC and London banks. The Department of Public Instruction operated a school from premises in Oxley Street. The Towers Drug Co. building contained the doctors' medical rooms and a residence, as well as Charles Wilson's photographic studio. A chemist shop at the front of the building dispensed the prescribed pills, elixirs and tonics. The hospital had been built twelve years earlier and contained two separate small cottages at the rear for isolating fever cases. Sanitary services included a pan-toilet system. The night-soil cart was a big iron tank, open at the top, the contents of which were emptied into ditches behind the cemetery.

Cobb & Co. manufactured coaches, buggies and wool wagons in their premises in Hope Street, while their stables and coach depot were located at the rear of a row of shops in Mitchell Street. Messages were either conveyed via the postal system or by telegraph (morse code). The local telegraph line was linked directly with Sydney and the smaller towns along the route communicated through the Bourke office. As well as being the dispatcher of letters and parcels, the post office was a great source of interest as it was here that the daily river heights were displayed for the interest of those involved in the river steamer industry.

Outback travellers utilised a variety of transport – bullock, horse, camel, coach and, if travelling in the general direction of a river-side station, boat. Cobb & Co. had developed a large network of coach services emanating from Bourke which linked the outlying western villages.

Provisions were hauled by either bullock, camel or horse teams from the township to the huge pastoral holdings west of the Darling, and wool was back-loaded to the Bourke railhead which was said to be the largest wool-loading centre in Australia at that time. Train services ran daily, except on Sundays, linking the town to Sydney and all the regions in between, in a comparatively comfortable and speedy manner.

The social life experienced by Lawson in Bourke would have equalled that of any western town and, despite his deafness, Lawson quickly came to know and enjoy the company of several men that he met about the various local hotels or in the course of his work. The social culture of 'mateship' was particularly well established within the ranks of the unionists. Unionism was on its way to great heights and the shearers' strike was still part of the industrial issue between the Pastoralists' Union and the Amalgamated Shearers' Union.

With a pub on almost every street corner, the core of social life for the men living in these country towns revolved around the hotels. Beer was supplied by Lindsay's Brewing Co. Limited, and was selling for fourpence a pint. Rum, whisky, Hennessy brandy and cognac were also preferred beverages. The hotels included the Central Australian, Shakespeare, Fitzgerald's Post Office Hotel, Caledonian, Gladstone, Royal, Carriers' Arms and the Great Western. The latter three were known as 'union' establishments and were patronised mainly by those affiliated with the unions and their ideals. The Carriers' Arms Hotel was also the Cobb & Co. staging post, and featured strongly in many of Lawson's poems and stories.

For two shillings, a boat trip could be enjoyed along the Darling on Sunday nights, to the accompaniment of music supplied by a band, piano, accordion or mouth organ. On Saturday evenings almost the entire population of the town congregated in Mitchell Street, parading up and down the footpaths participating in extended shopping hours, listening to the town bands. Football, cricket and rowing were popular sports. The Bourke Lyric Club staged productions in the Bijou Theatre.

Bourke was regarded as the virtual head of Darling River navigation, and an intercolonial steamer trade thrived between the town and numerous downriver ports during the 1890s. Though paddlesteamers had been taken over the Queensland border in times of flood, the river above Bourke was generally regarded as unnavigable. This was made even more so by the 'fisheries' at Brewarrina which Lawson described as the 'only national work performed by the blacks on the Darling. They threw a dam of rocks across the river — near Brewarrina, we think — to make a fish trap. It's there yet. But God only knows where they got the stones from, or how they carried them, for there isn't a pebble within forty miles.'[8]

The Darling is a slow-flowing river and has a fall of three inches in every mile (approximately 50 mm per km). It curls and turns, sometimes doubling back on itself, and from the air resembles a twisting snake. In times of good river height the river boats were cheaper and more comfortable than other forms of transport, and there was a steady flow of travellers between the South Australian port of Goolwa, situated at the mouth of the Murray River some 1500 river-miles (2400 km) away, and Bourke.

The river steamers, which mostly had side paddles, varied greatly in size. The '*Ethel Jackson*' was the largest, at 266 tonnes while, at 6 tonnes, the *Platypus* was the smallest. The *Florence Annie*, a Bourke-based hawking steamer, visited the various stations along the river and had on board a dry-goods shop, a fruit stand and a grocery store.

Steamers also hauled merchandise from the Murray River ports of Echuca, in Victoria, and Morgan in South Australia. They travelled via the Murray–Darling junction town of Wentworth, which lay 900 river-miles (1500 km) south-west of Bourke. Menindee was another important river port along the Darling at this time, as were Wilcannia and Louth.

Sheep stations downriver as far as Wilcannia, and within sixty miles (100 km) inland of the Darling and its tributaries, sent their wool to the river to be transported to the railhead at Bourke. Freight charges between Wilcannia and Bourke were £2 a tonne and the average steamer towing two barges could carry 300 tonnes.

Steam power for the engines was provided by burning long lengths of seasoned timber. Because the boats used a ton of wood for each one to two and a half hours steaming, depending on the size of the boat and the cargo, there were wood piles at regular intervals along the riverbank, at places where the steamers could easily pull in and take wood aboard with a minimum amount of fuss. Many of the woodcutters who manned these isolated posts were known for their strange behaviour. 'The Count' was a Frenchman who yelled obscenities from the riverbank towards the occupants of those boats that failed to stop at his landing. Danzig, a Dane, played a home-made banjo that had been manufactured from an old oil drum covered with kangaroo skin.

Despite the prolific river trade, there were no modern loading or unloading facilities at Bourke until 1897. Instead, wool and merchandise were hauled up and down the river bank, along wooden chutes, by steam-powered winches. Near the wharf stood the water pumping station and a large storage shed. The Gibson Engineering Works carried out plumbing and mechanical repairs to the river boats' steam engines.

The river trade employed great numbers of men and was a boon to the local Bourke economy. An average river boat crew generally consisted of a captain, engineer, mate, barge master, cook, fireman and deckhand. Multiply this figure by the eighty recorded steamers and barges on the Darling, and the number of employees is considerable. As New South Wales regulations forbade the loading and unloading of steamers on Sundays, the crews could often be found in the bars of the local hotels taking a little light refreshment on the Sabbath.

The riverboat men also generated a certain language of their own. Wives who helped on board were referred to as 'long-haired mates', and if a member of the crew was bad-tempered or angry he was said to have the 'Darling pea'. For the most part, the Darling was bordered by high banks, and the river was referred to as the 'trench' or the 'gutter'.

Some of the river steamers that plied the river around the time of Lawson's stay in the far west were the *Rob Roy, Emu, Pilot, Jandra, Brewarrina* and *Emily Jane*. The *Excelsior*, which had transported one hundred horses to safety during the 1890 flood, was cut adrift during 1892 by striking shearers at Bourke for transporting non-union labour. No damage was sustained. Another vessel, the *Pioneer*, saw her barge capsized with load of wool near Bourke, and the *Rodney*, a steamer which ran the Darling waterways during this time, was later burnt to the water-line by striking shearers in 1894.

Though the river at times was very low, the Darling was navigable from 1889 to 1895. However, by the beginning of the century, the protracted drought of 1901–02 resulted in fifteen months of no river trade. An economic decline in the whole western region of New South Wales, combined with the extensions of railway branch lines from

Nyngan to Cobar in 1897, and from Byrock to Brewarrina in 1901, saw the eventual reduction of the river steamer industry in the upper Darling.

The last river steamer to Bourke was the *J. G. Arnold* in 1931. Arriving on a rapidly falling river, her barge cargo of 1480 bales of wool was unloaded with great haste and as soon as the task was completed she steamed quickly down-river.

Lawson referred specifically to the Darling River and the associated paddlesteamer trade when he wrote 'Australian Rivers: On the Darling No. 1'. Lawson later added to the sketch and the title was later changed to 'The Darling River'.

AUSTRALIAN RIVERS: ON THE DARLING NO. 1[9]

The Darling — which is either a muddy gutter or a second Mississippi — is about six times as long as the distance, in a straight line, from its head to its mouth. The state of the river is vaguely but generally understood to depend on some distant and foreign phenomena to which bushmen refer in an off hand tone of voice as 'the Queenslan' rains,' and which phenomena seems to be held responsible, in a general way, for most of the out-back trouble.

It takes less than a year to go up stream by boat to Walgett or Bourke in a dry season, but after the first three months the passengers generally go ashore and walk. They get sick of being stuck in the same sort of places, in the same old way; they grow sick of seeing the same old 'whaler' drop his swag on the bank opposite whenever the boat ties up for wood; they get tired of 'len'in' ' him tobacco, and listening to his ideas, which are limited in number and narrow in conception, and which, from constant reiteration, become boreful to a painful degree.

It shortens the journey to get out and walk; but then, you will have to wait so long for your luggage — unless you hump it with you.

* * *

We heard of one man who determined to stick to a Darling boat and travel the whole length of the river. He was a newspaper man. He started on his voyage of discovery one Easter in flood-time, and a month later the captain got bushed between the Darling and the South Australian border. The waters went away before he could find the river again, and left his boat in a scrub. They had a cargo of rations, and the crew stuck to the craft while the tucker lasted; when it gave out they rolled up their swags and went to look for a station — they didn't find one. The captain would study his watch and the sun, rig up dials, and make out courses, and follow 'em without success. They ran short of water, and didn't sight any for a week; they suffered terrible privations, and lost three of their number, *not* including the newspaper liar. There are even dark hints concerning the drawing of lots in connection with something too horrible to mention. They crossed a thirty-mile plain at last and sighted a black-gin. She led them to a boundary rider's hut, where they were taken in and supplied with rations and rum.

Later on a syndicate was formed to explore the country and recover the boat, but where they found her was thirty miles from the river and about eighteen from the nearest waterhole deep enough to float her, so they left her there. She's there still, or else the man that told me about it is the greatest liar that ever the Lord created.

* * *

Imagine the hull of a North Shore ferry boat, blunted a little at the ends and cut off about a foot below the water-line, and parallel to it, then you will have something shaped somewhat like the hull of a Darling mud-rooter, but the river boat is much stronger. The boat we were on was built and repaired above deck after the different ideas of many bush carpenters, of whom the last seemed by his work to have regarded the original plan with a contempt which could only have been equalled by his disgust for the work of the carpenter who came before him. The wheel was boxed in, mostly with round sapling-sticks fastened to the frame with bunches of nails and spikes of all shapes and sizes, and most of them bent. The general result was decidedly picturesque in its irregularity, but dangerous to the mental welfare of any passenger who was foolish enough to try and comprehend the design, for it seemed as though every bush carpenter called upon to effect repairs or alterations had taken the opportunity to work in a little abstract idea of his own.

* * *

The way in which they 'dock' a Darling River boat is beautiful for its simplicity. They choose a place where there are two stout trees about the boat's length apart, and standing on a line parallel to the river. They fix pulley-blocks to the trees, lay sliding planks down to the water, fasten a rope to one end of the steamer and take the other end through the block attached to the tree, and thence back aboard a second steamer; then, likewise they carry a rope from the other end through the block on the second tree, and so aboard a third boat; then, at a given signal, one boat leaves for south, or Wentworth, and the other starts for the 'Queenslan', ' border. The consequence is that craft number one climbs the bank amid cheers of the local loafers, who congregate and watch the proceedings with great interest and approval. The crew pitch tents, and set to work on the hull, which looks like a big, rough, shallow box.

* * *

We once travelled on the Darling for a hundred miles or so on a boat called the 'Mud Turtle' — at least, that's what we called her. She might reasonably have haunted the Mississippi fifty years ago. She didn't seem particular where she went, or whether she started again or stopped for good after getting stuck. Her machinery sounded like a chapter of accidents, and she was always out of order; but she got along all the same, provided the steersman kept her off the bank.

Her skipper was a young man who looked more like a drover than a sailor, and the crew bore a greater resemblance to the unemployed than to any other body we know of, only they looked a

37

little more independent. They seemed clannish, too, with an unemployed or free labour sort of isolation. We have an idea that they regarded our personal appearance with contempt.

* * *

Above Louth we picked up a 'whaler,' who came aboard for the sake of society — and tobacco. Not that he hoped to shorten his journey; he had no destination. He told us many reckless and unprincipled lies, and gave us a few ornamented facts. One of them took our fancy, and impressed us — with its beautiful simplicity we suppose. He said: 'Some miles above, where the Darlin' an' the Warrygo runs inter each other, there's a billybong runnin' right across between the two rivers, an' makin' a sort of tryhangular hyland; 'n' I kin telyer a funny thing about it.' Here he paused to light his pipe. 'Now,' he continued, impressively, jerking the match overboard, 'when the Darlin's up and the Warrygo's *low*, the billybong runs from the Darlin' into the *Warrygo; and,* when the *Warrygo's* up and the Darlin' down, the water runs *from* the Warrygo 'n' inter the *Darlin'*.' What could be more simple?

* * *

The steamer was engaged to go up a billabong for a load of shearers from a shed which was cutting out, but the incidents of that trip can stand over till next week.

About four miles to the north, on the western side of the river, lay the satellite village of North Bourke. Since the erection of a bridge in 1883, which catered for the large numbers of passing drovers, teamsters, shearers and travelling public, the village had become an important river-crossing place.

Prior to the construction of the bridge, which contained an up-lifting span to allow paddle steamers to pass underneath, the only vehicular or pedestrian access to Bourke from the western side of the Darling River was via a punt, or ferry. At North Bourke, sheep were transported across the river on a pontoon owned by Mr Lunn. Cattle had to be swum across at North Bourke or further upstream at May's Bend.

North Bourke was also a depot and staging place for teamsters and drovers who often timed their arrival to coincide with nightfall, presumably so they could revive themselves at one of the four hotels before crossing their livestock the following morning. Large sheep yards, used for holding overnight stock, were situated on the Wanaaring–Hungerford road west of the slaughteryards.

The hotel closest to the bridge was owned by T. Manning and was later known as the Occidental Hotel. The location of this hotel, which was built before the bridge, was such that it interfered with the approach to the bridge on the western side. After the bridge had been built, the Department of Public Works offered to buy the pub so they could demolish it and so give better access for large bullock teams. The owner at the time, Isaac James, refused to sell and so a bend was put into the bridge on the western side in 1903 to compensate, so that the approach veered away from the hotel.

A short distance away was Murphy's Hotel, at the junction of the Barringun road and the Wanaaring–Hungerford road. Around the corner on the Barringun road, which was known as Darling Street, was the Bridge Hotel owned by James Maxwell, and the Overland Hotel owned by J. Willoughby.

The village also boasted a school, three stores, a fruit shop, butchery, hall, police station, dairy, slaughterhouse and cemetery. The Chinese grew vegetables in Lunn's garden and Mr Gorrie was the caretaker of the bridge. There were about seventeen private residences.

Even in 1892, two years after the fact, much of the talk in Bourke was of the 1890 flood. At a height above the river bed of 72' ½", the flood was at its peak on 18 April, the day the embankment broke and the water entered the town. Lawson wrote of the flood some time during 1893.

THE GREAT FLOOD OF '90

The press reporter has caused numbers of his unfortunate fellow men to be gaoled, flogged, and hanged in Australia and yet he isn't satisfied. He wants to drown the entire country. He wants to wash Australians off the face of the earth. As a boomer of murders, rapes, and fires he rises supreme; but when he is turned loose on a flood, he beats the United States of America.

We read about 'the floods in the country' until we can think of nothing else but a watery waste with chimneys sticking out of it here and there, and the population perching atop and coo-eeing. We read that Walgett, or Louth, or Crawlalong are 'under water'; and we take it all in good faith, and are impressed, and think — in short — that things must be pretty damp and uncomfortable up round there in the vicinity of those unfortunate towns. And we picture half dressed families, shivering on roofs, and clinging to each other; and mothers holding up their babes out of the water — or floating around with the babes on their ice-cold bosoms — and respectable married women in trees; and here and there a beautiful bush girl (with nothing on but a table cloth) being carried in the arms of a stalwart drover to a drier place — the drover having only a shirt and a pair of trousers on. And the lightning shows us picturesque heroes standing in stage attitudes in the bows of rescue boats while draggled cats and kittens, and dogs, and fowls float by on the furniture, and make 'good subjects for illustration'. And if we don't picture these things, the *Illustrated Smudge* does it for us, which amounts to the same thing.

But, as a matter of fact, we find that these aforementioned towns are not under water when they are supposed to be. Their back yards might be a little damp but that's all.

Furthermore — it would not intensify the prevalent depression to any appreciable extent if they *were* to go under water; and, moreover, if they stayed there till the day of judgement they wouldn't be missed. This is because these towns only consist of two pubs, a general store, and three weatherboard boxes with galvanised iron tops.

Every now and then we read of the town of Godforgotten being 'under water'; yet whenever we go there, we find it under whisky, but otherwise drier, dustier and thirstier than it was before.

Bourke had a flood in 1890, and the newspaper reports were enough to frighten Noah's ghost. Now, we were in Bourke last year, and we talked with men who came there shortly after the deluge, and the only sign they saw of the awful devastation was a dirty mark around the doorsteps where the water had been. Only one small brick house 'collapsed' (i.e., tumbled down) and that was chiefly because the rain softened the ground at the feet of some props which held the building up.

We were told in the city every day that the town of Bourke was in great danger, and we were reasonably impressed; but the chief danger was that the liquor would give out — the water having gotten into some of the pub cellars. We had read about the Bourke Flood Embankment till our imagination pictured something after the fashion of the Great Wall of China; but we knocked about the town for a week before we saw any sign of it; and then we didn't see it — we felt it. We wish we had seen it first. We jammed an ingrowing toenail against a rut one dark night, and asked our companion what the sheol* that was. He said it was the Bourke Flood Embankment; and so we marked the place and went out next morning to have a look at it. A drunken farmer could turn up a better dyke in a day with an old wooden plough and a blind bullock called 'Strawberry'.

We enquired after the heroes of the flood and found that most of the rescue work was done by a short man with his trousers tucked up and a bottle of whisky in his pocket.

We believed that some chaps did start to drag a boat through Mitchell Street, in order that they might say they had rowed through the principal street of the town during the flood — which they did say, and which they still tell jackeroos. But the boat bogged all the way; so they gave the job best and sent the craft back on a cart.

*Sheol: 'Hebrew Hades, place of the dead, the grave' (*Concise Oxford Dictionary*)

Lawson admitted to being 'pleasantly surprised' by Bourke. However the bank crashes, more shearers' strikes and other economic problems were still to follow. Had Lawson returned to Bourke in the late 1890s during the time of drought and recession, or after the 1901–02 drought, and observed what devastation had been wrought upon the land, his impressions would certainly have been quite different.

Carriers Arms Hotel — Bourke, NSW

CHAPTER 4

All Unyun Men

I met him in Bourke in the Union days — with which
  we have nought to do
(Their creed was narrow, their methods crude, but
  they stuck to the Cause like glue). [10]

As a fervent Labour supporter and a champion of the 'Cause', Lawson drifted naturally towards the leaders of the Bourke union movement and found pleasure in their company. These men symbolised the concept of mateship, the members drawn together by common objectives and their fight for what they considered to be fair issues. As a group, they embodied his radical political leanings. Lawson shared their ideals and dreams for the future. He saw himself as a worker, on their level, and felt he could relate to their problems.

The formation of the shearers' and labourers' unions in Bourke during the late 1800s were triggered by several incidents. The first was the appearance of the following advertisement in the *Australian* on 2 April 1886, signed by representatives of seventeen stations about the western district of New South Wales.

To Shearers.
The owners and managers of the undermentioned stations hereby

give notice that the price for shearing during the current year will be 17/6 per 100 sheep, but if any shearer is discharged for wilful bad shearing or other misconduct he shall accept payment at 15/- per 100 for all sheep shorn to date of discharge. The rations will be charged at a fixed rate, viz., flour £2 per bag, sugar 4d. per lb., tea 2/- per lb. and other articles at rates equally reasonable . . .

The pastoralists wanted to instigate a practice known as 'freedom of contract'. This meant that each worker was separately contracted by the station owner and the rate mentioned in the advertisement was 17s 6d ($1.75) per 100 sheep, a substantial decrease from the normal rate of 20s ($2) per 100.

The boss-of-the-board was in charge of the shearing shed and he decided the quality of the shearers' work. If only one sheep in an entire pen was affected by 'wilful bad shearing', the sheep shorn by that shearer had their backs marked, or 'raddled', and the shearer received the reduced rate for the whole pen. 'Misconduct' could mean anything from bringing alcohol onto a station (usually banned) to simply singing or whistling while working.

Shearers were not allowed to bring their own supplies and were required to purchase them from the station store at greatly inflated prices. A general complaint was the practice of overcharging. Although the pastoralists usually paid wholesale prices for their goods, a large mark-up was added before resale. As the shearers were not paid until 'cut out' (the end of shearing), the cost of provisions was deducted from their pay. Sometimes shearers were also paid by cheques that could only be cashed by city banks, hundreds of miles away.

The shearers considered the pastoralists' demands totally unacceptable. In retaliation they formed several unions, and the series of strikes and general industrial unrest that followed lasted for almost a decade.

One of the first unions established in the far west was the Shearers' Union. The first branch had been formed at Ballarat in June 1886; the second was formed in Bourke four months later, on 20 October 1886.

Twenty-one men joined at the inaugural Bourke meeting. Contributions for shearers and cooks were set at an annual rate of ten shillings; learner-shearers were required to contribute 2s 6d. Dugan's Shakespeare Hotel in Mitchell Street was the venue and the meeting was chaired by William G. Spence who was the Victorian founder and president of the union, and who had travelled from Melbourne for the occasion. The Victorian and New South Wales Shearers' Unions merged to form the Amalgamated Shearers' Union (ASU) in 1887, the following year.

The aim of the union was to obtain better shearing rates and conditions for its members, than those proposed by the pastoralists. In 1891 the Chairman of the Bourke branch of the ASU was Ben Stanley and the Secretary was William (Billy) Wood. John Andrews reportedly took over the position of Chairman in 1892. He was 'the youngest organiser ever to have set out to spread the ASU gospel'[11] and was associated for forty years with the ASU and the AWU In 1917 he took up residence in Sydney, where he died in 1958. Arthur Andrews, the father of John, was also associated with the A.S.U. in Bourke in the early 1890s and was said to have been its president in 1889.

The General Labourers' Union was formed in Bourke in February 1891, and represented all other shed and bush workers whose jobs did not come under the guidelines of the ASU. The General Secretary was William G. Spence, who was also national President of the ASU. In 1892 the elected Secretary of the Bourke branch was Thomas Hicks Hall and the fees ranged from 2s 6d to 7s 6d.

There were also two other groups represented at Bourke during these years: the Carriers' Union and the Coachbuilders' Union, the latter comprised mainly of workers from the Cobb & Co. factory.

The main strike years in Bourke were 1886, 1891 and 1894. The unrest was triggered not only by the demand for better wages and conditions but by the introduction of mechanical shearing methods. In 1888 the management of Dunlop Station, near Louth on the Darling River, installed steam-powered shearing machines in forty stands. The shearers retaliated by going on strike. After several weeks of

45

negotiations, the men were persuaded to commence shearing on a trial basis. With inducement, thirty shearers shore 180,000 sheep there that season. Dunlop was the first station to begin and complete the season's shearing by this method, and so became a part of the history of pastoralism in Australia.

As the decade of the 1890s began, the growing discontent between the Amalgamated Shearers' Union and the Pastoralists' Union began to manifest itself and strikes on a larger scale loomed ominously on the horizon. These strikes began in 1890 in the far north of Queensland. Eventually they continued on into New South Wales, along the entire Darling River and nearby districts.

The shearers rejected the pastoralists' demands that non-union labour was to be allowed into the sheds. In Sydney, carriers refused to carry 'black' wool (shorn by non-union shearers) from the railway to the wharves. Wharf labourers showed their support by refusing to handle the wool and maritime strikes in Melbourne and Sydney followed. However, by the end of the year the union carriers had resumed work.

During 1891, the year before Lawson's arrival, shearers and shed hands formed a large strikers' camp on the western side of the river at Bourke, and many other camps were formed near other townships along the Darling. Local pastoralists, concerned that their annual shearing season might not eventuate, arranged for representatives of the Pastoralists' Union to bring two contingents of non-unionists to several shearing sheds along the Darling and some off-river stations. The first group, numbering about 131, arrived at Bourke on 6 July 1891. The second group, consisting of 276 men, arrived a week later.

They were jeered by the strikers as they marched from the railway station to the river on the western side of town. A scuffle erupted and, as a result, two-thirds of the men were coerced into joining the unionists. The remaining third boarded the paddle steamer *Brewarrina*, which was waiting for them with steam up, and they were transported downstream to be employed in shearing sheds along the Darling. Eventually the shearers and pastoralists reached a compromise and the

1891 shearing season was completed. During this same year, the Australian Labour Party was formed in Barcaldine.

The strikes meant that the production of wool was often hampered by the constant interruption to shearing and the use of unskilled labour. However large consignments of wool steadily arrived at the Bourke railhead, brought by river and teams transport.

Early in 1892 approximately eight hundred striking shearers and shed hands formed another tent camp on the opposite side of the river at Bourke, between the ferry crossing and North Bourke. In town the mayor, Mr Gray, and the Inspector of Police kept a watchful eye on the camp and only a few striking shearers at a time were allowed to cross on the local punt to purchase supplies.

Although the local unions were very active during 1892, the shearing season was not marred by major disturbances, although it probably commenced later than normal. However effects from the disputes flowed on into other associated industries. The Teamsters' Union refused, for a time, to carry black wool and the Australian and English Maritime Unions refused to handle wool shorn in non-union sheds. Some steamer captains, mainly on those boats owned by large companies, refused to be intimidated by the unionists. Incidences of rocks and lighted sticks being thrown onto passing paddle steamers suspected of carrying 'scab' labour or 'black' wool were reported to police and many riverboat captains slung wire netting across the tops of their vessels as a precautionary measure.

The shearers were not only fighting the Pastoralists' Union. The day-to-day confrontations between the union shearers and 'scab' labour in the workplace provided a constant cause of antagonism. In 1893 Lawson put pen to paper regarding the issue of unionism versus free labour, and the resulting poem, 'All Unyun Men', was indicative of the tensions in the western shearing sheds at that time.

ALL UNYUN MEN

'Twas a big shed on the Darlin' —
The Unyuns know it well,

But mighty few in the Unyuns knew
About the thing I tell.
'Twuz a great shed for free labour,
As the chaps wuz all aware,
And the rep. wuz told that he'd best not try,
His funny bizzness there.

But the rep. wuz straight, an' the rep. hed grit,
He tried his funny biz:
He shoved the cause along a bit
With three square mates of his.
Their bunks stood in a corner —
'Twuz called the 'Unyun Den' —
And on the post they pasted
The sign: 'ALL UNION MEN'!

Now, 'twuz a shed where Unyun talk
Wuz answ'red with a vim,
An' each wuz told to take a walk,
An' take his swag with him.
They knew the boss had marked 'em —
They knew they'd git the sack —
And they risked their cheque for a convert:
Such men are found out back.

'Way down along the Darlin'
There tramped four Unyun men,
An' two-legg'd things from Whitely King's
Camped in the 'Unyun Den',
An' a jackaroo got up to do
A clever thing one day:
He started there, before 'em all,
To scrape that sign away.

Then up rose 'Jack the Dingo' —
A rough ole Darlin' slab —
Wuz known among the Unyuns
As 'Crawlin' Jack the Scab' —
At least, they called him 'Crawlin' Jack'
When he wasn't in the place —
They called him that behind his back,
But never to his face.

Then up got 'Jack the Dingo',
An' nasty was his tone —
He said, in shearing lingo:
'You let that sign erlone!
You've got a Unyun ticket,
You cur! An', what is more,
You've got a sneakin' ref'rence
From the last shed where you shore!
I hate the gory Unyun,
An' I'm game ter say I do,
But I think them chaps wuz better
Than a two-faced jackaroo!'

Four bunks stood in a corner —
'Twuz called the 'Unyun Den' —
An' on the post wuz written
Three words: 'All Unyun Men'.
Free labour thought a mighty lot,
But 'twuz not much it sed,
An' the sign stopped there while the 'Dingo'
Wuz shearin' in the shed.[12]

A careful scrutiny of microfilmed copies of Bourke newspapers at this time reveals little mention of the shearers' strikes, and it was left to the city papers to report the unrest. Possibly a voluntary censorship by the local media meant that the newspapers avoided being seen to take sides in the dispute, thus alienating readers.

By September 1892, strike problems along the Darling had begun to abate, though non-union labour was still being employed in local shearing sheds. During 1893 the upper Darling region remained free of any major incidents concerning union activity, and the tension that had existed during the previous year had marginally declined. In 1894 the Australian Workers' Union (AWU) was formed when the New South Wales and Victorian shed hands' unions merged with the shearers' unions.

The existence of the unions in Bourke during the pastoral unrest of the late 1800s meant that the town naturally became the first union administration centre for the upper Darling. The first union office of the Amalgamated Shearers' Union, and later the General Labourers' Union, was a small building in Mitchell Street and during the peak of union activity in 1892 the union officials and the unionists congregated there. After the amalgamation of the two unions in 1894 to form the Australian Workers' Union, a new site was purchased on the corner of Oxley and Sturt Streets.

The second office was a large wooden building with an iron roof, and contained a library where members could read the local and Sydney newspapers. Harry Smith, a later union official, recalled how the rooms 'reeked with tobacco fumes, and the yarns that were spun, scraps of which reached our ears, while busy in the office routine! . . . and friendly arguments as to the big-gun shearers, cooks, droughts and strike camps were much discussed, while race horses, the fistic arena, millionaire Jimmy Tyson, sheds, pack-horses, floods, camels, sheep dogs and opal fields and other topics received attention . . . '[13]

Such was the union scene in Bourke when Henry Lawson arrived in September 1892. The union officials were anxious to meet the young poet, who was a known sympathiser to their cause, hoping he would publicise the injustices being served upon them by the squatters. Billy Wood, the secretary of the local Amalgamated Shearers' Union, recalled that, after Lawson's arrival in the town, 'we of the union office got in touch with him, and for the rest of his stay he was on an intimate footing with Donald Macdonell, Thomas Hicks Hall, J. (John) Andrews, myself and a few others'.[14]

Lawson became friendly with four unionists in particular — Donald Macdonell, Billy Wood, Thomas Hicks Hall and Hugh Langwell — all of whom had been involved in the shearing industry in various capacities. Other unionists were John Andrews and his father Arthur, and the Currie brothers, Thomas and George. Jack Boreham, Teddy Thompson, 'Scotty' Anderson, Mick O'Brien, Con Barry, Bob Brothers, John (Jack) Merrick, Jack Meehan, Tommy White and Tommy Hurdis were also prominent members. Donald Macdonell, Jack Meehan and Tommy White were three former Bourke unionists who were still actively involved in union matters at the times of their deaths.[15]

Many of the unionists that Lawson met eventually appeared in his poems and short stories, some disguised, others not so. For instance, he based his main character 'The Giraffe', in 'Send Round the Hat', on local Bourke unionist Bob Brothers. Lawson also mentions unionists Billy Wood and Tom Hall in the same story, as well as in 'That Pretty Girl in the Army', another story set in Bourke around that time.

Lawson became involved in the union cause soon after his arrival in town, and he plunged immediately into wielding his pen in defence of the new Labour Party and the politicians and unionists who were involved in its progress in Bourke. Years later he became disillusioned with some aspects of the union movement. During 1894 he wrote several articles concentrating on the supposed plight of the bush workers and unionists. These were all published in the *Worker* and were probably triggered by the widespread shearers, strikes and violent clashes of that year. In 'A Word in Season' he reminded his readers to 'get rid of the idea that shearers are the only wronged men on earth and squatters the only tyrants'. And in 'The Stranger's Friend' Lawson wrote: 'I met him in Bourke in the Union days, with which we have nought to do. (Their creed was narrow, their methods crude, but they stuck to the Cause like glue)', suggesting a general later dissatisfaction with local unionism, but an admiration for their tenacity.

The union and political scenes in Bourke in the 1890s were very much enmeshed. Good representation in Parliament helped the union cause, though many elected representatives were seen by the shearers to 'sell out' after they had been elected to office. Because of its large size and the amount of travelling involved, the Bourke electorate comprised three seats during the 1880s and 1890s. Politicians were not paid a salary for their services, so it was necessary for intending candidates to possess substantial private funds.

The three member returned after the 1889 elections were William Walter Davis, William Nicholas Willis and Thomas Waddell and the number of votes each received was 343, 351 and 382 respectively.

William Walter Davis was a principal of the pastoral company Davis, Dale & Co., which owned Kerribree Station in the Fords Bridge district. Lawson later met Davis at Kerribree early in 1893 and subsequently based his main character in 'Baldy Thompson' on this well-known local.

William Nicholas Willis was the founder and owner of the Sydney *Truth* newspaper. Willis, who had been known to Lawson for several years and had previously published some of Lawson's caustic political poems, was a politician who promoted himself and his ambitions in his own publication. He was not a popular figure with the local unionists, who regarded him as a traitor to the Labour cause and believed that he had 'sold them out'. Willis remained as a representative for Bourke until the 1894 election, then he represented the Barwon electorate for the next ten years. Although he held a financial interest in a property in the Brewarrina district, he was never a resident of Bourke.

The representatives for the electoral district of Bourke returned in the July 1891 colonial elections were Hugh Langwell, William Willis and James Peter Howe. Howe, an absentee member, lived in Sydney and owned a footwear warehouse in Waterloo. During that same year he became involved in a spurious land deal and he and James Miller, a co-director of the Australian Loan and Guarantee Company, faced criminal proceedings and were found guilty. Howe was sentenced to seven years detention at Goulburn gaol and was forced to resign his seat on 21 October. Lawson later described Howe as a man who 'yelled for justice in the bush and robbed the poor in town.' [16]

A by-election, contested by Donald Macdonell and Thomas Waddell, was held to fill the vacant seat. Billy Wood, secretary of the ASU, recalled, years later, that '. . . there was an election on to fill the seat vacated by Mr James Peter Howe. The late Donald Macdonell was the Unions' candidate, Australian Shearers' Union and General Labourers' Union (G.L.U.), with the Carriers' Union coming in later. W. N. Willis had succeeded in getting the support of the coachbuilders against Donald Mac., and that just kept Donald out for that time.'[17]

On 16 December 1891, Thomas Waddell was the successful candidate for the same seat he had held until the previous July election. He was the absentee owner of Fort Bourke Station near Bourke, and a close friend of Samuel McCaughey who owned both Toorale and Dunlop stations. Waddell was not liked by the union men in Bourke. Lawson later wrote disparagingly of him when he penned the words 'Let us cull the person Waddle — (he is waddling to his fall)' and 'The only thing he's working for is covered by his hat'.[18] However Waddell, probably to the unionists' dismay, was not 'waddling to his fall'. He went on to become Premier of New South Wales from 1904 to 1907, after which he took up the post of Colonial Secretary.

Of all the local unionists and politicians that Lawson became acquainted with during his time in Bourke, his greatest friendships were probably forged with Donald Macdonell and Hugh Langwell. Langwell was one of the three serving members for the electorate of Bourke, though Macdonell's political aspirations had, so far, proved uneventful.

Irish by birth, Hugh Langwell was born in Belfast to Hugh Langwell and his wife Matilda, nee McCully. In 1861 the Langwells migrated to Victoria. By the age of twenty-one, Hugh was on his way north, working as a fencer, station-hand, well-sinker and shearer in western New South Wales and Queensland. A short, stocky man, he came to Bourke around 1886. After a lucky win in a Tattersall's lottery, he purchased a partnership in a newsagency which also incorporated a barber's shop and cigar shop. A billiard room was a later addition.

Langwell was a foundation member of the Amalgamated Shearers' Union in Bourke and represented the union at its annual conference in 1888. He was also a union force behind the 1891 shearers' strikes and was part of the committee involved in setting up the rules of the AWU. In 1890 he married Sarah Jane Brooks in St Andrew's Presbyterian Church, Bourke. Several children were born to the couple. A member of the Bourke Labour Electoral League, he was a successful candidate in the 1891 elections, becoming one of the few local politicians to reside in his constituency. After his election to parliament he also involved himself in local union affairs and was a vice-president of the ASU in 1892.

An advertisement in the Bourke *Western Herald* in September 1892 mentions a 'Tobacconists, Hairdressers, Booksellers & Newsagents' owned by Stevenson and Langwell in Mitchell Street. The newsagency was the proud supplier of 'All Sydney Daily and Intercolonial Weekly Papers' and a first-class billiard table was kept on the premises.

Langwell's participation in the local Bourke election on 25 June 1894 prompted Lawson to pen the poem 'Martin Farrell', which was published in the *Worker*. The poem tells of the attempts of a dying swagman west of the Darling to put his vote in for 'Hughie', as Lawson affectionately referred to the man who became a lifelong friend. Despite Lawson's vote of confidence, Langwell was unsuccessful in the election and was beaten by Edward Millen.

MARTIN FARRELL

Just before the last elections, and the chaps were
  fighting well
Round about the Paroo River, on the borderland of
  hell —
But the story of the struggle doesn't matter anyhow,
For a Parliament of angels couldn't save the country
  now.

But a poor old fellow struggled to a hut one broiling
    day,
And his ragged swag fell off him in a hopeless kind of
    way.
He was sick and very shaky, and his eyes were blurr'd
    and dim —
It was plain to all the fellows that 'twas nearly up with
    him.

He was stiff and out of tucker (all the fellows
    understood);
He wanted medicine and rest before he wanted food.
He was making for the border, underneath the blazing
    sun —
Old, and weak, and ill, he tottered, and but half his
    journey done.

'If I could put the time in up at Hungerford,' he said,
'Until after the election — I'd be ready to be dead.
I wouldn't care so much,' he sighed, 'my time is nearly
    past —
But I've got a vote for Hughie, and I s'pose 'twill be
    my last.'

And the rough and noisy bushmen gathered round.
    Their manner grew
In a moment soft and gentle, for their hearts, of
    course, were true;
And they said, 'What's up, old fellow?' and 'What
    can we do for you?'

Then he raised his head a moment, and the tired
    answer came:
'There is nothing you can do, lads, but I thank you,
    all the same;

I am pretty cronk and shaky — too far gone for hell or
heaven,
An' the chances are I'm goin' — that I'm goin' to 'do
the seven'.*

'But it isn't that that gripes me, an' I'll tell you what it
is,
Life ain't over bright and rosy, battlin' round in times
like this;
For many a year I've knocked round here, where livin'
is a crime,
An' couldn't get a vote — not once, tho' I tried it
every time.

But I got in on 'em this time, and when I did, said I,
This belongs to Hughie Langwell, an' I'll vote before I
die.
An' I can't reach Yantabulla — that's the thing that
makes me fret.
Chaps, I've got a vote for Hughie — but it ain't no
monte** yet.'

And it wasn't — chaps; he knew it. That same night
he 'did his seven',
But no doubt the swagman's name is safe upon the list
in heaven.

* *do the seven:* – die
** *monte:* – card game

After his appointment to the Legislative Council in 1900, Hugh Langwell left Bourke for Sydney. Two years later he resigned from this position and took up an appointment with the Western Land Board. In 1912 he was the Royal Commissioner in an enquiry into the Kentia palm seed industry on Lord Howe Island. He served on the Western Land Board from its inception until he retired in 1931, becoming its chief commissioner in 1922. He died in Bondi in May 1933.

Edward Millen, the man who defeated Langwell in the local 1894 elections, was born in Kent, England. Employed in a marine insurance office before migrating to Australia around 1880, he began a journalistic career in Walgett before moving to Brewarrina and taking up pastoral land after his 1883 marriage to Constance Flanagan. One son, Edward, was born in Brewarrina in 1884, but died there during that same year.

About 1887 Millen came to Bourke and obtained a position on the *Central Australian and Bourke Telegraph*, a local newspaper. Later he purchased the rival paper, The *Western Herald and Darling River Advocate*, probably in partnership with Philip Chapman, who was its editor. He became prominent in Bourke during the 1890s as a newspaper publisher and politician.

An unsuccessful candidate in the 1891 elections, Millen was elected to the Legislative Assembly for Bourke in June 1894, deposing Langwell from his seat. His criticism of Edmund Barton's leadership in the push for Federation cost him his seat in the next election. However, in April 1899 he was nominated to the Legislative Council after pledging new support for Federation. During the late 1890s he established a land, mining and financial agency and eventually ran an office in O'Connell Street, Sydney.

He resigned from the Council in 1901 and subsequently represented New South Wales in the Senate from 1901 until 1923, becoming opposition leader in the Senate in 1907. He was Minister for Defence at the outbreak of World War I, until the September election of 1914, and later Minister for Repatriation in 1917 under the leadership of Billy Hughes. During 1919 he was Acting Prime Minister for a time. In 1920, Millen attended the inaugural meeting of the General Assembly of the League of Nations at Geneva. He died in September 1923 and was buried at Rookwood Cemetery after being given a state funeral.

Lawson's other politically-aspiring Bourke friend, Donald Macdonell, was born at Richmond, Victoria, in 1865 to William

Macdonell and his wife Catherine, nee Andrew. His parents were hard-working people and Donald also experienced a hard life while working in shearing sheds and mining camps with his father. Eventually in the 1880s he came to western New South Wales as a shearer at Tinapagee, a large property on the Paroo River.

Macdonell, whom Lawson later described as a 'handsome giant of a man', was about six feet and three inches (190 cm) in height and possessed a wonderful personality. More than any other person in the West, apart from William Spence, he epitomised those unionists and politicians who struggled within the ranks of the Labour movement to obtain better living conditions for the working man.

In 1886 Macdonell became a foundation member of the Amalgamated Shearers' Union in Bourke and in 1891 he was active in the great shearers' strike. In the elections of that same year he was an unsuccessful candidate for the Bourke electorate, and continued on shearing in the district. At Belalie Station on the New South Wales – Queensland border in 1892, he sheared 214 sheep in one day while using hand-operated blade shears. Later that year he met up with Henry Lawson in Bourke and so began a long friendship between the two men.

In 1893 Macdonell was selected by the newly formed Bourke Labour League as their representative to the Labour Conference in Sydney, and the following year he was elected as the Secretary of the local ASU branch. In 1894 he contested the seat of Barwon, but without success, and was instrumental in the local amalgamation of the two Bourke unions into the Australian Workers' Union, of which he was Secretary. Never a quitter, he again unsuccessfully contested the seat of Barwon in both 1895 and 1898. Again in 1897 he was selected to represent the Bourke Labour League at the annual conference in Sydney.

Macdonell won the seat of Cobar in 1901. However union affairs continued to be part of his life and he also held the position of General Secretary of the AWU during this time. In 1910 he was awarded the Agriculture portfolio and the position of Colonial Secretary in the

McGowan ministry, which was the first Labour government in New South Wales. The following year he became Chief Secretary to the Cabinet.

In 1911, on hearing of the failure of the health of Donald Macdonell, Lawson penned a few verses to honour his friend's contribution to union and political affairs. Although the poem was composed in a rather elegiac style — which was considered by some to be in bad taste as Macdonell at that time was still alive — the verses revealed Lawson's great respect and admiration for the man who had promoted unionism in the west.

At the time of his death, at the age of forty-six, Macdonell was still serving as a member of Parliament. Shortly afterwards a memorial card was printed to notify friends and relations, as was the custom in those days. On the back of the card appeared a short elegy: the second verse of the poem 'Donald Macdonell'.

DONALD MACDONELL

Bourke in the Early Nineties —
Back in Ninety-One and Two —
Long Tom Hall and his villains,
Little Billy Woods and you.

Saddle-tweed suit and soft shirt,
Standing six-foot-three —
You long, slow, kindly smiling
Slab of Democracy!

Donald! Do you remember,
Back in the Dawn of Day
How we fought with our faces seaward
From Blackall, Bourke and Hay?

Fought with the Western Bushmen,
Fought for democracy,

Fought for the real Federation
And the things we knew must be.

They needed no banners to lead them,
They needed no drum to thump;
With long Tom Hall or with Donald
Macdonell 'on the stump'!

Then we ran the Worker for nothing,
And no man fought for hire;
When the orders went by 'Footmen',
And news by the 'Mulga Wire'.

'Twas the saddle strap belt they tightened,
(O the soft shirt, pants and coat!)
They fought in secret and danger,
And won with the Out Back Vote!

(It sounds like a song from the dying
To a living time and men,
But the bad, blind months are flying,
And the Spirit shall live agen.)

Donald! The Bushmen loved you,
And the Towneys loved you too;
And your colleagues more than respected,
As did all men when they knew.

Donald in ordered 'biled rags'
To suit his length and breadth
Yet true to his friends Truth and Justice,
As he'll be true to his death.
There was many a stone broke Bushman
Helped back not once nor twice;

There was many a quid and saxpence,
And kindly word of advice.

Donald the old mates vanish
From camp and tent and hut,
Some died or were forgotten
Some 'dropped their names and cut'.

Donald they tell us ill news
That flies through the wool and wheat —
There's grief on the wastes of Cobar
There's sorrow in Macquarie Street.

It goes by 'phone and Marconi
It's telegraphed to Nevertire —
Down the long barren creeks of Desolation
It is carried by Mulga Wire.

Donald they say you're ailing
They tell us the end is near
Donald they say that it's only
Your great heart keeps you here.

Donald, They say you're dying
God grant that it be not true;
But the sweep of the mulga's sighing —
Donald, in memory of you.

Over the years, Lawson continued to write about the unions and his days in Bourke. 'It Was Awful', which was published in the *Worker* on 29 September 1894, described union conditions about the town of Bourke at that time. The story concerns a trick played on an unsuspecting non-union 'new-chum' and how, with little inducement, he is persuaded to leave town on the next train.

IT WAS AWFUL

He was a tourist, and English, don't you know. He was on his way to pay a visit to his brother-in-law, a squatter on the Darling, and stayed over one night in a hotel in Tallytown. It was during the great strike. He said 'It was awful, don't you know.' In the morning he arose, and while he was fixing his collar he happened to glance out through the window and saw two bodies hanging to the limb of a tree across the road.

About three seconds later he tumbled down the back stairs on top of a Darling 'whaler', who rose up, collared him, and made inquiries in language totally unfit for publication.

'Oh, my God!' gasped the tourist, 'there's been a murder done!'

'What?'

'Murder! Run for the police. Fetch the police. There are two men hanging to a tree in front of the hotel. They've been lynched in the night. Oh, my God! it's awful.'

The tourist collapsed into a chair, and the whaler went to look. When he returned he seemed calmer and wore an interested expression.

'Well, have you informed the police?' gasped the new-chum, still trembling, and with a corpse-like face.

'No,' said the other sadly.

'Why? Why didn't you tell them?'

'Because it's no use. The Unionists hold this town. Those poor fellows are past all help now —'

'What — what do you mean?'

'Well, those men were non-Unionists; the boys caught them last night and choked 'em off. That's about it.'

'Great Scot! Does the law of this country allow men to be murdered in cold blood? . . . My God! it's awful!'

'Well, it seems so,' said the whaler, in reply to the first part of the question. Then an idea seemed to strike him.

'By the way,' he asked, in a hurried, anxious tone, 'have you got a ticket? Do you belong to the Union?'

'N — no. I — I don't know anything about it.'

'Well, you *will* soon, if you don't pull your wits together. Are you a jackaroo?'

'A what? I suppose I'm a new-chum, if that's what you mean.'

'Well, it amounts to the same thing: a jackaroo is a new-chum and a new-chum is a jackaroo. Now, those poor fellows hanging out there were jackaroos.'

'My God! it's awful.'

'It will be awfuller if you don't pull yourself together. Now, listen here, I'm a Union man, and true to my mates, but I don't like this business. I don't want any more choking off done. I like your looks, and I'll save you if I can —'

'My God! it's awful.'

'Don't interrupt me. There's no time to lose. Get your bag and get down to the station before the boys in the Union camp are up and on your track. There's a train in twenty minutes. Get your ticket and keep out of sight till she starts; then jump in.'

'I will. My —'

'Never mind that. Off with you, and do exactly as I tell you.'

'I will.'

And he did, and nearly got hauled up for boarding a train while in motion. He didn't visit his uncle; he came back to the city. Whenever he referred to the adventure he said it was awful.

The effigies of two notorious non-Unionists are hanging there yet.

Around 1920 Lawson wrote 'The Delegates', which referred to unionism in Bourke in 'ninety-two' and 'ninety-three'. It was published in the *Bulletin*.

THE DELEGATES: 1 THEN

I spent a year in Junee,
I spent a year in Bourke;

And one I spent revising
The year I spent in work.
They seemed so close together
They nearly broke my heart;
And yet those fateful two years
Were twenty years apart.

Oh, down the Lachlan River
Where father used to camp,
The old grey horse is missing
And I'm too old to tramp.

No Union flag was flying,
Because it never flew;
The cause was dead or dying
Round Bourke in 'ninety-two.
Through bogs of sodden black soil
We fell back, down and done,
Heart-broken from the battle
We'd lost in ninety-one.

From Union camps of hunger,
And cold and sodden beds,
Our leaders followed after;
Black-listed at the sheds,
They tramped and worked for tucker
To live for higher aims;
And round the furthest stations
Shore under other names.

Oh, greybeard meeting greybeard!
Oh, hearts of younger men!
'Tis long since I was called by
The name I 'went by' then.

We'd meet and know each other —
No matter how we knew;
We'd spies amongst the squatters
Right back in 'ninety-two;
And safer than the wireless,
Or any means for hire,
And surer were the messages
We sent by mulga wire.

Tall, gaunt and quaintly solemn,
To mask the lurking grin,
Matilda up at sunset,
Our delegate came in;
He'd look the rep. up (casual),
And, after tea, perhaps,
He'd say by light of slush-lamp
'A few words to you chaps'.

The few short words were spoken
And mulga'd further on;
The shed-bell rang at sunrise —
Our delegate was gone.
No par. was in the Herald,
He wrote not to the Sun
To tell the world what he had
Or what he had not done.

We had no grand head-office,
Where staffs are mild and meek
And bosses fight for freedom
On fifteen pounds a week;
Where pen-cranks blur the lessons
We'd learned in 'Ninety-three,
And well-dressed Union bullies
Bludge on Democracy.

Headquarters then were anywhere
Where headquarters might be —
The skillion of a shanty
Or underneath a tree.
In sheep or cattle country,
Drought-blaze or freezing rain,
Oh! there we fought the battles
We'll have to fight again!

Way down the Murrumbidgee
And up the Lachlan side
Are young bay horses saddled —
I'm not too old to ride.

Court House — Bourke, NSW

CHAPTER 5

The Poet
on the Central

Men of Bourke, and round about it, call your drinks,
   and put 'em down!
Here's a hand and here's a greeting from a new chum
   from the town;
You deserve to thrive and prosper if you worry through
   the drought,
And the Darling doesn't drown you or the devil wipe
   you out.[19]

At the time of Lawson's arrival in Bourke, the qualities and capabilities of the three elected parliamentary representatives were the topics for lively and heated debate in the town. William Willis and Thomas Waddell, who were local absentee landowners, gained much of their support from the pastoralists. However the unions undoubtedly regarded them as 'the enemy' during the bitter strikes and confrontations between the pastoralists and the shearers. Willis, in particular, was thought by the unionists to have discarded the promises under which he had been elected, while Waddell, as owner of Fort Bourke Station, had been involved in bringing non-union labour to the area the previous year. The unions favoured Hugh Langwell, a former shearer, and the only local member who resided in the electorate.

Although the local Bourke newspapers had published little of the ongoing battles between the pastoralists and the union shearers, this was about to change. One of the first people to meet Lawson after his arrival in Bourke was Phil Chapman, editor of the *Western Herald and Darling River Advocate*.

Born in Colac in Victoria in 1860, Chapman had worked as the sub-editor of the Sydney *Evening News* before coming to Bourke about 1887. His first position in the town was as editor and co-owner, with Edward Millen, of the *Central Australian and Bourke Telegraph* newspaper. Eventually the two men sold their interests and purchased the rival newspaper, the *Western Herald and Darling River Advocate*. With Millen's departure into politics in the mid 1890s, Chapman assumed greater control over the newspaper, which he operated until about 1918.

Chapman saw great potential in Lawson's presence in town. Without delay, he requested a meeting between the poet and a group of local unionists, in order to give Lawson 'some points for a political poem'. Lawson must have been impressed with the plight of these men and, armed with this new information, he immediately began setting their issues to rhyme.

Lawson's work for the *Western Herald* has been well documented over the years. He referred to it himself when he informed Aunt Emma that he was writing '*sub rosa* for the *Western Herald*'. And later reminiscences by Lawson's friends, Billy Wood and Edwin Brady, also gave important clues as to the existence of the verses. Researchers, assuming that no relevant copies of the *Western Herald* remained, believed they had come to a dead end in their search. However, old copies of the *Western Herald*, stored in Bourke and reasonably preserved by the dry climate, *had* survived and were eventually sent to the Mitchell Library in Sydney for microfilming.

These poems have never been published in their entirety outside the Bourke area, and the majority of them have not been published since they first appeared in the *Western Herald* in the latter months of 1892, over a hundred years ago. Here, for the first time, they are presented collectively.

The 28 September edition of the *Western Herald* reveals much coverage of local news and events, a host of advertisements, but only one poem. In fact, a careful scrutiny of previous issues of the newspaper highlights the curiosity value of the verse, as it was certainly not normal practice for the newspaper to print poetry at all. A stirring political poem which no doubt resulted in more heated local discussion, it was titled 'Our Members Present and Future'.

OUR MEMBERS PRESENT AND FUTURE

Dear Mr Editor — Will you favour me by publishing the following verses, written on a gidgea log, after supper: –

> *There was joy along the Darling when the labour war*
> *   begun,*
> *An' Labour whoop'd for triumph in the year of ninety-*
> *   one.*
> *Three men we sent to Parliament — three men who*
> *   promised fair,*
> *We sent 'em out to fight for us; but only one 'got*
> *   there'.*
> *There were Huey, Howe an' Nich'las, all eager for*
> *   the fray,*
> *And the latter two were going for the 'tyrant' straight*
> *   away.*
>
> *There was swearing on the Darling ere the dawn of*
> *   ninety-two,*
> *For the western men were angry at the man who*
> *   wasn't true.*

An' the man no doubt was boasting how he did the
  bushmen brown
While he fought against oppression in the private bars
  of town.
The principles of Labour had been left out in the cold,
An' it riled the shearers when they thought how they'd
  been sold.

Now Willis yelled for 'Labour's rights' an' howled for
  'Libertee';
He wouldn't know a dummy if he saw it — no, not he.
He seemed to love the workers all, but cared a curse
  for none.
An' now he's fighting boldly in the cause of
  NUMBER ONE.
For though he praised the sons of toil, an' d—d
  [damned] the sons of Pelf,
He's not a Labour member, he is member for himself.

He pretends to be ignorant at the actions of 'His
  Nibs',
An' joins the Opposition in the interests of Dibbs.
He walks against the country, at the country's
  expense,
An' tries to dodge the crisis just by sitting on the fence.
Tho' Nich'las fights for Number One, he thinks it not
  a crime
To yell for 'Rights o' Labour' when it's near election
  time.

He worked against McDonnell [sic] with his influence
  and tin,
An' the shearers' man was broken while a railer
  waddled in.

70

Let us cull the person Waddle — (he is waddling to his
    fall),
An' he'll favour sword and rifle, if they killed the
    people all,
He'll uphold the constitution till he pumps his dying
    breath
An' he'll yell for Law-an'-Order, if the people starved
    to death.
The only thing he's working for is covered by his hat,
An' Davis had to stand aside for such a man as that!
(Oh it's 'claim the Law's protection' when greedy
    deeds are done,
An' it's whoop for 'Law-an'-Order' when you fight for
    Number One).

An' Howe was down on Greed an' Wrong, a friend of
    toil was Howe,
But 'twasn't that which sent him where he spreads his
    bluey now.
He yelled for justice in the bush, an' robbed the poor in
    town,
But let him rest, it's rather mean to kick a man that's
    down.
If others went where they deserve, we'd play a lively
    tune;
We'd have a new election on the Darling pretty soon.

But plucky Huey Lancy, well — he did his very best
To save the tatter'd colours that he carried from the
    West,
For when the Labour Party fell, an' comrades turned
    about,
He strove to save the honour of the man who sent him
    out.

71

An' if his speech is rather 'free' — his manner
    somewhat rough,
We know his heart is big and true an' made of sterling
    stuff.
But he struggled single-handed, an' he fought agin the
    fates,
He was handicapped and humbugged for the want of
    better mates.

There's 'Watty of the Future' throwing us his little
    sop,
He's another friend of Labour when the Labour dog's
    on top,
An' if western men remember how he served 'em in
    the past,
He'll be 'Watty of the Future' — of the future till the
    last.
He is fishing now for Labour, but the fishes ought to
    know,
How he baited hooks for Willis, not so very long ago.
Better Jack of the 'Great Western'; he at least is
    straight and true,
An' he always does for Labour what he thinks it's best
    to do.
He's the sort of man that's wanted at election times out
    back,
So while cheering honest fellows, let us give a whoop
    for Jack.

Then it's whoop for Huey Langwell, who's a straight
    an' honest man,
An' a bushman an' a shearer from the ranks o'
    Labour's van.
They know him down the Murray, an' away up in the
    north,

As one who'd free his country from the rule of George
  the Fourth.
An' when the next election comes we'll send him back
  agen,
And take good care his mates shall be the proper kind
  of men.

Better men than 'Nick' and 'Waddle' are a-camping in
  the gums,
An' we'll easy find a couple when the next election
  comes;
There's 'William Walter Davis', and there's half-a-
  dozen more;
There's the open-hearted owner of the station with the
  bore;
There's Millen of 'The Western', an' plenty honest
  men,
An' two must go with Hughey when we send him back
  again.
Let 'em stand and fight together, spite of influence and
  'tin';
Let 'em come straight out for honour, and send the
  best man in!

Yours &c,
Tally
Down River,
September 27, 1892.

To a reader not familiar with the local Bourke political and union scene, some of the names appearing in the above poem would appear confusing, especially as Lawson used pseudonyms or nicknames for many of his characters. The list on the following page gives some of these names and their real counterparts.

Willis	William Nicholas Willis, Bourke MLA
Nich'las	as above
Dibbs	George Dibbs, Premier of New South Wales
McDonnell	Donald Macdonell, Bourke unionist
Waddle	Thomas Waddell, Bourke MLA
Davis	William Walter Davis, former Bourke MLA
Howe	James Peter Howe, former Bourke MLA
Hughey Lancy	Hugh Langwell, Bourke MLA
Watty	Watson Braithwaite, proprietor Carriers' Arms Hotel
Jack	John Lennon, proprietor Great Western Hotel
Millen	Edward Millen, owner of the *Western Herald*

Few people, apart from the unionists and his host at the Great Western Hotel, were aware of Lawson's presence in Bourke. Phil Chapman, editor of the *Western Herald*, had offered to publicise his arrival however the poet 'preferred to keep dark for a while', no doubt to gauge the reaction to his first poem. In order to conceal his identity and presence in town he used the pseudonym of 'Tally' for the above poem.

The use of the pseudonym comes as no great surprise to those who are familiar with Lawson's writing, as over the years he used many such fictitious names. The first was 'Youth', followed in later years by 'Caliban', 'HAL' (his initials), 'Joe Swallow', 'Rumfellow' and 'Jack Cornstalk'. Earlier in 1892 he used the name 'Cervus Wright' for a series of almost-libellous political poems that were printed in William Willis's *Truth* newspaper.

Lawson left a riddle behind in the use of Tally, and the precise derivation of the name is unknown. In shearers' terms 'tally' means the number of sheep shorn in one day. Lawson had yet to visit any of the shearing sheds about the Darling River, but the expression probably came from his close association with the local unionists involved in the wool industry.

In one of his short stories, 'That There Dog O' Mine', Lawson names the dog 'Tally'. This story was written in Wellington, New

Zealand in December 1893 and found its way into the *New Zealand Times* during that same month. Another use of the name is found in Lawson's short poem 'Tally Town', which was supposedly written with Bourke in mind and published in the *Freeman's Journal* during 1893.

TALLY TOWN

A shearer tramped from Borderland
When Sunset shed cut out;
He scarcely felt the miles of sand,
The hot plains baked with drought.
His cheque was in his ragged clothes,
The future wore no frown,
When blazing white before him rose
The roofs of Tally Town.

From Tally Town the shearer fled
When Christmas time was past;
His cheeks were drawn, his eyes were red,
His breath came rough and fast;
Along the creek he ran and yelled
Till devils struck him down.
The landlord banked the cheques he held
That day in Tally Town.

The second of Lawson's *Western Herald* poems was published on Saturday, 1 October. More in keeping with his usual style of bush verse, 'A Stranger on the Darling' recorded Lawson's impressions of Bourke and was granted the distinction of being printed on the front page.

Possibly because of the change of theme, Lawson chose to use the pseudonym 'Joe Swallow'. Joe Swallow was a name well associated with Lawson. He first used it in 1890 while living in Western Australia, where he contributed freelance verse and prose, which was confined to union, social and political themes, to the newly established Albury *Observer*, at a payment of one penny per line. Lawson was always vocal on such matters and was seemingly unafraid to voice his opinion, especially when writing under a fictitious name.

The origin of the name Joe Swallow went back to Lawson's childhood days at Mudgee. An old imperial ex-convict by that name had owned land opposite the Lawsons at Sapling Gully, on the other side of the Mudgee–Gulgong road. However Lawson could never have known him well. He died in 1872, when Lawson was only five years old. Yet the impressions of the old man, and certainly his name, must have remained in his mind over the years.

'A Stranger on the Darling' appears to be a public announcement of Lawson's (the 'new-chum') arrival in town. Though the use of the name Joe Swallow may have revealed to Lawson's avid followers his true identity, there was nothing in the verse to suggest he was in any way connected to the political poem that had been published three days earlier.

A STRANGER ON THE DARLING

When a fellow strikes the Darling, after coming from
    the East,
He will mostly take his bearing for a day or two at
    least;
And the roving rhymer always notes his first
    impressions down
For a life along the Darling isn't like the life in town.

Prominent among the matters that will strike a
    stranger first,
Are the awful Annanius* and most decided thirst;
And the thirst is all-pervading, it is regular and strong
'Twould be worth a lot in Sydney, where the beers are
    cheap and long.

The liar is a novel and refreshing kind of bore,
With his wild and wondrous stories of the stations
    where he shore.

And nothing suits him better than to case his mighty
    mind,
When he buttonholes a 'greeny' like the guileless
    undersigned.

I have lied against a sailor, I have lied against the
    press,
An auctioneer and poet,** with considerable success;
I have lied against a Yankee, a bagman and the rest,
But I had to strike my colours to a liar from the west.

He's a ranger and a rooster, and his name is mostly
    'Jim',
And you'd think that all the squatters in the country
    wanted him;
He can lick the whole creation, in the bush or in the
    town,
And it's good to hear a bushman size him up and take
    him down.

Men of Bourke, the world is moving, and you're
    moving with it, too,
And you live a little faster than your fathers used to
    do;
But although the bush was lonely, and the life was
    rather slow,
Don't forget the vanished seasons on the Darling long
    ago.

And the way you shift your cargo, and a lot of other
    ways,
Somehow seem to remind a fellow of the good old
    roarin' days —
Of the Mis'sipi pilot, and the things we read about,

And tell us that the early days have not quite drifted
out.

You're a trifle gone on sporting, you are over fond of
beer,
But you pull yourself together when election time is
near,
And altho' you often blunder, yet you do your very
best
For to send a decent fellow to mis-represent the west.

Men of Bourke, and round about it, call your drinks,
and put 'em down!
Here's a hand and here's a greeting from a new chum
from the town;
You deserve to thrive and prosper if you worry through
the drought,
And the Darling doesn't drown you or the devil wipe
you out.

The Darling's rather muddy and the plains a trifle
bare,
But your girls are fairly pretty, and your liquor's pretty
fair,
Just go on as you are going, you have only got to try,
And you'll have a tidy city on the Darling by-and-by.

Yours truly
Joe Swallow

*ananias: 'a liar' (Concise Oxford Dictionary). Lawson's use of 'annanius' possibly
denotes the plural form. In fact Lawson appeared to be preoccupied, and extremely
unimpressed, with the 'bush liars' he had encountered since his departure from the
city. He dwells on this fact, not only in this poem, but in his first letter to Aunt Emma
and the prose work 'In a Dry Season'.
** Probably refers to his duel of verse with Banjo Paterson.

During this time many of the townspeople were actively organising the second Eight Hour Day parade to be held in Bourke. On 3 October, two days after the publication of 'A Stranger on the Darling', the whole town turned out for the festivities. No doubt Lawson attended, as he had been present at the similar Eight Hour Day marches in Sydney in 1891.

The parade was a well-organised affair involving local coachbuilders, mechanics, carpenters, wheelwrights, blacksmiths, carriers and unionists. According to the Wednesday 5 October edition of the *Western Herald*, the activities commenced with a march that began at the western end of Mitchell Street opposite the Amalgamated Shearers' Union office at nine o'clock. The parade, in which each local union was represented, progressed from Mitchell Street through the town, across the billabong, to a vacant block of land. The order of procession was: Grand Marshall; Bourke Town Band; Amalgamated Coachbuilders, Carpenters, Blacksmiths and Wheelwrights Committee; Carriers' Committee; Half Holiday Association; Bourke Mechanics' Band; Amalgamated Shearers' Union Committee, comprising Messrs Andrews, Wood, Hall and Currie; General Labourers' Union. Billy Wood was marshal of the parade and the music was provided by the Town Band and the Mechanics Band, the latter mainly made up of employees of the Cobb & Co. factory.

Several large banners were carried in the parade and most prominent was that of the Amalgamated Shearers' Union, and there were reportedly three hundred representatives of the shearers' and labourers' unions present. One of their members, recorded only as 'Bogan' in the local newspaper reports, was dressed in typical bush attire and rode a horse and led another which carried a pack saddle. Possibly this is the man who became Lawson's character 'One-eyed Bogan' in his later Bourke-based stories. Watty Braithwaite, representing the Carriers' Committee, also participated in the march.

Meanwhile, 'Our Members Present and Future' had created much excitement in Bourke, a town whose sympathies were already divided between the squatters and the shearers. To add to the controversy, there was also an existing rivalry between the two local newspapers. The two co-owners of the *Western Herald and Darling River Advocate*, Phil Chapman and Edward Millen, had been the original proprietors of the *Central Australian and Bourke Telegraph*, which was now the opposition and operating under the editorship of Horace K. Bloxham.

No doubt fuelled by this rivalry, the *Central Australian* was quick to publish a reply to 'Our Members Present and Future', which was penned by an unknown writer–poet using the pseudonym 'Smoko'. Unfortunately no relevant copies of the *Central Australian* have survived, so the exact content of the poem will never be known. John Hawley, a local contractor who employed Lawson as a house painter for a time during his stay in Bourke, later recalled that Smoko's poem began with the words 'The "Herald" has a poet, The "Central" has one too'.[20]

Reverting to the pseudonym of Tally, Lawson retaliated in the best way he knew how — with his pen — using every ounce of sarcasm and contempt he could muster upon his literary opponent, Smoko. The result was the rather lengthy 'The Poet on the Central', which was published on 5 October. We can only surmise what the hapless Smoko wrote from Lawson's retort. Billy Wood, the local unionist, reinforced the assumption that Lawson's identity was still well concealed from the locals. 'Henry Lawson', he stated, 'wrote some political verses in answer to something that appeared in the columns of the *Central Australian* newspaper. Henry's were published in the Bourke *Western Herald*, under a *nom de plume* . . . The verses were very effective too, and none of the other side had any idea of Henry's being in Bourke.'[21]

THE POET ON THE CENTRAL

*There's a poet on the Central, and his verses are
    sublime,
In their independent metre, and their disregard for
    rhyme;
Well, he did his best, I fancy, tho' he only could abuse,
For a lamer poetaster never 'rassled' with the muse;
But I'm really very sorry that I kept him out of bed*

With a pen between his fingers and a towel around his
    head.

Said the Super on the Central, ere the paper went to
    press,
'Have you read the Western Herald?' and the poet
    answered 'Yes.'
Said the Super of the Central, and the poet grinned the
    while —
'Go to work and give it to 'em in your most sarcastic
    style;
Paint 'em all as black as Satan; put the enemy to
    route,
And you'll get the little billet that you're worrying
    about,
Try and let us have some verses, make 'em rough and
    make 'em good,'
And the poet grinned and nodded for he rather thought
    he could.

Armed with pen and paper, and a table and a chair,
Sat the bard with inky fingers, clutching wildly at his
    hair,
And he called the muse to aid him, but the muse was
    deaf and dumb;
So he yanked her by the tresses when he saw she
    wouldn't come.
Oh it's good to hear the rhymer with his rhymes of
    'wealth' and 'pelf',
In a sheet to which the Member telegraphs about
    himself.
And we chuckled a little chuckle as we listened to the
    whoop
Of a crippled poet yelling that a man was 'in the
    whoop'.

'In the whoop' is very pretty, but it doesn't rhyme with
    'route',
Though perhaps it suites the tooting of a tootler with a
    toot.
You are foolish, Mr 'Smoko'; better go and learn a
    trade
Than be writing at the bidding of the Number One
    Brigade;

You are fishing like the others in the service, it is true,
But you mightn't get the billet for the dirty work you do.

All that you can say of Huey, when we put the lot on
    top,
Is about his billiard table and his book and 'baccy'
    shop.
With his 'barber's pole', you fancy you have given him
    a dose,
But he'll shave a certain party, and he'll shave 'em
    pretty close.
And you think that selling papers is an easy way to
    live —
Well, he doesn't sell the Central, so the angels will
    forgive.
And you say Levein is brainy — 'tis a foolish thing to
    say,
How did H—[Huey] speak of Willis in the House the
    other day?

What had Huey done for Labour? You should
    moderate your tone,
There are little things in Hansard that are better left
    alone,
For they tell us of the city, and they tell us of the bush

How a certain member voted for the military push;
And the member wasn't Huey, it was one that you
    adore —
So you'd better not refer us back to Hansard any
    more.

You are harmless in your sneaking little dab at Tommy
    White,
For the labourers have tried him and they find that he's
    all right.
With regard to Phil and Edward, your impotent 'allee
    same',
And you say of Hall and Andrews that they're living
    on the game.
You are foolish when you said it, and you went a bit
    too far,
I can only say in answer 'you're a liar,' there you are;
You only go for Wood because he isn't of your tribe,
And he isn't hunting rabbits for he wouldn't take the
    bribe.
And the honest Currie Brothers wouldn't be of any use
To the followers of Willis, hence the Central crowd's
    abuse.

And you say, in spite of grammar, that 'the western
    press shriek high';
You will find that we are whooping to some purpose,
    by-and-by.
But we never 'swore at Lennon's' nor 'repeated it to
    Drew',
And we do not care a candle if ' 'twas heard by
    Donohoe',
What his principles amount to would be very hard to tell,
For at times he follows Willis and at other times
    Waddell.

You were near it when you told us that the stalwart
    shearers swore,
'They had had enough of humbug and of promises
    galore'.
We had had enough for certain — you have struck the
    truth, my lad —
We are sick of being humbugged, we are tired of being
    had,
But the days of 'talk' are dying — times have changed,
    my brother bard,
For the men along the Darling have been thinking very
    hard,
And when certain 'Labour Members' come agen to
    'talk them fair',
They will wink at one another, and they'll mutter
    'We've been there.'
With regard to Hall and Andrews, you should really
    be discreet,
They are not the sort of fellows to be humming for a
    seat;
But they won't remain inactive, neither will they speak
    in vain,
When a certain gang of traitors try for Parliament again.

Yours &c TALLY
Down River

P.S.
We were rather rough on Watty — rather hasty, we'll
    allow,
But he ought to know the colour of the crowd he
    follows now.
Let him break away with Willis and repudiate the
    push,

> *Let him prove that he is loyal to the shearers and the*
> *   bush.*
> *Let him come straight out for Labour — true in deed*
> *   as well as word!*
> *And he'll hear along the Darling such a cheer he never*
> *   heard.*

Some additional characters were revealed in this second poem:

Tommy White	member of the ASU, Bourke
Phil	Phil Chapman, editor of *The Western Herald*
Edward	Edward Millen, owner of The *Western Herald*
Hall	Thomas Hicks Hall, Secretary of the GLU, Bourke
Andrews	John Andrews, Chairman of the ASU, Bourke
Currie Bros	George and Thomas Currie, Bourke unionists
Donohoe	Licensee of the Gladstone Hotel, Bourke
Wood	Billy Wood, Secretary of the ASU, Bourke
Drew	Licensee of the Telegraph Hotel, Bourke
Lennon's	John Lennon, manager of the Great Western Hotel

Lawson was no stranger to confrontations and debates of the written kind and during the previous twelve months he had had much practice in writing sarcastic and scornful replies to other poets. Only months before, he had been involved in a similar duel of verse with his contemporary, 'Banjo' Paterson. And earlier in the year he had written several scathing anti-establishment poems for John Norton, editor of *Truth*. The caustic verses included 'The House of Fossils', 'More Echoes from the Old Museum', and 'Wales the First'.

Thus Lawson's brutal attack on Smoko was not without precedent, and the events that followed soon rivalled Lawson's comparable recent city experiences. Not to be outdone, the 'poet on the Central' (Smoko), after missing one issue of the *Central Australian*, penned another retort. Lawson's fourth poem — 'The Poet by Telegraph' — was another blast at the cheeky Smoko. It appeared on 15 October. The word 'Telegraph' in the title refers to the full name of the opposition newspaper — *The Central Australian and Bourke Telegraph*.

THE POET BY TELEGRAPH

Oh, the cheek of poetasters! Oh, the self conceit of men!
Here's the poet of the Central on the wallaby agen;
But their poet missed an issue, they are rather short of
    rhyme,
And they telegraph to Sydney for their verses ev'ry
    time.

Now the editor is sorry, for he sought to make it
    known,
That the verses were a clever little effort of his own,
Oh, there's nothing so transparent as his paltry little
    shams;
But I'm sorry that I cost him much a sum in
    telegrams.

But in cases where the message is delayed they make
    pretence
To reply with printed nonsense that has no rhyme or
    sense.
What's the Central's dirty linen, or its rhymer's
    meaner dirt,
Got to do with Wood, the poet, and a song about the
    shirt?
And they say I chummed with Smoko and we shared
    our bread and beer;
I was never more insulted in the course of my career
For his metre runs as smoothly as the language of a
    chow,
And his sense is not apparent, and his rhyme would
    jolt a cow.

And they say the 'Herald' rhymer writes the 'Central'
    stuff as well

'Tis the lie that suits the 'Central' like the other lies
    they tell;
There's a stock of lies for 'Smoko', there are plenty on
    the shelves,
But they can't persuade the people that they blacked
    their eyes as well.

'Twould be like the dirty dodges that the Central people
    play,
If I wrote for both the papers, and from each received
    my pay.
Let them shuffle as they must, and let them slander as
    they will,
I was always true to Labour, and am loyal to it still.

Mr Smoko, you should never speak of 'parting with
    the tin',
There are some who never do it till the bailiff saunters
    in.
Mr Smoko, you should never speak of 'living on the
    game',
While your masters get their living in a manner much
    the same.

'Never argue with a liar', will in future be my rule;
More especially in cases where the liar is a fool.
I, myself, can fib a little, but I rather think I'd pause,
Ere I'd slander honest fellows who are loyal to the
    cause.

There are tartars to be caught, and there are lessons to
    be learnt,
So you'd better drop it, 'Smoko', ere you get your
    fingers burnt.

'Poets are for peace', you tell me, and I never like a
row,
But you'd better drop it, 'Smoko', and you'd better
drop it now.

Yours &etc
Tally
Coming up from Down River.

P.S.
You are sneering too at Millen, but he is laughing at
such as you,
For to rhyme his name with 'fillin' is as much as you
can do.
And what Huey did for Labour is a tidy lot indeed
For he did as much for Labour as the others did for
greed.

Lawson's notation to the above poem, 'Coming up from Down River', suggests that he was in the process of making his way back to Bourke from a downriver station. However this is unlikely as he appears not to have left Bourke until the end of November. Instead, the statement could have been written to fool the general public in respect of his true identity.

By this time, the greater part of the local population was speculating on the identities of the two poets, Tally and Smoko, and the controversy probably prompted many bar-room fights in the local pubs. Protected by the realms of unionism, Lawson's secret was safe, however he theorises, in 'The Poet by Telegraph', on Smoko's true identity. First he suggests that the editor of the *Central Australian* had 'sought to make it known that the verses were a clever little effort of his [the editor's] own'. Then he implies that a Sydney poet was responsible for the verse, and apologises for costing the editor 'much a sum in telegrams.'

Some of the local residents believed that Tally and Smoko were the same person. Lawson was obviously aware of the talk and, in this latest poem, he went to considerable effort to discount the theory, scorning the rumour that he was a friend of Smoko and that 'the "Herald" rhymer writes the "Central" stuff as well'. In a huff, he responded angrily to the insinuations, saying 'I was never more insulted in the course of my career'.

However John Hawley held a different view on the subject when he wrote:

> Henry Lawson told me he had written a poem each for the two local papers, the 'Western Herald' and the 'Central'. Through them ran a competitive strain as one poet writing against another poet ... Henry Lawson showed me a letter from Brady expressing surprise that Lawson had managed to get the two inserted. Brady had recognised his style. [22]

Lawson certainly wrote with a distinctive technique, and the supposed beginning of Smoko's first poem, 'The "Herald" has a poet, The "Central" has one too,' certainly has a certain 'Lawson' ring to it. However the true identity of Smoko will probably be never known and the whole topic is open to conjecture.

Two more poems followed in quick succession in the *Western Herald* on 22 October. They were 'What Huey Didn't Do' and 'Have You Heard'. 'What Huey Didn't Do' concerned the virtues of Hugh Langwell, the Independent Labour representative for the Bourke electorate and a man for whom Lawson held much respect.

WHAT HUEY DIDN'T DO

'What's Huey done for Labour?'
Is asked by Huey's foes;
I see no good in telling
What everybody knows.
If I read 'Hansard' inch by inch,
And here retold the tale,

My readers each would give a pinch
For tidings that are stale.
I'd hear them recommending me
To 'stretch' my blooming legs,
Or teach my aged grand-ma-ma
The art of sucking eggs.

For 'Smoko's' sake, and for the sake
Of writing something new,
I'll give a list of shady things
That Huey didn't do:
I will not mention any names;
I will not give a clue;
I'll only speak of certain things
That Huey didn't do.

He will not break in Parliament
The pledges made in Bourke;
Nor yet, with public billets, pay
For dirty, private work.
He didn't hire a shady push
To keep him in the swim —
To trap and slander honest men,
And lie and whoop for him.
I do not say that others did —
Although I knew a few —
I only mention certain things
That Huey didn't do.

He never joined the Labour cause
To sell it in the end;
He didn't work a cruel wrong
On one who was his friend.
He's not a saint — we're sinners all —

He's had a lark or two;
But someone did a cruel deed
That Huey wouldn't do.
(At least they say that someone did —
They do not tell me who;
I only speak of dirty things
That Huey didn't do.)

And if he had no work to do
And scarce enough to eat,
And workmen lent a pound or two
And helped him on his feet,
He'd not forget in better days
To thank them for the deed;
He would not write against the man
Who helped him in his need.
And yet they say another did —
I don't know if it's true —
I only speak of crawling things
That Huey didn't do.

He didn't jump another's claim,
He never made a bid
For Labour votes, by claiming praise,
For work another did.
He didn't wait for backs to turn
Before he'd throw a stone,
Nor did he advertise or puff himself
In papers of his own.
I cannot say that others did —
I wouldn't if I knew —
I simply speak of shady things
That Huey didn't do.

(Save where I speak of other things
That Huey wouldn't do.)

Yours &c
Tally
     P. S.
     There's 'Smoko' down in Sydney
     And 'Smoko' here in Bourke;
     They found the Sydney poet
     Not equal to his work.
     I thought I fought a single fool;
     I find I'm fighting two,
     And that's a thing I fancy
     That Huey wouldn't do.

     P. P. S.
     I slander none. I hope that I'm
     Distinctly understood;
     For, it be known, I only rhyme
     And prose for Labour's good.
     I haven't mentioned names, or said
     A thing that isn't true;
     I've just confined myself to deeds
     That Huey didn't do.
     To things that Huey didn't
     And Huey wouldn't do.
     Let 'Smoko' give a list of things
     His master wouldn't do.
  T.

The poem contained thinly veiled innuendoes of improper dealings by other local politicians, supposedly Waddell and Howe. And Lawson undoubtedly refers to William Willis when he mentions the man who liked to 'advertise or puff himself in papers of his own'. His wrath was also directed to the *Central Australian* newspaper and Smoko, stating the inferior quality of the poet's work.

The accompanying poem was entitled 'Have You Heard'. By granting the subject of his poem anonymity, Lawson cleverly avoided libelling him. However he lays certain clever clues that would have readily identified his 'certain Labour member' to the local Bourke readers. Given the political situation and the unionists disregard for all the local politicians except Langwell, the subject of this poem was probably William Nicholas Willis.

HAVE YOU HEARD

Did you hear in last September how a certain 'Labour'
    member —
One whose name I didn't mention, for there isn't any
    need —
How a certain politician got a government commission
To betray the Opposition in the interests of greed?
Oh! The shearers heard a story, and their adjectives
    were gory,
For they knew what he was doing, and they saw what
    he had done.
He had promised to uphold them; but in spite of all he
    told them,
He betrayed them and he sold them for the sake of
    Number One.
He got in on false pretences, and he sat upon the
    fences,
Till his interests induced him to get down the other
    side.
But there'll be no insurrection, if he comes for re-
    election;
And he better bring a gattling* if he wants to save his
    hide.
Better seek another section, where they have no
    recollection,

Of the way he sold the shearers, and the awful way he
     lied.
Tally
*gatling: Gatling — a crank-operated multi-barrel machine gun patented by its
American inventor Richard Gatling in 1862

The last two poems appeared in the *Western Herald* on 29 October. The first, 'Old Labour and the Echo', extolled the virtues of those who supported the interests of the unionists, namely Davis, Langwell, Currie and Millen. On the other hand, Lawson blatantly threw all caution aside and went on to name those who he considered stood in the way of fair play and truth and 'Freedom'. Willis was labelled a 'traitor' who worked a 'double game' and Watty (Watson Braithwaite, proprietor of the Carriers' Arms Hotel) was derided for being undecided in his political leanings.

OLD LABOUR AND THE ECHO

I heard old Labour call across
The dusty flats and hollows;
I heard an echo in reply,
'Twas pretty much as follows —

Who is this traitor, to his shame,
Who tried to sell and kill us?
Who tried to work a double game?
And the Echo answered 'Willis'.

And who replies, when ere the soul
Of Freedom send us a cooey?
Who answers to the roll?
The Echo shouted 'Huey'.

Who'll bring in future Parliaments,
Pull many a Peoples' Bill in?

The thoughtful Echo paused awhile
And then it shouted 'Millen'.

Who'll help us when the struggle comes?
Who'll do his best to save us?
Who'll help us from the other side?
The Echo shouted 'Davis'.

Who must decide which road to take?
Who mustn't now be scotty?
Who is this man who hesitates?
And the Echo answered 'Watty'.

Who keeps his head when other heads
Are lost in wild delirium?
The Echo nearly broke its jaws,
With shouting 'Megatherium'. **

And who to march in Labour's van
Is always in a hurry?
Who proved himself a shearers' man?
The Echo shouted 'Currie'.

(And here the funny Echo said,
Its answer to embellish:
'It is the sort of currie too
That Willis doesn't relish.')

Who runs behind his master like
A truck behind a loco?
Who wouldn't take a friendly hint?
'Why,' Echo answered, 'Smoko'.

And who has made, with 'Tally's' aid,
His paper very fillen?

95

The Echo answered, 'Chapman, sure —
And not forgetting Millen.'*

Who writes the rugged rhymes?
Who's Labour's unknown ally?
Who keeps himself so very dark?
And Echo answered:
Tally

* Rhyme borrowed from 'Smoko'
** *megatherium*: 'extinct kind of huge herbivorous sloth-like animal' (*Concise Oxford Dictionary*).

The subject of the last political Bourke poem, "The Lissington Verdict', was the large pastoral holding of Lissington, situated in the Bourke–Enngonia district. Like most sheds in the region, it was involved in some kind of industrial action and the shearers there were most critical of one of their local parliamentary representatives, who appears to have failed them rather than acted as they thought that a local representative should. This poem reveals a condemnation of William Willis, MLA.

THE LISSINGTON VERDICT

They say thirteen at Lissington,
Have Willis doomed to die.
We say fifty at Lissington
Have uttered that same cry.
For he had failed them in their need,
When they required their aid,
Four thousand of us now endorse
What Lissington then said.
From Southern bank and Northern side
Of Darling River wide,
The news has gone, he proven false,
He'll never more be tried.
From first to last we trusted him

But now he's proved our foe;
Should any doubt what Labour means
Let future actions show.

In times to come we'll know our friends
Our foes too, quite as well;
The former help, the latter show
That treachery so fell.
As he who sold us in the fight
When Labour stood at bay,
Shall meet the fate a traitor should,
No more with us can stay.

When time goes by and Parliament
Is on the country thrown . . .

'The Lissington Verdict' originally contained four complete verses. Unfortunately, as a result of the newspaper file being damaged prior to the contents being microfilmed at the Mitchell Library in Sydney, the last six lines of this poem are missing. Therefore, no signature remains to claim penmanship of the verse. The poem, compared to the previous seven, appears clumsy in parts. And though it cannot be said for certain that it was written by the secretive 'Tally', it has been included for the sake of chronology and interest.

This series of poems completes the series of verse written by Lawson in September and October 1892 for the express use of the *Western Herald and Darling River Advocate.* Contemptuous and derisive, almost libellous in nature, the verse undoubtedly helped to fuel what was already an explosive situation between the Labour ranks and the unionists. Lawson had done his job well.

CHAPTER 6

Lawson Meets James Gordon

There used to be two young fellers knockin' about Bourke and West-o'-Bourke named Joe Swallow and Jack Mitchell in those old days.[23]

James William Gordon was born at Creswick in Victoria on 23 October 1874, at a spot known locally as 'Bloody Gully',[24] where his father, a Scottish gold digger, was prospecting at the time. After completing his schooling, James obtained work at Kongbool Estate near Hamilton in Victoria, where he later became overseer before deciding to set off by himself to see more of the countryside.

Jim, as he was more usually known, was eighteen years old when he met Henry Lawson in Bourke in 1892. In his contribution to the book *Henry Lawson by His Mates*, Gordon described the event:

Looking backwards through the mists of the years of a quarter of a century, I can visualise him as I saw him first, a tall and angular stripling, eager-eyed and hopeful with ambition beginning to awaken in him. A reckless spirit he was ever in those days, quick to feel the smart of a slight, impatient at small obstacles, and when the mood was with him, morose, almost to grumpishness — a character which, by the way, entirely disappeared in later years. But withal, an affectionate and sincere friend, and, although easily led by those he trusted, the man or woman was not born who could not drive him.

Although Jim Gordon did not specify when he first met Henry Lawson, it was probably after the publication of Lawson's last Bourke-based political poem on 29 October. In his reminiscences Gordon certainly never mentioned Lawson writing for the *Western Herald*, and it is doubtful that he had any knowledge of the real identity of the controversial poet known locally only as Tally.

The scene was Mitchell Street in Bourke. Gordon observed a man striding along, seemingly oblivious to his surroundings. Apparently in one of his pensive moods, Lawson paced continually along one section of the street, up one side of the footpath down the length of a town block, crossed the road and walked back along the other side towards his original starting point. After watching the strange antics for a while, Gordon, who had recently arrived in town and later admitted to feeling somewhat homesick and lonely, approached the stranger and bid him 'Good-day'. Lawson, who had probably been working out matching rhymes for another poem, appeared suddenly embarrassed at being caught thus engrossed.

A conversation followed, with Gordon admitting that he was short of money and in desperate need of work. Lawson, who had left the Great Western Hotel by this stage, offered to share the facilities in his own home. Shortly, Gordon claimed, 'with two Swedes or Norwegians, he and I were camped in a small house over the billabong on the western side of Bourke'.[25]

The house was possibly one of those built during the boom of the 1880s when Bourke was expanding to the west, beyond Horsfalls Billabong which divided the town. A small, three-roomed dwelling, it was well built and contained not only an open fireplace but a stove as well. Firewood was either in short supply or the occupants of the house had no funds to purchase any, so dried cow-dung was substituted instead.

Besides Lawson, the house was inhabited by two other men, Scandinavians, according to Gordon, either Swedes or Norwegians, who were confirmed socialists and happy to share their meagre supplies. Soon the four men were partaking in a meal of sardines, supplied by Gordon, and cold corned beef supplied by the others.

The cottage did not contain any luxuries. There were no beds or chairs and the only cooking utensils were a billy and frying pan which were owned by Lawson's companions. After a restless and uncomfortable night, Gordon woke to find that his mate had already left the house before breakfast. It was only then that he was informed, to his amazement, that his new-found friend was Henry Lawson, the well-known Sydney poet.

Lawson had been out early in search of work. By this time he had been in Bourke for over five weeks and, apart from payments for the verse for the *Western Herald*, he had received no regular income. The £5 provided by J. F. Archibald had long since been spent in the local hotels, either on board or grog, and funds were in short or non-existent supply.

Gordon set out for the main street and soon he saw Lawson swinging excitedly along towards him. As the two men met, the poet asked: 'Can you paint?'

Gordon, remembering that his friend was the renowned poet, was confused. 'Pictures?' he asked, surprised.

'Pictures be B— !' Lawson rapped back. 'Houses, fences, anything of wood and corrugated iron?' [26]

Lawson, who had previously trained as a railway coach painter at Hudson Brothers factory at Clyde in Sydney, had obtained a job house painting. As Gordon later wrote:

> The town was booming at that time, and one Heseler, a well-to-do German, had bought half a block in its centre and built a big brick hotel on one corner — (it was at that time called the Great Western, but later on, the Empire). On the other allotments he erected five or six small cottages, and it was at these places that Lawson and I got a job painting. [27]

During the 1870s and 1880s Edward Otto Heseler had built several large brick buildings in Bourke, including two churches, the hospital, public school, Telegraph Hotel and two prominent bond stores. In 1884 he built the Great Western Hotel in Richard Street, which was licensed in 1892 by John Lennon. Additionally Heseler built several cottages near this hotel, and it was here that Lawson and his mate Gordon worked for a short time.

John Hawley, a local building contractor who was employed by Heseler to oversee the work, confirmed his employment of Lawson in a letter published in the *Sydney Morning Herald* on 20 February 1939. The occasion for the letter is unknown. However, after Lawson's death, many of his friends and acquaintances were happy to confirm events, via the media, of the poet's life. It is these reminiscences that now help us to piece together otherwise obscure details.

'To the Editor of the Herald', he wrote. 'Sir, When I was in charge of construction work in Bourke in 1892, two years after the Bourke flood, the late Henry Lawson asked me if I could put him on as a house painter. I did so, although not aware at the time of his identity.'

As the days passed Lawson grew discontented. Life in Bourke was uncertain and there was little other work to be found. He had come west to see the bush. Instead he was spending his time painting houses and had not ventured past the confines of the town. He wanted to write, but he required money. He needed to gain outback experience which in turn would provide the literary material requested by the *Bulletin*. Lawson was undecided what to do next. One day he was all for heading off into the bush, the next he was sick of the west and determined to return to Sydney. Finally he threw down his paint brushes and walked from his job.

It was probably about this time that the two men decided to look for work in the shearing sheds. Although September was the usual time for the commencement of shearing — and by late November the task would normally have been completed — the season was still in full swing, delayed by union strikes and general pastoral unrest. Gordon himself suggested that he was the instigator of the idea, stating: 'I decided to make out to one of the big shearing sheds — and Lawson, eager for the bush, and wanting a mate, made up his mind to come with me.' [28]

Meanwhile a cheque from the *Bulletin* arrived for Lawson. This was probably payment for 'In a Dry Season', the first article he had written since he had come to Bourke, which Archibald had published in the *Bulletin* on 5 November. Then, according to Gordon, the pair waited a week in Bourke before heading off into the bush. The delay was probably to wait for news of available work, the selection of which would have been aided by Lawson's union friends.

Along with Archibald's £5, since Lawson's arrival in Bourke he had earned possibly in excess of £8 for his poems published in the *Western Herald*, as well as payment for the several weeks' house painting he had completed for John Hawley. Although this was a considerable sum of money in 1892, undoubtedly most of it had been spent in the local bars. Prior to the arrival of the *Bulletin*'s cheque, Lawson, true to his usual form, was penniless and in urgent need of funds.

In preparation for his search for work in the Darling River shearing sheds, Lawson joined the Bourke branch of the General Labourers' Union on 23 November. The union ticket — number 2581 — was valid until 31 December 1893 and Lawson paid the sum of 10 shillings for the privilege. [29] It was issued by the secretary of the union, Thomas Hicks Hall, a man who Lawson immortalised in later stories such as 'Send Round the Hat'. Gordon, who had worked in the bush for several years, was probably already ticketed by the union.

Lawson's last task before setting off was to write a letter to his friend Arthur Parker.

Bourke.
24th November 1892

Dear Arthur,
I didn't call to see you lately. I am five hundred miles from Sydney.
I left in a hurry and hadn't time to let you know. I will be down at

*Xmas and bring back your books; they are perfectly safe. I start
down river today, in about an hour. I haven't much time to write,
also I am pretty drunk, so you'll excuse me. I expect to get a job in
a shearing shed. Will write a long letter in about two weeks' time.
My mate is a socialist and including a grand little fellow. Love to
Charley and all the Bummer push. Write c/o Thos. Hicks-Hall,
G.G., Workers' General Union*, Bourke, and he will forward
letters.*

Yours truly,
Henry Lawson
* General Labourers' Union

Henry Lawson and Arthur Parker first met about 1887 when they were
introduced by a mutual friend who knew that Parker had a shotgun to
sell and Henry wanted to purchase one. The sale of the gun never
eventuated, but instead a lifelong friendship was formed. Later they
worked together on cottages in the Blue Mountains; Henry as a painter
and Arthur as a plasterer. Parker later recollected that when Lawson
'went to Bourke, in 1892, I [Parker] wanted to go with him as his mate,
but I could not manage it then.' [30]

Although Jim Gordon was seven years younger than Lawson, the
two men quickly became friends. Gordon was a knowledgeable young
man, and his education was undoubtedly equal, if not superior, to
Henry Lawson's. By 1892, he had already gained considerable bush
experience. In later years he also became a writer of poetry, using the
pseudonym of Jim Grahame. Though he developed a somewhat
individual style of his own, a careful study of his work reveals, at times,
Lawson's influence. Two of his books of poems survive as testimony to
his craft: *Under Wide Skies* and *Call of the Bush*.

In later years, Gordon eventually recorded some of his impressions
of the time he spent with Lawson in Bourke and the surrounding areas
during the spring and summer of 1892–93. These took the form of
letters to the editor which were published in the *Bulletin*, and his

contribution to *Henry Lawson by His Mates* — 'Amongst My Own People'. Lawson made little reference in his subsequent writings to Jim Gordon, or anyone else for that matter, accompanying him on his wanderings about the Bourke district. Although certain discrepancies arise in Gordon's accounts, these reminiscences allow us, in part, to reassemble those missing months. It was not until 'By the Banks of the Murrumbidgee' was published in the *Bulletin* on 13 May 1916 that Lawson publicly acknowledged Gordon's presence at Bourke in 1892, when he wrote: 'My mate, James Grahame . . . We first met in Bourke some twenty-five years ago . . . '

Catholic Church — Bourke, NSW

CHAPTER 7

The Union Buries Its Dead

The dead bushman's name was Jim, apparently; but they found no portraits, nor locks of hair, nor any love letters, nor anything of that kind in his swag — not even a reference to his mother; only some papers relating to union matters.[31]

Four days before Lawson departed for the shearing shed alluded to in his letter to Arthur Parker, a stockman was drowned in a billabong at North Bourke while crossing a team of horses. A report of the fatality appeared in the next issue of the *Western Herald* on Wednesday 23 November.

A drowning fatality occurred on Sunday, to which an additional element of regret was attached by the fact that it transpired in broad daylight and within reach of willing assistance, had the necessity for it been known. The unfortunate victim was known as James Tyson, though at present it is not certain whether that was his real name or a *sobriquet* which from long use had been generally adopted. He had engaged with others to proceed to Beemery and from thence take sheep to Buckanbie, Mr W. Ross being in charge. Deceased was camped with his mates opposite the town near the punt and on Sunday the horses were collected for the purpose of starting to Beemery. The punt being underwater, the party had to proceed round by the North Bourke bridge, to gain which they had to cross a flooded warrambool. They swam the loose horses over, and proceeded to follow. Deceased's horse plunged when in the water, apparently coming over on Tyson, both going under. Deceased came to the surface, and gave a cry for help, and a mate, John Evans, swam to his assistance and succeeded in clutching him, but failed to hold him. Three times Tyson rose and each time his mate caught hold of him, but was not able to maintain his grip, and after sinking the third time Tyson rose no more. By this time the boats in the vicinity had reached the spot, and some of the occupants proceeded to dive, but without success. Upon receiving information the police set to dragging, and continued operations unsuccessfully till dark. Resuming next morning, they were ultimately rewarded in bringing the body to the surface about noon. It was found about 70 yards from the spot where deceased was drowned. Behind the left ear was a nasty gash, evidently the result of a kick from a horse. Deceased was apparently about twenty-five years of age. The coroner, Mr Daniell, held an inquiry ... and a finding of accidentally drowned was returned. Since the above [information] was in type, from papers in the deceased's swag, it has been ascertained that his real name was John Hallahan and his address is given as Mort's Estate, Toowoomba (Q). Several Queensland union tickets, voting rights and receipts for money given to the recent strikers were also found in the swag. Nothing was known of him locally.

This incident was immortalised in Lawson's 'A Bush Funeral', subtitled 'A Sketch from Life', which was published in *Truth* on 16 April 1893 while Lawson was still living in Bourke. It was renamed 'The Union Buries Its Dead' at a later date, possibly for its inclusion in *The Country I Come From* in 1901.

During the late 1800s, it was a common practice for many bush workers, for reasons known sometimes only to themselves, to adopted a 'new name' while working in the western woolsheds and stations of New South Wales. It is interesting to note that the alias used by this young drover was James Tyson, the same name as the well-known pastoralist who at that time owned the equally well-known Tinnenburra Station of 2,000,000 acres in the Cunnamulla district.

Although the young man's name was John Hallahan, New South Wales death records show that he was actually buried under the name of James Tyson, and the accompanying details are 'died Bourke 1892, parents unknown'.

Lawson claimed to have met the young man just before the accident as he walked along the riverbank. Whether it was the fact that he was one of the last to see the man alive, or that the death of the stranger at a similar age to his own evoked some sense of mortality in Lawson, he certainly went to great lengths to report the meeting and the eventual funeral.

Lawson's story reveals in great detail how the funeral procession wound its way from the Roman Catholic Church, along Mitchell Street, before turning into Richard Street and heading southwards, finally disappearing over the railway line in the direction of the cemetery, which was about a mile out of town. The priest officiating at the burial service was the Reverend Father Patrick Treacy.

Although he did not mention Lawson's actual attendance, Billy Wood, a union official and Lawson's friend, later claimed

> I was present with other union officials at the funeral described by Henry Lawson in 'The Union Buries Its Dead' and still remember many of the incidents which he so humorously describes ... The band would pray the deceased to the grave with dead marches and on the way back to town would give more lively airs. The cemetery was a good step from town and many of the mourners developed a good strong thirst before the pub was met on the way back. [32]

The first pub encountered on the way back into town was the Central Australian Hotel, on the corner of Richard and Anson Streets.

THE UNION BURIES ITS DEAD

While out boating one Sunday afternoon on a billabong across the river, we saw a young man on horseback driving some horses along the bank. He said it was a fine day, and asked if the water was deep there. The joker of our party said it was deep enough to drown him, and he laughed and rode farther up. We didn't take much notice of him.

Next day a funeral gathered at a corner pub and asked each other in to have a drink while waiting for the hearse. They passed away some of the time dancing jigs to a piano in the bar parlour. They passed away the rest of the time skylarking and fighting.

The defunct was a young union labourer, about twenty-five, who had been drowned the previous day while trying to swim some horses across a billabong of the Darling.

He was almost a stranger in town, and the fact of his having been a union man accounted for the funeral. The police found some union papers in his swag, and called at the General Labourers' Union Office for information about him. That's how we knew. The secretary had very little information to give. The departed was a 'Roman', and the majority of the town were otherwise — but unionism is stronger than creed. Drink, however, is stronger than unionism; and, when the hearse presently arrived, more than two-thirds of the funeral were unable to follow. They were too drunk.

The procession numbered fifteen, fourteen souls following the broken shell of a soul. Perhaps not one of the fourteen possessed a soul any more than the corpse did — but that doesn't matter.

Four or five of the funeral, who were boarders at the pub, borrowed a trap which the landlord used to carry passengers to and from the railway station. They were strangers to us who were on foot, and we to them. We were all strangers to the corpse.

A horseman, who looked like a drover just returned from a big trip, dropped into our dusty wake and followed us a few hundred yards, dragging his pack-horse behind him, but a friend made wild and demonstrative signals from a hotel verandah — hooking at the air in front with his right hand and jobbing his left thumb over his shoulder in the direction of the bar — so the drover hauled off and didn't catch up to us any more. He was a stranger to the entire show.

We walked in twos. There were three twos. It was very hot and dusty; the heat rushed in fierce dazzling rays across every iron roof and light-coloured wall that was turned to the sun. One or two pubs closed respectfully until we got past. They closed their bar doors and the patrons went in and out through some side or back entrance for a few minutes. Bushmen seldom grumble at an inconvenience of this sort, when it is caused for a funeral. They have too much respect for the dead.

On the way to the cemetery we passed three shearers sitting on the shady side of a fence. One was drunk — very drunk. The other two covered their right ears with their hats, out of respect for the departed — whoever he might have been — and one of them kicked the drunk and muttered something to him.

He straightened himself up, stared, and reached helplessly for his hat, which he shoved half off and then on again. Then he made a great effort to pull himself together — and succeeded. He stood up, braced his back against the fence, knocked off his hat, and remorsefully placed his foot on it — to keep it off his head till the funeral passed.

A tall, sentimental drover, who walked by my side, cynically quoted Byronic verses suitable to the occasion — to death — and asked with pathetic humour whether we thought the dead man's ticket would be recognised 'over yonder'. It was a GLU ticket, and the general opinion was that it would be recognised.

Presently my friend said:

'You remember when we were in the boat yesterday, we saw a man driving some horses along the bank?'

'Yes.'

He nodded at the hearse and said:

'Well, that's him.'

I thought awhile.

'I didn't take any particular notice of him,' I said. 'He said something, didn't he?'

'Yes: said it was a fine day. You'd have taken more notice if you'd known that he was doomed to die in the hour, and that those were the last words he would say to any man in this world.'

'To be sure,' said a full voice from the rear. 'If ye'd known that, ye'd have prolonged the conversation.'

We plodded on across the railway line and along the hot, dusty road which ran to the cemetery, some of us talking about the accident, and lying about the narrow escapes we had had ourselves. Presently someone said:

'There's the Devil.'

I looked up and saw a priest standing in the shade of the tree by the cemetery gate.

The hearse was drawn up and the tail-boards were opened. The funeral extinguished its right ear with its hat as four men lifted the coffin out and laid it over the grave. The priest — a pale, quiet young fellow — stood under the shade of a sapling which grew at the head of the grave. He took off his hat, dropped it carelessly to the ground, and proceeded to business. I noticed that one or two heathens winced slightly when the holy water was sprinkled on the coffin. The drops quickly evaporated, and the little round black spots they left were soon dusted over; but the spots showed, by contrast, the cheapness and shabbiness of the cloth with which the coffin was covered. It seemed black before; now it looked a dusky grey.

Just here man's ignorance and vanity made a farce of the funeral. A big, bull-necked publican, with heavy, blotchy features and a supremely ignorant expression, picked up the priest's straw hat and held it about two inches over the head of his reverence during the whole of the service. The father, be it remembered, was standing in

110

the shade. A few shoved their hats on and off uneasily, struggling between their disgust for the living and their respect for the dead. The hat had a conical crown and brim sloping down all round like a sunshade, and the publican held it with his great red claw spread over the crown. To do the priest justice, perhaps he didn't notice the incident. A stage priest or parson in the same position might have said: 'Put the hat down, my friend; is not the memory of our departed brother worth more than my complexion?' A wattlebark layman might have expressed himself in stronger language, none the less to the point. But my priest seemed unconscious of what was going on. Besides, the publican was a great and important pillar of the Church. He couldn't, as an ignorant and conceited ass, lose such a good opportunity of asserting his faithfulness and importance to his Church.

The grave looked very narrow under the coffin, and I drew a breath of relief when the box slid easily down. I saw a coffin get stuck once, at Rookwood, and it had to be yanked out with difficulty, and laid on the sods at the feet of the broken-hearted relations, who howled dismally while the grave-diggers widened the hole. But they don't cut contracts so fine in the West. Our grave-digger was not altogether bowelless, and, out of respect for that human quality described as 'feelin's', he scraped up some light and dusty soil and threw it down to deaden the fall of the clay lumps on the coffin. He also tried to steer the first few shovelfuls gently down against the end of the grave with the back of the shovel turned outwards, but the hard, dry, Darling River clods rebounded and knocked all the same. It didn't matter much — nothing does. The fall of lumps of clay on a stranger's coffin doesn't sound any different from the fall of the same things on an ordinary wooden box — at least I didn't notice anything awesome or unusual in the sound; but, perhaps, one of us — the most sensitive — might have been impressed by being reminded of a burial of long ago, when the thump of every sod jolted his heart.

I have left out the wattle — because it wasn't there. I have also neglected to mention the heart-broken old mate, with his grizzled head bowed and great pearly drops streaming down his rugged cheeks. He was absent — he was probably 'Out Back'. For similar reasons I have omitted reference to the suspicious moisture in the eyes of a bearded bush ruffian named Bill. Bill failed to turn up, and the only moisture was that which was induced by the heat. I have left out the 'sad Australian sunset' because the sun was not going down at the time. The burial took place exactly at mid-day.

The dead bushman's name was Jim, apparently; but they found no portraits, nor locks of hair, nor any love letters, nor anything of that kind in his swag — not even a reference to his mother; only some papers relating to union matters. Most of us didn't know the name till we saw it on the coffin; we knew him as 'that poor chap that got drowned yesterday'.

'So his name's James Tyson,' said my drover acquaintance, looking at the plate.

'Why! Didn't you know that before?' I asked.

'No; but I knew he was a union man.'

It turned out, afterwards, that J.T. wasn't his real name — only 'the name he went by'.

Anyhow he was buried by it, and most of the 'Great Australian Dailies' have mentioned in their brevity columns that a young man named James John Tyson was drowned in a billabong of the Darling last Sunday.

We did hear, later on, what his real name was; but if we ever chance to read it in the 'Missing Friends Column', we shall not be able to give any information to heart-broken Mother or Sister or Wife, nor to anyone who could let him hear something to his advantage — for we have already forgotten the name.

CHAPTER 8

The Trek to Toorale

A shearing-shed is not what city people picture it to be — if they imagine it at all; it is perhaps the most degrading hell on the face of this earth. Ask any better-class shearer.[33]

With the experience of the drover's funeral behind them, Henry Lawson and Jim Gordon prepared themselves for their downriver trek.

Armed with their newly acquired union tickets, they rolled their swags, filled their water and tucker bags and finally departed from the 'metropolis of the great scrubs' on 24 November 1892.

Their destination was the shearing shed at Toorale Station, situated downriver from Bourke. Here they planned to join the large seasonal work force that descended annually on the property. Positions as shed hands awaited them, no doubt arranged by Lawson's union mates in Bourke. James Gordon later wrote: '. . . one chilly morning Lawson and I . . . crossed the punt and headed for Fort Bourke Station . . . We were at Fort Bourke station for about three weeks . . .'[34]

Gordon's description of the weather poses a mystery. As anyone who has ever lived in the western outback area of New South Wales knows, November weather could never be described as 'chilly'. In another recollection, from a different source, Gordon contradicted himself when he wrote: 'We crossed on the punt and tramped down the river to Toorale Station, then owned by Sam. McCaughey, afterwards Sir Samuel, and secured a job at picking up wool on the shearing board.' [35] Here there is no mention of Fort Bourke, although it is possible that that station had been their intended destination, hence Gordon's mistaken reference to spending three weeks there. A lack of work may have forced the men further downriver to Toorale, which would be confirmed by events and personalities that Lawson later depicted in his shearing poems.

Although it is doubtful whether the two men spent any significant time in the Fort Bourke shearing shed, the first section of their journey on the western side of the river certainly led them past the station homestead. At that time the Fort Bourke pastoral holding consisted of approximately 300,000 acres (120,000 hectares). It was owned by Thomas Waddell, MLA, whom Lawson had satirised several weeks earlier in his poems 'Our Members Present and Future' and 'The Poet on the Central'.

A few miles past the Fort Bourke homestead, Lawson and Gordon passed the station shearing shed. Then, some forty miles downriver, they came to the Toorale shearing shed which was situated near the junction of the Darling and Warrego Rivers. Toorale was owned by the renowned pastoralist Samuel McCaughey at the time of Henry Lawson's visit, and comprised over 1,000,000 acres (400,000 hectares). Though several resumptions had taken place in 1885, it was still the largest pastoral holding in the Bourke Land Board District. Normally about a quarter of a million sheep were shorn there annually, though yearly fluctuations occurred depending on the climatic conditions. Droughts dramatically reduced the stock numbers just as the natural increase in breeding in good seasons boosted the total.

McCaughey, who also owned Dunlop Station which adjoined Toorale to the south, was the owner of more pastoral land in New

South Wales than any pastoralist in history. He did not live at any time at either Toorale or Dunlop stations, but at his mansion at Yanco in the Riverina. In 1892 the manager of Toorale was Samuel McCaughey's brother, John. Well known for his efficient methods of station management, he held the position from 1882 until 1898.

Toorale was a natural choice as a place of employment for Lawson and Gordon. The property was relatively close to Bourke and the shearing season was still in progress, although it was nearing its end. As it took approximately three months to complete the Toorale shearing during an average season, Lawson and Gordon participated in only a small portion of the shearing at that shed. No official station log books remain to authenticate their presence, however Lawson claimed in a later letter to Arthur Parker that he had spent 'a month' there. Certainly he appears to have stayed long enough to become familiar with the shearers' terminology.

The two trekkers enrolled at the shearing shed as rouseabouts. The duties of their new job consisted of picking up shorn fleeces from the board and putting them in large baskets which were dragged to the classing tables. There the fleeces were spread for the process of sorting by the wool classer. Lawson never learned to shear sheep, and most certainly time would not have permitted him to acquire such a skill. Jim Gordon wrote: 'It has often been written that Lawson was a fast shearer, and remarks have been made of the big cheques he could and did make at that work. Henry Lawson never shore a sheep in his life. Like myself, in those days, he was always a rouseabout.' [36]

The large shearing shed at Toorale was built during the 1880s. In 1889, three years prior to Lawson's arrival, it had been equipped with forty-six mechanical steam-operated shearing stands to align it with its sister property Dunlop. The shed was also furnished with a steam-powered generator to provide electric lighting when natural visibility was poor. As a rule, shearing sheds, because of their design and construction material — generally corrugated iron — tended to be dark inside.

During a shearing season at Toorale, an estimated one hundred men were employed, in addition to the shearers. These included shed hands, stockyard men, musterers and cooks. The musterers worked from camps established over most of the holding, which extended some 75 miles (120 km) from the shearing shed on the Darling River to the Nocolechie boundary near Kulkyne Creek. Here they rounded up the scattered mobs of sheep and slowly herded them towards the massive holding yards at the shearing shed. A large wool-scouring plant had also been established around 1880 by the previous owner, Samuel Wilson, an uncle of the McCaughey brothers.

For the first time, Henry Lawson experienced life in the western shearing sheds with a group of toughened men from the bush. Never before had he seen sheep shorn on such a large scale, and the experience stimulated his senses. He spent hours taking notes and jotting ideas for future writing.

Meanwhile, Lawson's moods fluctuated. Although the experience was providing good 'copy', he disliked working in the shed and considered the life uncivilised and lacking in culture. His partial deafness set him apart from the others and he spent most of the evenings lying on his bunk. To his dismay, the Sydney poet found he had little in common with the rough bush workers.

Jim Gordon offered some insight when he wrote: 'In those days his deafness rather served him well, as he could lie on his bunk in a rouseabouts' hut amidst the clatter and rattle of dish-washing and the babble of the tongues of the yarn-spinners and card-players after tea, and write until he was sleepy'.[37] But there were darker moments.

Henry was moody most of the evenings, as a rule lying on his bunk from tea time until lights were out, talking very little and gazing at the cobwebby corrugated iron roof ... There were nights, though, when he would suggest a walk, and we might stroll a mile or so by some dusty bush track, at times meeting the Royal Mail Coach on its long night journey to Wanaaring. Lawson often seemed moved and a little excited as in a cloud of dust and with a rattle and clocking of axles and the creak of leather, the mail rolled past.[38]

It is difficult to imagine what Gordon was actually referring to with the Wanaaring coach. The coach did not pass either Fort Bourke or Toorale shearing sheds. Instead it followed the Bourke–Wanaaring road for the whole distance of 120 miles (190 km) and took two nights and one day of travelling to complete the journey, one way. The only time the pair would have seen the Wanaaring road was when they later trekked from Goonery, an outstation of Toorale, to the Gumbalie Hotel on the Warrego.

J. F. Archibald was obviously privy to Lawson's whereabouts and plans. On 1 December he wrote to the poet, asking if he intended returning to Sydney or if he planned on trekking until he reached the Gulf of Carpentaria.[39] The letter found Lawson at Toorale, where the shearing season was all but finished. Whether Lawson bothered to reply or not is unknown.

While in the shearing shed and tramping the western tracks, Lawson's mate was Gordon. It was in these outback shearing sheds that the culture of mateship manifested itself in those early years of unionism. And along with loyalty to the great cause of Labour, it was the sense of mateship and bush camaraderie that became the core of unionism and solidarity. However no mateship existed, nor was any love lost, between the unionists and non-unionists, or the unionists and pastoralists during those years of strike activity in eastern Australia. Lawson explained:

> A Bushman always has a mate to comfort him and argue with him, and work and tramp and drink with him, and lend him quids when he's hard up, and call him a b— fool, and fight him sometimes; to abuse him to his face and defend his name behind his back; to bear false witness and perjure his soul for his sake; to lie to the girl for him if he's single, and to his wife if he's married; to secure a 'pen' for him at a shed where he isn't on the spot . . . And each would take the word of the other against all the world, and each believes that the other is the straightest chap that ever lived — 'a white man!' And next best of your mate is the man you're tramping, riding, working or drinking with . . . When a man drops mateship altogether and takes

to 'hatting' in the Bush, it's a step towards a convenient tree and a couple of saddle-straps buckled together.[40]

Thus Lawson defined mateship. Though he was a dedicated supporter of the ideals of mateship, it is interesting to note that the characters in his writings are often solitary souls, even when in the company of others. Many, particularly those inhabitants of the bush, seem to carry some great burden of sorrow or despair, or suffer some great and monstrous misfortune from which they never recover. In some ways they seem to mirror Lawson's own life and the way he regarded himself as a loner within society.

Jim Gordon elaborated on the fact that, apart from his sense of isolation within society, Lawson had a great affinity with his fellow men — his mates — who worked both in Bourke and the Bush: 'He was a stalwart mate, generous and unselfish, and ever ready and willing to take more than his own share of the hardships — and God knows there were plenty.' [41]

A good example of Lawson's views of mateship can be found in 'A Sketch of Mateship', which was published in *Children of the Bush* in 1902.

A SKETCH OF MATESHIP

Bill and Jim, professional shearers, were coming into Bourke from the Queensland side. They were horsemen and had two packhorses. At the last camp before Bourke Jim's packhorse got disgusted and homesick during the night and started back for the place where he was foaled. Jim was little more than a new-chum jackaroo; he was no Bushman and generally got lost when he went down the next gully. Bill was a Bushman, so it was decided that he should go back to look for the horse.

Now Bill was going to sell his packhorse, a well-bred mare, in Bourke, and he was anxious to get her into the yards before the horse sales were over; this was to be the last day of the sales. Jim was the best 'barracker' of the two; he had great imagination; he was a very entertaining story-teller and conversationalist in social life, and a glib and most impressive liar in business, so it was decided that he should hurry on into Bourke with the mare and sell her for Bill. Seven pounds, reserve.

Next day Bill turned up with the missing horse and saw Jim standing against a verandah post of the Carriers' Arms, with his hat down over his eyes, and thoughtfully spitting in the dust. Bill rode over to him.

' 'Ullo, Jim.'

' 'Ullo, Bill. I see you got him.'

'Yes, I got him.'

Pause.

'Where'd yer find him?'

' 'Bout ten mile back. Near Ford's Bridge. He was just feedin' along.'

Pause. Jim shifted his feet and spat in the dust.

'Well,' said Bill at last. 'How did you get on, Jim?'

'Oh, all right,' said Jim. 'I sold the mare.'

'That's right,' said Bill. 'How much did she fetch?'

'Eight quid;' then, rousing himself a little and showing some emotion, 'An' I could 'a' got ten quid for her if I hadn't been a dam' fool.'

'Oh, that's good enough,' said Bill.

'I could 'a' got ten quid if I'd 'a' waited.'

'Well, it's no use cryin'. Eight quid is good enough. Did you get the stuff?'

'Oh, yes. They parted all right. If I hadn't been such a dam' fool an' rushed it, there was a feller that would 'a' given ten quid for that mare.'

'Well, don't break yer back about it,' said Bill. 'Eight is good enough.'

'Yes. But I could 'a' got ten,' said Jim, languidly, putting his hand in his pocket.

Pause. Bill sat waiting for him to hand over the money; but Jim

119

withdrew his hand empty, stretched, and said:

'Ah, well, Bill, I done it in. Lend us a couple o' notes.'

Jim had been drinking and gambling all night and he'd lost the eight pounds as well as his own money.

Bill didn't explode. What was the use? He should have known that Jim wasn't to be trusted with money in town. It was he who had been the fool. He sighed and lent Jim a pound, and they went in to have a drink.

Now it strikes me that if this had happened in a civilised country (like England) Bill would have had Jim arrested and gaoled for larceny as a bailee, or embezzlement, or whatever it was. And would Bill or Jim or the world have been any better for it?

Over the years, many people claimed mateship with Lawson during his days in Bourke. These were the men he met in the western towns and woolsheds, and 'on the track'. One such man was Jimmy Gibbs. Gibbs was known as a 'gun' shearer and during his shearing career he created many records for the number of sheep shorn in individual sheds. He made a name for himself as one who shore over the longest period of time, both in sheds in New South Wales and Queensland. In later years he claimed that he had shorn a total of 1,600,000 sheep during his shearing career.

Gibbs was well known in western circles and he made his permanent home in Bourke while shearing in the general region of the upper Darling. He appears to have had a regular stand at Toorale shearing shed, later claiming that he shore there in 1890 for twenty weeks, and again in 1891 for a period of six months when forty-four shearers supposedly shore the unprecedented number of 382,000 sheep. Gibbs also claimed that he shore 18,000 himself at Toorale during the 1891 season which he maintained was a record for any one man at one shed.

In the early 1900s an unknown poet recorded the deeds of Jimmy Gibbs when the following poem.

JIMMY GIBBS THE SHEARER

He is known by all the woolmen
Who travel out for the sheds,
The 'Bidgee, Lachlan, Bogan, Paroo,
Darling and Warrego heads;
He is not a giant in stature,
But he is a regular terror to work,
And he is going strong and willing
At 'Toorale' not far from Bourke.

May he live to pen some hundreds
Of sovereigns — aye and more.
And drop the scorching Boggi*
And be wealthy instead of poor;
And shearers and men of the future,
As they belt wool from weathers' ribs
Will be telling the tales of old hands
And be asking: 'Did you know Jimmy Gibbs?'

* *Boggi*: shearer's handpiece

Jimmy Gibbs later wrote in his memoirs:

. . . I knew Henry Lawson for many years; he used to be a wool-roller at 'Toorale' on the Darling River near Bourke for 4 seasons, while I shore there. I also shore in other sheds that he worked in for a number of years too. He was a very quiet man and when he and his mate finished a shed they used to get drinking at the first town or roadside pub they came to and spent every bob and not even buy clothes. He always had old clothes on and well patched-up and nearly always wore a cotton shirt with the sleeves undone at the wrist. He carried his swag all over Queensland and N.S.W. too, mostly wool-rolling in woolsheds. He knew all the stations in both states, roadside rules, and towns. I travelled a lot myself shearing, from one shed to another, and I have met him and his mate in dozens of different places on the track for hundreds of miles around the Bourke district, and beyond Wanaaring to the Paroo, and also in

121

the Charleville and Cunnamulla country, and there was not many that knew him much better than I did and there is no doubt he was a great bush poet . . . [42]

While it is possible that Jimmy Gibbs met Lawson at Toorale during the 1892 shearing season, and the pair could have renewed their acquaintance on the Paroo River early in 1893, Lawson certainly did not spend four seasons around the Darling and never worked at Charleville or Cunnamulla. Jimmy Gibbs left Bourke about 1908. He died in the Toowoomba district during the early 1940s.

Although Lawson grew up in the central west of New South Wales, he wrote little to suggest that he had, at any time, a natural affinity with the bush. This was confirmed after Lawson's return from Bourke to the city by A. G. Stephens.

Lawson hates the bush, he is blind to its beauty, deaf to the cheerful strain heard continuously through the sighing of the wilderness. His six months journey to the Queensland border in 1892, the basis of all he has written of Australia's outback, was like the journey of a damned soul swaggering through purgatory, and Lawson persisted in looking at Australia through the memories of these six months.

Stephen's estimation of the time spent by Lawson on the western tracks was an exaggeration. Altogether his travels would have taken no more than eight weeks out of the nine months he spent in Bourke and the region west of the Darling.

Edwin Brady and Jim Gordon held a different opinion to Stephen's. Brady, a long-time friend of Lawson's, once wrote 'If you search certain lines of Lawson's verse you will find therein a burning country love.'[43] Jim Gordon, in describing Lawson's attitude toward the bush, reveals the same view.

Lawson loved the bush and mostly all it contained therein — its rivers and old homesteads with their straggling bridle paths and winding tracks. He saw beauty in the plain with its cruel mirages, and found charm in the great silences of the nights of the Never-

Never. None of them were lost romances to him, and although he knew the tragedy and pathos that inevitably follow the footsteps of those who pioneer new lands, amongst it all he found content and friendship. [44]

Apart from Edwin Brady and Jim Gordon, no other person who lived or worked with Lawson claimed that Lawson held any great affinity with Australia's outback in general. Knowing Lawson's changeable moods, Gordon's assessment of Lawson's love of the bush was probably quite valid if all was going in the poet's favour. But as Lawson and Gordon later struggled along the lonely tracks west of the Darling, under the most adverse conditions, the situation was not always agreeable.

Love or hate, Lawson rarely wrote of the beauty of the bush, preferring instead to dwell on its harshness and, particularly where Bourke and its surrounding districts was concerned, its bitter aspects of life and great isolation. Later Lawson defended his views, saying:

I have been accused of painting the bush in the darkest of colours from some equally dark personal motives. I might be biased — having been there; but it is time the general public knew the back country as it is — no one who has not been there can realise the awful desolation of Out Back in ordinary seasons. [45]

The physical adversities Lawson encountered during his time in the west eventually became the central theme of his many outback-inspired poems and stories, and in 'Some Popular Australian Mistakes', he set out to correct any disillusions that city folk may have had about the bush.

SOME POPULAR AUSTRALIAN MISTAKES
[published in the *Bulletin*, 18 November 1893]

1. An Australian mirage does not look like water; it looks too dry and dusty.

2. A plain is not necessarily a wide, open space covered with waving grass or green sward, like a prairie (the prairie isn't necessarily that way either, but that's an American mistake, not an Australian one);

it is either a desert or a stretch of level country covered with wretched scrub.

3. A river is not a broad, shining stream with green banks and tall, dense eucalypti walls; it is more often a string of muddy waterholes — 'a chain of dry waterholes', someone said.

4. There are no 'mountains' out West; only ridges on the floors of hell.

5. There are no forests; only mongrel scrubs.

6. Australian poetical writers invariably get the coastal scenery mixed up with that of 'out back'.

7. An Australian Western homestead is not an old-fashioned, gable-ended, brick-and-shingle building with avenues and parks; and the squatter doesn't live there, either. A Western station, at best, is a collection of slab and galvanised-iron sheds and humpies, and is the hottest, driest, dustiest, and most God-forsaken hole you could think of; the manager lives there — when compelled to do so.

8. The manager is not called the 'super'; he is called the 'overseer', — which name fits him better.

9. Station-hands are not noble, romantic fellows; they are mostly crawlers to the boss — which they have to be. Shearers — the men of the West — despise station-hands.

10. Men tramping in search of a 'shed' are not called 'sundowners' or 'swaggies'; they are 'trav'lers'.

11. A swag is not generally referred to as a 'bluey' or 'Matilda' — it is *called* a 'swag'.

12. No bushman thinks of 'going on the wallaby' or 'walking Matilda', or 'padding the hoof'; he goes on the track — when forced to it.

13. You do not 'hump bluey' — you simply 'carry your swag'.

14. You do not stow grub — you 'have some tucker, mate'.

15. (Item for our Australian artists) A traveller rarely, if ever, carries a stick; it suggests a common suburban loafer, back-yards, clothes-lines, roosting fowls, watch dogs, blind men, sewer pipes, and goats eating turnip-parings.

16. (For artists). No traveller out back carries a horse-collar swag — it's too hot; and the swag is not carried by a strap passed round the chest but round *one* shoulder. The nose (tucker) bag hangs over the other shoulder and balances the load nicely — when there's anything in the bag.

17. It's not glorious and grand and free to be on the track. Try it.

18. A shearing-shed is not what city people picture it to be — if they imagine it at all; it is perhaps the most degrading hell on the face of this earth. Ask any better-class shearer.

19. An Australian lake is not a lake; it is either a sheet of brackish water or a patch of dry sand.

20. Least said about shanties the better.

21. The poetical bushman does not exist; the majority of the men out back now are from the cities. The real native out-back bushman is narrow-minded, densely ignorant, invulnerably thick-headed. How could he be otherwise?

22. The blackfellow is a fraud. A white man *can* learn to throw the boomerang as well as an aborigine — even better. A blackfellow is *not* to be depended on with regard to direction, distance, or weather. A blackfellow once offered to take us to better water than that at which we were camping. He said it was only half-a-mile. We rolled up our swags and followed him and his gin five miles through the scrub to a mud-hole with a dead bullock in it. Also, he said that it would rain that night; and it didn't rain there for six months. Moreover, he threw a boomerang at a rabbit and lamed one of his dogs — of which he had about 150.

23, etc. Half the bushmen are *not* called 'Bill', nor the other half 'Jim'. We knew a shearer whose name was Reginald! Jim doesn't tell pathetic yarns in bad doggerel in a shearers' hut — if he did, the men would tap their foreheads and wink.

In conclusion. We wish to heaven that Australian writers would leave off trying to make a paradise out of the Out Back Hell; if only out of consideration for the poor, hopeless, half-starved wretches who carry swags through it and look in vain for work — and ask in vain for tucker very often. What's the good of making a heaven of a hell when by describing it as it really is we might do some good for the lost souls there.

'Bush Terms' was a short piece written along similar lines as 'Some Popular Australian Mistakes'. It was published in the *Worker*.

BUSH TERMS

Swagmen are called 'travellers' out back. The word 'sundowner' is only used by squatters and people who know little about the bush, and is an insult. Men travelling on foot are 'footmen', as distinguished from 'horsemen'. 'Humping bluey' is referred to as 'carrying your swag', and 'padding the hoof' is simply 'tramping'. The 'super' is called the 'overseer' — and it fits him better. Bushmen don't 'go on the wallaby', they 'go on the track'. And so on.

The old bush terms have died out with the old poetical bushman — who never existed; and the country has lost nothing, except poetry. The scenery out back isn't like Illawarra. And so on without limit.

All of which might be new, interesting, and perhaps startling to most Australian poets. We found it was also painful.

'Trav'ler comin', mate!'

According to Lawson, he never visited the village of Louth, although he was only a few miles from it during his time at the Toorale shearing shed. However, in retrospect he recorded how he imagined (or perhaps had been told) the village to be. The resulting sketch, 'Louth, On the Darling', was published in the *Worker* on 29 July 1893.

LOUTH, ON THE DARLING

We never saw Louth. We started to hump bluey there once — it was in the drought of eighty something — but we gave it best, just in time, and started back, carrying the swag thirty miles a day, and sustained only by a wild hope that reason would stick to her throne till such time as we sighted a policeman and got him to lock us up for our own protection, as a person unfit to be at large. We don't know whether reason clung as desperately to her seat as we to the hope, which was all we had to cling to. We are not even now sure that she wasn't jolted off that time — certain enemies and friends seem to think that she was.

However, we can imagine Louth — especially on a Sunday afternoon. Two or three wooden humpies, badly in need of paint — a scrimpy swag here and there under a tree along the river bank, and maybe a tent, or a bag — and the mia-mia — and a sad and dusty sheepdog — a primitive steamboat — and perhaps a barge tied up to the river bank — severe dry rot above the waterline everywhere, and the other rot below — the usual pub, with warped and cracked weatherboards, suffering from dry rot — and half-a-dozen men standing at the end, by the uncertain chimney, playing pitch-and-toss, and one or two others sitting on their heels against the wall and spitting in semi-circles, all more or less dry rotted.

Blazing drought overhead and all round, burning the Darling banks to ashes, and audibly baking the land for a depth of several feet.

We can even hear — though in a drowsy, faraway murmur — the language of the interior of our native land:

'Heads a quid — heads half-a-quid — heads a crown — a caser heads — heads half-a-caser — *heads half-a-crown!* Well, such a — lot of — I blanky well never seen! What yer frightened of? . . . Heads a crown — heads a half — heads another half! . . . Look out behind! Heads one! . . . Look out behind! Tails! No, that sort of tossin' won't do — spin 'em up again, proper . . . Look out behind! Heads one! . . . Look out behind! HEADS!'

'Heads a quid — heads half-a-quid — heads a crown, etc.'

'Come on and have a drink, all you chaps!'

Our attention was first directed to Louth by a letter to the *Out Back Advocate*. We saw the printers' copy. It came wrapped in a tract, and it said:

'DEAR SUR,

Kindly alow me to traspis on yur valeable spase and oblige. Ther is no chirch at Lowth and very little pleese supervison. The roughest charactres congratulate here on Sunday evening larst the quite of the Sabarth was broken by the sounds of a fiddel and the scufling of feat dancing from one of the howses and, what is more a comeic song. Its known to be a bad howse and the man is a bad charactre, and what was worse ther was woman ther some is supposed to be rispectabel gurls what are parents doing is the Lod's day to be disgrazed in this manner I will trispas no more on yor valubel spaze a chirch is badly neded in Lowth also more pleese what's the law doin that it ain't done nothing towords perventing Sarbath Breaking which is on the panefull increaze in australia. Thanking you for trespazing on yor valubel spaze I remane yors truely

A GOD FEARING CHRISTHEN'

We were surprised, but not exactly by the awful depravity of Louth, as exposed by the Christian — we are afraid that our sympathy was inclined towards the wrong parties. They could find a ray of pleasure, then, even there; when the drought and rabbits were ruining all the land, and when the Unionists sadly shouldered their swags and tramped away, penniless and hungry, from the hopeless, one-sided fight they lost.

We are haunted, too, but not exactly in the right way, by the 'sounds of the fiddle' and the 'scuffling of feet and dancing', and the 'comic song', and we can even find a small place in the corner of our heart for the 'hard case' who kept that shanty. God forgive us all — the 'Christian' included.

Contrary to Lawson's portrayal, Louth of the early 1890s was a flourishing village. It was a river port where local wool was collected and taken by boat upstream to the railhead at Bourke. Consignments of copper ingots were also brought from nearby Cobar by bullock teams, to be transported downriver by steamer and barge to Morgan in South Australia

Besides a substantial brick post office and residence which had been erected during the 1880s, Louth possessed a school, police station and the Dan O'Connell Hotel, which had been built by Thomas Mathews, the founder of the town. A large ferry operated across the river for the crossing of sheep, Cobb & Co. coaches and the travelling public, and the electric telegraph had already been extended, via Louth, along the entire Darling River. In 'Louth, on the Darling', Lawson embroidered his tale with drab and dismal scenes, instead of describing the village as it really was. The sketch is a prime example of his use of exaggeration to emphasize his long-held views on the bush.

Court House — Bourke, NSW

CHAPTER 9

Of Rouseabouts and Shearing Sheds

For Wool, Tallow and Hides and Co.,
For Wool, Tallow and Hides —
Over the roofs of hell we go
For Wool, Tallow and Hides.[46]

The shearing sheds provided work for shearers and rouseabouts, wool classers and pressers, foremen and 'experts' who were in charge of sharpening the combs and cutters and keeping the massive steam engines running. The all-important cooks were usually criticised by the shearers for their somewhat sub-standard culinary endeavours. Associated workers were the wool-scourers (wool-washing) and the stockmen employed in mustering and lamb marking.

Although Henry Lawson worked in the shearing sheds of the Bourke district for only a few weeks, the experience gave him a wonderful insight into the life of the outback shearer. While his writings show alternately a respect for these men, coupled with a sense that they often overstated their own importance, Lawson saw the men of the outback sheds as a breed of their own. As he later wrote in 'Crime in the Bush', which was published in the *Bulletin*:

> The shearer is a social animal at his worst; he is often a city bushman
> — *i.e.*, a man who has been through and round and between the
> provinces by rail and boat. Not unfrequently he is an English public
> school man and a man of the world; so even the veriest out-back
> bushie, whose metropolis is Bourke, is brought in touch with outside
> civilisation.

Despite his partial deafness, Lawson was an astute listener and managed to absorb the idiom of the shearers quickly. This is demonstrated in an excerpt from a later poem 'Years After the War In Australia' which was published in *Verses Popular and Humorous*:

> *The big rough boys from the runs Out Back were first*
> *   where the balls flew free,*
> *And yelled in the slang of the Outside Track: 'By*
> *   God, it's a Christmas spree!'*
> *'It's not too dusty' — and 'Wool away! — stand clear*
> *   of the blazing shoots!'*
> *'Sheep O! Sheep O!' — 'We'll cut out today' —*
> *   'Look out for the boss's boots!'*
> *'What price the tally in camp tonight!' — 'What price*
> *   the boys Out Back!'*
> *'Go it, you tigers, for Right or Might and the pride of*
> *   the Outside Track!' —*
> *'Needle and thread!' — 'I have broke my comb!' —*
> *   'Now ride, you flour-bags, ride!'*
> *'Fight for your mates and the folks at home!' —*
> *   'Here's for the Lachlan side!'*
> *Those men of the West would sneer and scoff at the*
> *   gates of hell ajar.*

*And oft the sight of a head cut off was hailed by a yell
of 'Tar!'*

At Toorale Lawson found a setting which formed his scenario for the outback shearer and the culture of the Australian shearing shed. He was often tardy in writing about those things he had seen in the bush, however he stored his Toorale research material, bringing it out years later to compose a series of shearing-based poems and stories — 'The Boss's Boots', 'The Boss Over the Board' and so on. Most of the shearing sequence appears to have been written during the late 1890s, long after Lawson had departed from Bourke. And while Lawson's 1892–93 writings concerning the bush were full of the misery of the outback, it is interesting to note that the later shearing series, written perhaps in a mood of nostalgia when time had softened his views, exhibits an unusual mixture of comedy and pathos. Lawson discovered during his time at Toorale that shearers were men of great stamina who managed, despite the harsh living conditions of the times, to find humour in everyday life.

The shearing sheds of the 1890s provided anything but a peaceful working environment and an abrasive situation existed between the shearers and management. Apart from the ever-present threat of strike action and employer–employee friction, the pressure of hot western summers and poor working conditions in the stuffy corrugated-iron shearing sheds meant that the Australian shearer considered himself abused and unappreciated. The conditions in the quarters where the shearers and shed-hands slept, ate their meals and spent their leisure hours also left much to be desired.

In 1892 Jimmy James held the position of superintendent of Toorale shearing shed, under the instruction of the manager, John McCaughey. In shearing terms this position was generally known as 'boss-of-the-board'. Jimmy was a short, energetic man who regularly walked briskly up and down the full length of the shearing board so he could check on the standard of work. He personally penalised any shearer who did not shear in a clean and proper manner by marking his sheep with raddle (coloured chalk). Such shearing would be paid at a lesser rate and the amount deducted from the shearer's tally.

It was Jimmy James who provided Lawson with the inspiration for his poem 'The Boss's Boots'. Jim Gordon confirmed this when he wrote: 'Jimmie James was boss-of-the-board — small and dapper, with neat, well-kept boots. It was from him Henry got the idea for the "Boss's Boots":- "The shearers squint along the pens, they squint along the shoots . . ."' [47]

Local legend claimed that Jimmy James wore highly-polished, elastic-sided boots, or sidesprings as they were more commonly known. The shearers, as they crouched over their sheep, regularly cast sideways glances at every pair of shoes that appeared near them to make sure they were not those belonging to the boss-of-the-board on a tour of inspection.

As a keen observer of human behaviour, Lawson noted the situation, filed the information away for further use, and later used the scene to compose 'The Boss's Boots'. Published in the *Bulletin* on 11 December 1897, this poem contains a considerable element of humour which distracts from the harshness of the shearing shed administration.

THE BOSS'S BOOTS

The shearers squint along the pens, they squint along
the 'shoots';
The shearers squint along the board to catch the Boss's
boots;
They have no time to straighten up, they have no time
to stare,
But when the Boss is looking on, they like to be aware.

The 'rouser' has no soul to save. Condemn the
rouseabout!
And sling 'em in, and rip 'em through, and get the
bell-sheep out;
And skim it by the tips at times, or take it with
the roots,

But 'pink' 'em* nice and pretty when you see the
    Boss's boots.

The shearing super sprained his foot, as bosses
    sometimes do —
And wore, until the shed cut out, one 'side-spring' and
    one shoe;
And though he changed his pants at times — some
    worn-out and some neat —
No 'tiger' there could possibly mistake the Boss' feet.

The Boss affected larger boots than many Western
    men,
And Jim the Ringer swore the shoe was half as big
    again;
And tigers might have heard the boss ere any harm was
    done —
For when he passed it was a sort of dot and carry one.

But now there comes a picker-up who sprained his
    ankle, too,
And limping round the shed he found the Boss's cast-
    off shoe,
He went to work, all legs and arms, as green-hand
    rousers will,
And never dreamed of Boss's boots — much less of
    Bogan Bill.

(Ye sons of sin that tramp and shear in hot and
    dusty scrubs,
Just keep away from 'headin' 'em' and keep away
    from pubs,
And keep away from handicaps — for so your
    sugar scoots —

And you may own a station yet and wear the
　　Boss's boots.)

And Bogan by his mate was heard to mutter through
　　his hair:
'The Boss has got a rat to-day; he's buckin'
　　everywhere —
He's trainin' for a bike, I think, the way he comes an'
　　scoots,
He's like a bloomin' cat on mud the way he shifts his
　　boots.'

Now Bogan Bill was shearing rough and chanced to
　　cut a teat;
He stuck his leg in front at once, and slewed the ewe a
　　bit;
He hurried up to get her through, when, close beside
　　his shoot,
He saw a large and ancient shoe, in mateship with a
　　boot.

He thought that he'd be fined all right — he couldn't
　　turn the 'yoe';
The more he wished the boss away, the more he
　　wouldn't go;
And Bogan swore amenfully — beneath his breath he
　　swore —
And he was never known to 'pink' so prettily before.

And Bogan through his bristling scalp in his mind's eye
　　could trace
The cold, sarcastic smile that lurked about the Boss's
　　face;
He cursed him with a silent curse in language known
　　to few,

He cursed him from his boot right up, and then down
    to his shoe.

But while he shore so mighty clean, and while he
    screened the teat,
He fancied there was something wrong about the
    Boss's feet;
The boot grew unfamiliar, and the odd shoe seemed
    awry,
And slowly up the trouser went the tail of Bogan's eye.

Then swiftly to the features from a plaited green-hide
    belt —
You'd have to ring a shed or two to feel as Bogan felt —
For 'twas his green-hand picker-up (who wore a
    vacant look),
And Bogan saw the Boss outside consulting with his
    cook.

And Bogan Bill was hurt and mad to see that
    rouseabout;
And Bogan laid his 'Wolseley'** down and knocked
    that rouser out;
He knocked him right across the board, he tumbled
    through the shoot —
'I'll learn the fool,' said Bogan Bill, 'to flash the Boss's
    boot!'

The rouser squints along the pens, he squints along the
    shoots,
And gives his men the office when they miss the Boss's
    boots.
They have no time to straighten up, they're too well-
    bred to stare
But when the Boss is looking on they like to be aware.

The rouser has no soul to lose — it's blarst the
rouseabout!
And rip 'em through and yell for 'tar' and get the
bell-sheep out.
And take it with the scum at times or take it with
the roots,
But 'pink' 'em nice and pretty when you see the
Boss's boots.

* *pink 'em*: shear them
** *Wolseley*: shearer's handpiece

The job of boss-of-the-board was a lonely one. Although regarded by the station owner as a mere employee, the shearers did not consider the holder of the position as part of their own shearing fraternity. Any principled union shearer automatically hated the boss, not necessarily because he was an unlikable character but because of what he stood for — the dominance over the shearers by the pastoralists. Or, as Lawson so aptly put it in 'A Rough Shed': 'We hate the boss because he *is* the boss' and 'We hate the boss-of-the-board as the shearers' slushy hates the shearers' cook. I don't know why. He's a very fair boss.'

'The Boss Over the Board' illustrates the problems of those who worked in Australian shearing sheds under the trying conditions of an outback summer (even spring weather could be most uncomfortable). The poem concerns a fist-fight between the supervisor and a union shearer and reveals the hatred and aggression that existed in the sheds at that time. Lawson writes of the shed as being 'a blacklisted shed down the Darling', which Toorale was at the time. It was also considered to be a rough shed, having been involved in a fair share of strike activity in the past, and was unpopular because it employed a mixture of union and non-union shearers. The boss could have been the same Jimmy James from 'The Boss's Boots'.

THE BOSS OVER THE BOARD

When he's over a rough and unpopular shed,
With the sins of the bank and the men on his head;

And he musn't look black or indulge in a grin,
And thirty or forty men hate him like Sin —
I am moved to admit — when the total is scored —
That it's just a bit off for the Boss-of-the-board.
  I have battled a lot,
    But my dreams never soared
To the lonely position of Boss-of-the-board.

'Twas a black-listed shed down the Darling: the Boss
Was a small man to see — though a big man to cross.
We had nought to complain of — except what we
      thought,
And the Boss didn't boss any more than he ought;
But the Union was booming, and Brotherhood soared,
So we hated like poison the Boss-of-the-board.
  We could tolerate 'hands',
    We respected the cook;
But the name of the Boss was a blot in our book.

He'd a row with Big Duggan — a rough sort was Jim —
Or, rather, Jim Duggan was 'laying' for him!
Jim's hate of Injustice and Greed was so deep
That his shearing grew rough, and he ill-used the
      sheep.
And I fancied that Duggan his manliness lower'd
When he took off his shirt to the Boss-of-the-board.
  For the Boss was ten stone,
    And the shearer full-grown,
And he might have, they said, let the crawler alone.

Though some of us there wished the fight to the strong,
Yet we knew in our hearts that the shearer was wrong.
And the crawler was plucky, it can't be denied,
For he had to fight Freedom and Justice beside;

But he came up so gamely, as often as floored,
That a black-leg stood up for the Boss-of-the-board!
  And the fight was a sight,
  And we pondered that night —
'It's surprising how some of those blacklegs can fight!'

Next day at the office, when sadly the wreck
Of Jim Duggan came up like a lamb for his cheque,
Said the Boss, 'Don't be childish! It's all past and
    gone;
I'm short of good shearers. You'd better stay on.'
And we fancied Jim Duggan our dignity lower'd
When he stopped to oblige a damned Boss-of-the-
    board.
  We said nothing to Jim —
  Such a joke might be grim,
And the subject, we saw, was distasteful to him.

The Boss just went on as he'd done from the first,
And he favoured Big Duggan no more than the worst;
And when we'd cut out and the steamer came down —
With the hawkers and spielers — to take us to town,
And we'd all got aboard, 'twas Jim Duggan, good
    Lord!
Who yelled for three cheers for the Boss-of-the-board.
  'Twas a bit off, no doubt —
  And with Freedom about —
But a lot is forgot when a shed is cut out.
With Freedom of Contract maintained in his shed,
And the curse of the Children of Light on his head,
He's apt to long sadly for sweetheart or wife,
And his views be inclined to the dark side of life.
Then Truth must be spread and the Cause must be
    shored —

But it's just a bit rough on the Boss-of-the-board.
I am all for the Right,
But perhaps (out of sight)
As a son or a husband or father he's white.

Women were generally not received favourably by shearers into their workplace. The shed, they considered, was a man's domain and the catchcry of 'ducks on the pond' was often used to herald an unwelcome female arrival. Regarding women as a distraction, the men were also embarrassed at their own dirty, sweaty appearance after working for hours in the heat. Lawson's short sketch, 'Ladies in the Shed', was published in the *Worker* on 4 November 1893. It was later re-written as verse, re-named 'When the Ladies Come to the Shearing Shed', and published in the *Bulletin* on 11 December 1897 and later in *Verses Popular and Humorous*.

WHEN THE LADIES CAME TO THE SHEARING SHED

'The ladies are coming,' the super says
To the shearers sweltering there,
And 'the ladies' means in the shearing-shed:
'Don't cut 'em too bad. Don't swear.'
The ghost of a pause in the shed's rough heart,
And lower is bowed each head;
And nothing is heard, save a whispered word,
And the roar of the shearing-shed.

The tall, shy rouser has lost his wits;
And his limbs are all astray;
He leaves a fleece on the shearing-board,
And his broom in the shearer's way.
There's a curse in store for that jackaroo
As down by the wall he slants —
And the ringer bends with his legs askew
And wishes he'd 'patched them pants'.

They are girls from the city. (Our hearts rebel
As we squint at their dainty feet.)
And they gush and say in a girly way
That the 'dear little lambs' are 'sweet'.
And Bill, the ringer, who'd scorn the use
Of a childish word like 'damn',
Would give a pound that his tongue was loose
As he tackles a lively lamb.

Swift thoughts of homes in the coastal towns —
Or rivers and waving grass —
And a weight on our hearts that we cannot define
That comes as the ladies pass.
But the rouser ventures a nervous dig
In the ribs of the next to him;
And Barcoo says to his pen-mate: 'Twig
The style of the last un, Jim.'

Jim Moonlight gives her a careless glance —
Then he catches his breath with pain —
His strong hand shakes, and the sunbeams dance
As he bends to his work again.
But he's well disguised in a bristling beard,
Bronzed skin, and his shearer's dress;
And whatever Jim Moonlight or hoped or feared
Were hard for his mates to guess.

Jim Moonlight, wiping his broad, white brow,
Explains, with a doleful smile;
'A stitch in the side', and 'I'm all right now' —
But he leans on the beam awhile,
And gazes out in the blazing noon
On the clearing, brown and bare —
She had come and gone, like a breath of June,
In December's heat and glare.

The bushmen are big rough boys at the best,
With hearts of a larger growth;
But they hide those hearts with a brutal jest,
And the pain with a reckless oath.
Though the Bills and Jims of the bush-bard sing
Of their life loves, lost or dead.
The love of a girl is a sacred thing
Not voiced in a shearing-shed.

In 'That Pretty Girl in the Army', Lawson identified one of his characters in the poem, Jack Moonlight, when he wrote:

> . . . I caught sight of a swagman coming along the white, dusty road . . . It was John Merrick (Jack Moonlight), one time Shearers' Union Secretary at Coonamble, and generally 'Rep' (Shearers' Representative) in any shed where he sheared. He was a 'better-class shearer', one of those quiet, thoughtful men of whom there are generally two or three in the roughest of rough sheds, who have great influence, and give the shed a good name from a Union point of view . . . I had worked in a shed with Jack Moonlight . . .

While working at Toorale, Lawson came in contact with many types of men, all with different reasons for leaving the towns and cities and heading for the outback. In 'The Ballad of the Rouseabout', he examines the men and their motives, describes their existence, and predicts little for their future. It was published in *Verses Popular and Humorous*.

THE BALLAD OF THE ROUSEABOUT

A rouseabout of rouseabouts, from any land — or
* none —*
I bear a nick-name of the Bush, and I'm a woman's
* son;*
I came from where I camp'd last night, and, at the
* day-dawn glow,*
I rub the darkness from my eyes, roll up my swag, and
* go.*

*Some take the track for bitter pride, some for no pride
    at all —*
*(But to us all the world is wide when driven to the
    wall)*
*Some take the track for gain in life, some take the
    track for loss —*
*And some of us take up the swag as Christ took up the
    Cross.*

*Some take the track for faith in men — some take the
    track for doubt —*
*Some flee a squalid home to work their own salvation
    out.*
*Some dared not see a mother's tears nor meet a father's
    face —*
*Born of good Christian families some leap, head-long,
    from Grace.*

*Oh, we are men who fought and rose, or fell from
    many grades;*
*Some born to lie, and some to pray, we're men of
    many trades;*
*We're men whose fathers were and are of high and low
    degree —*
The sea was open to us, and we sailed across the sea.

*And — were our quarrels wrong or just? — has no
    place in my song —*
*We seared our souls in puzzling as to what was right or
    wrong;*
*We judge not and we are not judged —'tis our
    philosophy —*
*There's something wrong with every ship that sails
    upon the sea.*

From shearing shed to shearing shed we tramp to make
*   a cheque —*
Jack Cornstalk and the ne'er-do-well — the tarboy
*   and the wreck.*
We learn the worth of man to man, and this we learn
*   too well —*
The shanty and the shearing shed are warmer spots
*   than hell!*

I've humped my swag to Bawley Plain, and further
*   out and on;*
I've boiled my billy by the Gulf, and boiled it by the
*   Swan —*
I've thirsted in dry lignum swamps, and thirsted on the
*   sand,*
And eked the fire with camel dung in Never-Never
*   Land.*

I know the track from Spencer's Gulf and north of
*   Cooper's Creek —*
Where falls the half-caste to the strong, 'black velvet'
*   to the weak —*
(From gold-top Flossie in the Strand to half-caste and
*   the gin —*
If they had brains, poor animals! we'd teach them how
*   to sin).*

I've tramped, and camped, and 'shore' and drunk with
*   many mates Out Back —*
And every one to me is Jack because the first was
*   Jack —*
A 'lifer' sneaked from gaol at home — the 'straightest'
*   mate I met —*
A 'ratty' Russian Nihilist* — a British Baronet!

I know the tucker tracks that feed — or leave one in
   the lurch —
The 'Burgoo' (Presbyterian) track — the 'Murphy'
   (Roman Church)
But more the man, and not the track, so much as it
   appears,
For 'battling' is a trade to learn, and I've served seven
   years.

We're haunted by the past at times — and this is very
   bad,
And so we drink till horrors come, lest, sober, we go
   mad
So much is lost Out Back, so much of hell is realised —
A man might skin himself alive and no one be
   surprised.

A rouseabout of rouseabouts, above — beneath
   regard,
I know how soft is this old world, and I have learnt
   how hard —
A rouseabout of rouseabouts — I know what men can
   feel,
I've seen the tears from hard eyes slip as drops from
   polished steel.

I learned what college had to teach, and in the school
   of men
By camp-fires I have learned, or, say, unlearned it all
   again;
But this I've learned, that truth is strong, and if a man
   go straight
He'll live to see his enemy struck down by time and
   fate!

We hold him true who's true to one however false he
    be
(There's something wrong with every ship that lies
    beside the quay);
We lend and borrow, laugh and joke, and when the
    past is drowned
We sit upon our swags and smoke and watch the world
    go round.

*Billy Wood, Bourke unionist, later referred to Lawson's friendship with a man named Ernest De Guinney, who was 'a supposed Russian turned nihilist'. Perhaps Lawson is also referring to the same person here.

As the countryside around Bourke was used mainly for wool production, it was natural that the meat from sheep was the main constituent of the shearers' diet. Not for them a nice juicy lamb roast or a tender lamb-loin chop, but copious quantities of tough, stringy meat from aged sheep, known as 'mutton'. Minced, curried, stewed, fried or boiled: by the end of the shearing season the men were heartily sick of the sight of it and longed for a piece of beef or pork.

'The Greenhand Rouseabout' was published in *Verses Popular and Humorous*. The poem tells how a shearer, after 'cut-out', ordered a long-awaited beef meal in a city restaurant. While he is waiting, he reminisces about the shearing season. Finally his meal is put before him and he discovers, much to his disgust, that he has been mistakenly served with mutton.

THE GREENHAND ROUSEABOUT

Call this hot? I beg your pardon. Hot! — you don't
    know what it means.
(What's that waiter? lamb or mutton! Thank you —
    mine is beef and greens.
Bread and butter while I'm waiting. Milk? Oh, yes —
    a bucketful.)
I'm just in from west the Darling, 'picking-up' and
    'rolling wool'.

146

Mutton stewed or chops for breakfast, dry and
  tasteless, boiled in fat;
Bread or brownie, tea or coffee — two hours' graft in
  front of that;
Legs of mutton boiled for dinner — mutton greasy-
  warm for tea —
Mutton curried (gave my order, beef and plenty greens
  for me).

Breakfast, curried rice and mutton till your innards
  sacrifice,
And you sicken at the colour and the smell of curried
  rice.
All day long with living mutton — bits and belly-wool
  and fleece;
Blinded by the yolk of wool, and shirt and trousers stiff
  with grease,
Till you long for sight of verdure, cabbage-plots and
  water clear,
And you crave for beef and butter as a boozer craves
  for beer.

Dusty patch in baking mulga — glaring iron hut and
  shed —
Feel and smell of rain forgotten — water scarce, and
  feed-grass dead.
Hot and suffocating sunrise — all-pervading, sheep-
  yard smell —
Stiff and aching, green-hand stretches — 'Slushy' rings
  the bullock-bell —
Pint of tea and hunk of brownie — sinners string
  towards the shed —
Great, black, greasy crows round carcass — screen
  behind of dust-cloud red.

147

Engine whistles. 'Go it, tigers!' and the agony begins,
Picking up for seven devils out of Hades — for my
  sins;
Picking up for seven devils, seven demons out of Hell!
Sell their souls to get the sheep-bell — half-a-dozen
  Christs they'd sell!
Day grows hot as where they come from — too
  damned hot for men or brutes;
Roof of corrugated iron, six-foot-six above the shoots!

Whiz and rattle and vibration, like an endless chain of
  trams;
Blasphemy of five-and-forty — prickly heat — and
  stink of rams!
'Barcoo' leaves his pen-door open and the sheep come
  bucking out;
When the rouser goes to pen them, 'Barcoo' blasts the
  rouseabout.
Injury with insult added — trial of our cursing
  powers —
Cursed and cursing back enough to damn a dozen
  worlds like ours.

'Take my combs down to the grinder, will yer?' 'Seen
  my cattle pup?'
'There's a sheep fell down in my shoot — just jump
  down and pick it up.'
'Give the office when the boss comes.' 'Catch that
  gory sheep, old man.'
'Count the sheep in my pen, will yer?' 'Fetch my
  combs back when yer can.'
'When yer get a chance, old feller, will yer pop down
  to the hut?
Fetch my pipe — the cook'll show yer — and I'll let
  yer have a cut.'

*Shearer yells for tar and needle. Ringer's roaring like a
  bull:
'Wool away, you (son of angels). Where the hell's the
  (foundling) WOOL!!'*

*Pound a week and station prices — mustn't kick
  against the pricks —
Seven weeks of lurid mateship — ruined soul and four
  pounds six.*

*What's that? waiter! stuffed mutton! Look here,
  waiter, to be brief,
I said beef! you blood-stained villain! Beef — moo-
  cow — Roast Bullock — BEEF!'*

Not only was the unenviable, endless diet of mutton offered by the
usually surly cook, the meat was butchered in an unhygienic temporary
slaughterhouse nearby. The rouseabouts' hut contained the kitchen,
dining area and sleeping quarters all under one roof. Rough,
uncomfortable bunks were a poor excuse for beds. There were no
proper laundry facilities.

Originally published as 'A Rouseabout of Rouseabouts' in the
Bulletin on 13 January 1900, 'A Rough Shed' provides a valuable
insight into the living conditions of the shearers at the time.

A ROUGH SHED

A hot, breathless, blinding sunrise — the sun having appeared
suddenly above the ragged edge of the barren scrub like a great disc of
molten steel. No hint of a morning breeze before it, no sign on earth
or sky to show that it is morning — save the position of the sun.

A clearing in the scrub — bare as though the surface of the earth
were ploughed and harrowed, and dusty as the road. Two oblong huts
— one for the shearers and one for the rouseabouts — in about the
centre of the clearing (as if even the mongrel scrub had shrunk away

from them) built end-to-end, of weatherboards, and roofed with galvanised iron. Little ventilation; no verandah; no attempt to create, artificially, a breath of air through the buildings. Unpainted, sordid — hideous. Outside, heaps of ashes still hot and smoking. Close at hand, 'butcher's shop' — a bush and bag break-wind in the dust, under a couple of sheets of iron, with offal, grease and clotted blood blackening the surface of the ground about it. Greasy, stinking sheepskins hanging everywhere with the blood-blotched sides out. Grease inches deep in great black patches about the fireplace ends of the huts, where wash-up and 'boiling' water is thrown.

Inside, a rough table on supports driven into the black, greasy ground floor, and formed of flooring boards, running on uneven lines the length of the hut from within about six feet of the fireplace. Lengths of single six-inch boards or slabs on each side, supported by the projecting ends of short pieces of timber nailed across the legs of the table to serve as seats.

On each side of the hut runs a rough framework, like the partitions in a stable; each compartment battened off to about the size of a manger, and containing four bunks, one above the other, on each side — their ends, of course, to the table. Scarcely breathing space anywhere between. Fireplace, the full width of the hut in one end, where all the cooking and baking for forty or fifty men is done, and where flour, sugar, etc., are kept in open bags. Fire, like a very furnace. Buckets of tea and coffee on roasting beds of coals and ashes on the hearth. Pile of 'brownie' on the bare black boards at the end of the table. Unspeakable aroma of forty or fifty men who have little inclination and less opportunity to wash their skins, and who soak some of the grease out of their clothes — in buckets of hot water — on Saturday afternoons or Sundays. And clinging to all, and over all, the smell of dried, stale yolk of wool — the stink of rams!

'I am a rouseabout of the rouseabouts. I have fallen so far that it is beneath me to try to climb to the proud position of "ringer" of the shed. I had that ambition once, when I was the softest of green-hands; but then I thought I could work out my salvation and go home. I've got used to hell since then. I only get twenty-five shillings a week (less station store charges) and tucker here. I have been seven years west of the Darling and never shore a sheep. Why don't I learn to shear, and so make money? What should I do with more money? Get out of this and go home? I would never go home unless I had enough money to keep me for the rest of my life, and I'll never make that Out Back. Otherwise, what should I do at home? And how should I account for the seven years, if I were to go home? Could I describe shed life to them and explain how I lived? They think shearing only takes a few days of the year — at the beginning of summer. They'd want to know how I lived the rest of the year. Could I explain that I "jabbed trotters" and was a "tea-and-sugar burglar" between sheds. They'd think I'd been a tramp and a beggar all the time. Could I explain *anything* so that they'd understand? I'd have to be lying all the time, and would soon be tripped up and found out. For, whatever else I have been, I was never much of a liar. No, I'll never go home.

'I become momentarily conscious about daylight. The flies on the track got me into that habit, I think; they start at daybreak — when the mosquitoes give over.

'The cook rings a bullock bell.

'The cook is fire-proof. He is as a fiend from the nethermost sheol, and needs to be. No man sees him sleep, for he makes bread — or worse, brownie — at night, and he rings a bullock bell loudly at half-past five in the morning to rouse us from our animal torpors. Others, the sheep-ho's or the engine drivers at the shed or wool-wash, call him, if he does sleep. They manage it in shifts, somehow, and sleep somewhere, sometime. We haven't time to know. The cook rings the bullock bell and yells the time. It was the same time five minutes ago — or a year ago. No time to decide which. I dash water over my head and face, and slap handfuls on my eyelids — gummed over aching eyes — still blighted by the yolk o' wool — grey, greasy-feeling water from a cut-down kerosene tin which I sneaked from the cook and hid under my bunk and had the foresight to refill from the cask last night, under cover of warm, still, suffocating darkness. Or was it the night before last? Anyhow, it will be sneaked from me to-day, and from the crawler who will collar it tomorrow, and "touched" and "lifted" and "collared" and recovered by the cook, and sneaked back again, and cause foul language, and fights, maybe, till we 'cut-out'.

'No; we didn't have sweet dreams of home and mother, gentle poet — nor yet of babbling brooks and sweethearts, and love's young dream. We are too dirty and dog-tired when we tumble down, and have too little time to sleep it off. We don't want to dream those dreams out here — they'd only be nightmares for us, and we'd wake to remember. We *mustn't* remember here.

'At the edge of the timber a great galvanised-iron shed, nearly all roof, coming down to within six feet six inches of the "board" over the "shoots". Cloud of red dust in the dead timber behind, going up — noonday dust. Fence covered with skins; carcasses being burned; blue smoke going straight up as in noonday. Great glossy (greasy-glossy) black crows 'flopping' around.

'The first siren has gone. We hurry in single file from opposite ends of rouseabouts' and shearers' huts (as the paths happen to run to the shed) gulping hot tea or coffee from a pint-pot in one hand and biting at a junk of brownie in the other.

'Shed of forty hands. Shearers rush the pens and yank out sheep and throw them like demons; grip them with their knees, take up machines, jerk the strings; and with a rattling, whirring roar the great machine-shed starts for the day.

'"Go it, you — tigers!" yells a tar-boy. "Wool away!" "Tar!" "Sheep Ho!" We rush through with a whirring roar till breakfast time.

'We seize our tin plate from the pile, knife and fork from the candle-box, and crowd round the camp-oven to jab out lean chops, dry as chips, boiled in fat. Chops or curry-and-rice. There is some growling and cursing. We slip into our places without removing our hats. There's no time to hunt for mislaid hats when the whistle goes. Row of hat brims, level, drawn over eyes, or thrust back — according to characters or temperaments. Thrust back denotes a lucky absence of brains, I fancy. Row of forks going up, or jabbing, or poised, loaded, waiting for last mouthful to be bolted.

'We pick up, sweep, tar, sew wounds, catch sheep that break from the pens, jump down and pick up those that can't rise at the bottom of the shoots, "bring-my-combs-from-the-grinder-will-yer", laugh at dirty jokes, and swear — and, in short, are the "will-yer" slaves, body and soul, of seven, six, five or four shearers, according to the distance from the rolling tables.

'The shearer on the board at the shed is a demon. He gets so much a hundred; we, twenty-five shillings a week. He is not supposed, by the rules of the shed, the Union, and humanity, to take a sheep out of the pen *after* the bell goes (smoke-ho, meals, or knock-off) but his watch is hanging on the post, and he times himself to get so many sheep out of the pen *before* the bell goes, and *one more* — the "bell sheep" — as it is ringing. We have to take the last fleece to the table and leave our board clean. We go through the day of eight hours in runs of about an hour and twenty minutes between smoke-ho's — from six to six. If the shearers shore 200 instead of 100, they'd get £2 a day instead of £1, and we'd have twice as much work to do for our twenty-five shillings per week. But the shearers are racing each other for tallies. And it's no use kicking. There is no God here, and no Unionism (though we all have tickets). But what am I growling about? I've worked from six to six with no smoke-ho's for half the wages, and food we wouldn't give the sheep-ho dog. It's the bush growl, born of heat, flies and dust. I'd growl now if I had a thousand a year. We *must* growl, swear, and some of us drink to D.T.s, or go mad sober.

'Pants and shirts stiff with grease as though a couple of pounds of soft black putty were spread on with a painter's knife.

'No, gentle bard! — we don't sing at our work. Over the whirr and roar and hum all day long, and with iteration that is childish and irritating to the intelligent greenhand, float unthinkable adjectives and adverbs, addressed to jumbucks, jackeroos and mates

indiscriminately. And worse words for the boss-over-the-board —
behind his back.

'I came of a Good Christian Family — perhaps that's why I
went to the Devil. When I came out here I'd shrink from the man
who used foul language. In a short time I used it with the worst. I
couldn't help it.

'That's the way of it. If I went back to a woman's country again I
wouldn't swear. I'd forget this as I would a nightmare. That's the way
of it. There's something of the larrikin about us. We don't exist
individually. Off the board, away from the shed (and each other) we
are quiet — even gentle.

'A great-horned ram, in poor condition, but shorn of a heavy
fleece, picks himself up at the foot of the "shoot", and hesitates, as if
ashamed to go down to the other end where the ewes are. The most
ridiculous object under heaven.

'A tar-boy of fifteen, of the bush, has a mouth so vile that a
street-boy, same age (up with a shearing uncle), kicks him behind —
having proved his superiority with his fists before the shed started.
Of which unspeakable little fiend the roughest shearer of a rough
shed was heard to say, in effect, that if he thought there was the
slightest possibility of his becoming the father of such a boy he'd —
take drastic measures to prevent the possibility of his becoming a
proud parent at all.

'Twice a day the cooks and their familiars carry buckets of
oatmeal-water and tea to the shed, two each on a yoke. We cry,
"Where are you coming to, my pretty maids?"

'In ten minutes the surfaces of the buckets are black with flies.
We have given over trying to keep them clear. We stir the living
cream aside with the bottoms of the pints, and guzzle gallons, and
sweat it out again. Occasionally a shearer pauses and throws the
perspiration from his forehead in a rain.

'Shearers live in such a greedy rush of excitement that often a
strong man will, at a prick of the shears, fall in a death-like faint on
the board.

'We hate the boss-of-the-board as the shearers' "slushy" hates the shearers' cook. I don't know why. He's a very fair boss.

'He refused to put on a traveller yesterday, and the traveller knocked him down. He walked into the shed this morning with his hat back and thumbs in waistcoat — a tribute to man's weakness. He threatened to dismiss the traveller's mate, a bigger man, for rough shearing — a tribute to man's strength. The shearer said nothing. We hate the boss because he *is* the boss, but we respect him because he is a strong man. He is as hard up as any of us, I hear, and has a sick wife and a large, small family in Melbourne. God judge us all!

'There is a gambling-school here, headed by the shearers' cook. After tea they head 'em, and advance cheques are passed from hand to hand, thrown in the dust until they are black. When it's too dark to see with nose to the ground, they go inside and gamble with cards. Sometimes they start on Saturday afternoon, heading 'em till dark, play cards all night, start again heading 'em Sunday afternoon, play cards all Sunday night, and sleep themselves sane on Monday, or go to work ghastly — like dead men.

'Cry of "Fight"; we all rush out. But there isn't much fighting. Afraid of murdering each other. I'm beginning to think that most bush crime is due to irritation born of dust, heat and flies.

'The smothering atmosphere shudders when the sun goes down. We call it the sunset breeze.

'Saturday night or Sunday we're invited into the shearers' hut. There are songs that are not hymns, and recitations and speeches that are not prayers.

'Last Sunday night: slush lamps at long intervals on table. Men playing cards, sewing on patches — nearly all smoking — some writing, and the rest reading *Deadwood Dick*. At one end of the table a Christian Endeavourer endeavouring; at the other a cockney Jew, from the hawker's boat, trying to sell rotten clothes. In response to complaints, direct and not chosen generally for Sunday, the shearers' rep. requests both apostles to shut up or leave.

'He couldn't be expected to take the Christian and leave the Jew, any more than he could take the Jew and leave the Christian. We are just amongst ourselves in hell.

'Fiddle at the end of rouseabouts' hut. Voice of Jackeroo, from upper bunk with apologetic oaths: 'For God's sake chuck that up; it makes a man think of blanky old things!'

'A lost soul laughs (mine) and dreadful night smothers us.'

Old Boot

CHAPTER 10

Wandering About the Warrego

The season is over;
The shearing is done;
The wages are paid; and
The 'sprees' have begun.[48]

By mid-December the shearing season was virtually finished at Toorale. As Lawson later wrote in 'Lord Douglas', 'the big shearing sheds within a fortnight of Bourke cut out in time for the shearers to reach the town and have their Christmas dinners and sprees — and for some of them to be locked up over Christmas Day'.

In 1925, three years after Lawson's death, Jim Gordon wrote:

After Toorale shed cut out, we started to walk to Queensland and followed a track that led to Goonery, the out-station of Toorale. (I forgot to mention that there was a third man with us for a while. His name doesn't matter, as he was only with us for a few days.) [49]

Goonery was close to the Bourke–Wanaaring road, west of the Warrego River, and the third person accompanying them was probably a shearer or shed-hand who had met up with them at Toorale. If Queensland was indeed their destination, then the route they were on would eventually have led them to the New South Wales–Queensland border town of Hungerford. Unfortunately little is known of the entire course taken by Lawson and his co-trekkers. Lawson himself wrote nothing of his tramping around the countryside north-west of Bourke prior to the Christmas of 1892. Gordon was the only one to do so, though his notes, written thirty-three years later, contain details that are sketchy and chronologically confusing. The party's precise movements from the time they left the shearing shed at Toorale will probably never be known.

The availability of water was of utmost importance to those who travelled the region. This was especially so along the Travelling Stock Routes, where livestock depended solely upon accessible supplies. The countryside was arid and many watercourses that were officially known as 'rivers' were merely seasonal streams that flowed only after heavy and constant rain. Near Bourke, the Darling River normally contained a supply of fresh water. It was fed from the east by the Culgoa, Barwon and Bogan Rivers, and south of Bourke by the Warrego. Even in drought conditions, the water holes remaining along the river bed meant that the townspeople did not go thirsty. Normally it was from here that all intending travellers drew their water supply before heading out on the track.

By the 1890s, an assured supply of water for the drovers, teamsters and travellers existed along various western tracks in the form of Public Watering Places. Established by the New South Wales Colonial Government, these facilities consisted of bores — either artesian flowing or sub-artesian — and ground tanks (otherwise known as 'dams'). These bores and tanks, surrounded by saltbush and Mitchell grass, were a welcome sight to thirsty travellers.

The need for a constant supply of fresh water meant that Lawson and Gordon had to travel within close proximity to the Government bores or flowing watercourses in the area, limiting the route they could have taken. As a result of studying old pastoral maps of the Bourke district, aided by Gordon's recollections and Lawson's poems, the probable course can be calculated.

The first section of Lawson's journey from the Toorale woolshed to Goonery outstation was along the Warrego River, past the Travellers' Rest Hotel. From there the group progressed towards the Toorale homestead, several miles from the station shearing shed. Here they branched off westwards.

By following the dray tracks left by the mustering camp employees, and travelling between the various water supplies such as Red Tank and Toorale bores Nos. 3 and 4, at last they came to the Goonery outstation which was close to the Goonery Bore and Murphy's Exchange Hotel. About this time the group was employed (probably only for a day) at a small shearing shed used expressly for the shearing of 'stragglers' — those sheep which had inadvertently been missed during the general shearing muster.

From Goonery, the trio travelled eastwards along the Bourke–Wanaaring road towards its junction with the Warrego River. Here they came across a vast, treeless plain. It was known either (unofficially) as Eight-mile Plain or (officially) as Poison Point Plain, and is the largest of its kind found between the Darling and Paroo Rivers. It was undoubtedly this landscape Lawson had in mind when he penned 'The Great Grey Plain', which was published in the Brisbane *Worker* on 7 October 1893.

THE GREAT GREY PLAIN

Out West, where the stars are brightest,
Where the scorching north wind blows,
And the bones of the dead gleam whitest,
And the sun on a desert glows —
Yet within the selfish kingdom
Where man starves man for gain.
Where white men tramp for existence —
Wide lies the Great Grey Plain

No break in its awful horizon,
No blur in the dazzling haze,
Save where by the bordering timber*
The fierce, white heat-waves blaze,
And out where the tank-heap rises
Or looms when the sunlights wane
Till it seems like a distant mountain
Low down on the Great Grey Plain.

No sign of a stream or fountain,
No spring on its dry, hot breast,
No shade from the blazing noontide
Where a weary man might rest.
Whole years go by when the glowing
Sky never clouds for rain —
Only the shrubs of the desert
Grow on the Great Grey Plain.

From the camp, while the rich man's dreaming,
Comes the 'traveller' and his mate,
In the ghastly dawnlight seeming
Like a swagman's ghost out late;
And the horseman blurs in the distance,
While still the stars remain,
A low, faint dust-cloud haunting
His track on the Great Grey Plain.

And all day long from before them
The mirage smokes away —
That daylight ghost of an ocean
Creeps close behind all day
With an evil, snake-like motion
As the waves of a madman's brain:
'Tis a phantom not like water
Out there on the Great Grey Plain.

There's a run on the Western limit
Where a man lives like a beast;
And a shanty in the mulga
That stretches to the East;
And the hopeless men who carry
Their swags and tramp in pain —
The footmen must not tarry
Out there on the Great Grey Plain.

Out west, where the stars are brightest,
Where the scorching north wind blows,
And the bones of the dead seem whitest,
And the sun on a desert glows —
Out back in the hungry distance
That brave hearts dare in vain —
Where beggars tramp for existence —
There lies the Great Grey Plain.

'Tis a desert not more barren
Than the Great Grey Plain of years,
Where a fierce fire burns the hearts of men —
Dries up the fount of tears;
Where the victims of a greed insane
Are crushed in a hell-born strife —
Where the souls of a race are murdered
On the Great Grey Plain of Life!

*This is an example of poetic licence. There were no trees of any kind growing near the plain and no doubt there never had been for thousands of years. The drovers and teamsters, who often had to camp out on the plain at night, always made sure they carried their own firewood with them.

Continuing on past the 'great grey plain', the three men eventually arrived at the Gumbalie Hotel, which was situated on a flood plain on the western side of the Warrego River and the Bourke–Wanaaring road, about forty miles (65 km) from Bourke. The licensee was Mary Baker. A hotel had existed at Gumbalie from as early as 1873 to cater for the drovers and travellers passing along the Warrego River. However, the Gumbalie Hotel of Lawson's time was probably built during the 1880s and was constructed of corrugated iron. It was also a horse-changing station, and a stop-over for the Bourke–Wanaaring coach service where passengers could buy a meal. Perhaps it was here that Lawson and Gordon saw the Wanaaring coach.

The men set up camp near the hotel and rested for a few days before continuing their journey. By this time it was probably mid-December. Jim Gordon later remembered:

> After leaving Goonery we reached the Wanaaring–Bourke road, and camped for a couple of days at a small wayside pub called Gumbalie. It was there, I think, that Lawson saw for the first time aboriginals in a semi-wild state. That is to say, a big camp of them together, depending mostly on game and fish for an existence. A few of them came to our camp, expecting, I suppose, tucker, tobacco or drink. They got a little of each. Before they were with us long, Lawson showed signs of excitement, and said to me almost hysterically: 'They're a dying race, Jim, and they know it. I can read it in their eyes — I can read it in their eyes. I was suckled on a black breast, Jim.' This last remark I took with a grain of salt, as the saying is, which was the right way to take it, as I proved later when we were camped with an old hawker, a Spaniard, who had a bottle or two in his van. After the third or fourth round Henry began to recite
>
> > My father was a Spaniard,
> > My father was a Spaniard,
>
> in such the same tone as he had previously mentioned the black breast. [50]

It is interesting to note that, during his lifetime, Lawson wrote virtually nothing of the Australian Aborigine. However Gordon's words echo the prediction of many — that the Aborigine, as a pure race, was doomed for extinction. Owing to a lack of regular diet and a compulsive addiction to alcohol, which was supplied to them by the white settlers, their health was generally deteriorating. Part de-tribalisation and domination by European society had left them landless and robbed of their culture. Like the Asians, Afghans and Indians, who by that stage had arrived in Australia in relatively large numbers, they were not allowed to join local unions and were forbidden employment in the sheds. Despite these strict union attitudes and his own union involvement, Lawson had a high regard for the Afghan cameleers who operated their teams along the outback tracks under the command of Gunny Khan & Co. of Bourke, and later under the command of Abdul Wade and his well known Bourke Carrying Company.

Whether the above outburst was caused by sheer excitement, or whether Lawson had been drinking at the time, remains a mystery. He obviously held some recurring fixation about the subject, as he wrote in 'A Bush Publican's Lament', which was published in *Children of the Bush*: 'an ole gin nursed me an' me mother when I was born, an' saved me blessed life —'.

At this stage, Lawson, Gordon and their unknown companion were still intent on heading towards the Queensland border. Forgoing the quickest and most direct route back to Bourke via the Wanaaring road, they continued on a north-easterly course along the Warrego River in the general direction of Fords Bridge. The route lay along another section of the Warrego River, which meant a steady supply of fresh water. At this stage of their journey, the men were still within the boundaries of the vast Toorale holding, near its northern limit. However, some distance from the village of Fords Bridge the original plan to walk to Queensland seems to have been cancelled and the group decided to return to Bourke. They left the Warrego River track and headed east across country towards the Hungerford road.

One reason for the change of plan could have been Lawson's previous letter to Arthur Parker of 24 November, which stated quite firmly that he intended to be back in Sydney by Christmas. This suggests that Lawson had had no intention of participating in any outback wanderings but simply wanted to spend a few weeks in a shearing shed before heading back to the city.

Mindful of the need for fresh water, according to Gordon their intended destination was Sutherland's Lake and the nearby official Public Watering Place known as Kelly's Camp Bore.

> The day was warm, the water-bag empty, and we were tired and thirsty, so we stopped some distance back at the tank that was filled by an oil-engine pump, to keep the troughs supplied. Our other mate was in the lead, and he clambered up and filled a billy and handed it down to us. We both had a long pull. Then he said: 'Come up and have a look.' There was a carpet snake about six feet long floating, dead and swollen! Henry's eyes flashed as he said: 'He's a blanker of a mate. Come on, we'll leave him.' As we lifted our drums to move on the man said, 'Where yer goin'? Ain't we goin' to camp here?' Lawson dropped his swag hurriedly and made a step or two towards him, and answered: 'We are going on, but you are staying here.' He stayed, and I never saw him after. Thinking over the incident now I do not fancy that he saw the snake till after we drank the water, and on the spur of the moment invited us to look. Still, it may have been his idea of humour. [51]

As Jim Gordon observed, the water was pumped from the sub-artesian bore with the aid of an oil engine (an early type of diesel engine) to a raised reserve tank. From there it gravitated to a trough for the use by travelling stock and team animals. It was probably from the reserve tank that Lawson and Gordon's co-trekker 'climbed up and filled a billy'. Lawson and Gordon continued on their way, leaving the astonished man standing alone. He was never mentioned by Lawson or Gordon in their later writings.

The availability of fresh water on the track was a constant source of worry. Lawson wrote of the problem, adding a touch of humour in the sketch 'That's What It Was', published in the *Worker*.

THAT'S WHAT IT WAS

The two travellers were lost on a lignum plain all day without water, and when they struck the track they were ten miles from the Government tank. They were pretty thirsty when they got there. The water in the tank was not fit to drink, but the caretaker's wife had some in a barrel which she had 'cleared'. The two mates drank as much as they could hold; then they rolled out their swags and lay down, each with a billy-full alongside him. They drank the cask very low. Towards morning they began to get uneasy. First one would retire a little distance from the camp and then come back and sit on his swag and think; then the other would go and have a look at the country, and come back after a while and sit down on his swag and think. They compared notes, and tried to remember what had disagreed with 'em. They couldn't make it out. By-and-by one went up to the house to get a bit o' meat, and, in the course of the conversation he asked:

'What did yer clear that blanky water with, Mum?'

She said, 'Epsom's salts.'

The caretaker's children were healthy enough, but they looked a trifle thin and tired.

As Lawson and Gordon continued their walk along the outback track, they were undoubtedly passed by a variety of alternative transport. A mail coach owned and operated by Bill Doyle ran weekly from Bourke to Wanaaring. It was of the standard Cobb & Co. design and had probably been manufactured at the steam-operated factory in Bourke. Doyle operated this service for thirty-three years until 1917, when the advent of the motor transport industry, pioneered in this area by W. L. Green, caused its eventual demise. During those years it is estimated that Doyle covered 400,000 (50,000 km) miles in his coach. The men would have watched this coach pass and Gordon later recalled it in his poem 'Across the Warrego'.

> And through the night I saw a light,
> That crossed the Warrego;
> The battered lights, the spattered lights
> The lights of Cobb & Co.
> The coach went creeping through the sand
> That skirts the mulga ridge,
> And rattled down the stoney track
> That leads towards the bridge.[52]

About this time, the camel trains were beginning to emerge in the area as serious competition for the traditional bullock teams. Afghan cameleers carried supplies to the outback stations and villages, their beasts laden with bales of wool bound for the railway station at Bourke. Gordon acknowledged them in the same poem:

> And in my dream a camel team
> Was wandering in and out;
> With swinging packs and blistered backs
> The messengers of the drought.
> And as they crossed the sandy ridge,
> The sun went down below;
> I saw them on the sky-light then
> Beyond the Warrego.

Hauling along the wool routes west of the Darling, with up to eighty bales on board, the bullock teams followed the rutted wheel tracks through the scrub, across the black soil plains, the elevated red soil country and the treacherous sandhills. It was this heavy red sand that presented problems and, on the Bourke–Wanaaring Road, the sandhills at Goonery posed a great challenge to the teamsters and their wagons and they often became bogged. One particular trouble spot was called the 'Gin Bottle'. Here the heavy box-chains running between the bullocks dragged along the ground as the beasts struggled knee-deep through the sand.

Left: Tommy White, Bourke unionist and later General Secretary of the A.W.U. He is mentioned in Lawson's 'Bourke' poems.

Below: Remains of shearers' huts at Toorale Station, 1995.

Above: The Carriers' Arms Hotel, Bourke. Although this photograph was taken in the 1930s, the hotel had remained virtually unchanged since the late 1800s.

Below left: Phil Chapman was a union supporter who published eight of Lawson's poems in the *Western Herald* between September and October 1892.

Below right: Horace Bloxham was the proprietor of the rival Bourke newspaper, the *Central Australian & Bourke Telegraph* which printed the rhymes of the anonymous Smoko. Bloxham later became an author himself, writing *On the Fringe of the Never-Never* and *The Double Abduction*.

Left: It is commonly believed that the character of Baldy Thompson, in the story of the same name, was based on William Walter Davis, local Bourke grazier and occasional Member of Parliament.

Below centre: Henry Lawson and Jim Gordon spent the New Year of 1893 at Fords Bridge. The local pub was the Salmon Ford Hotel.

Below: The old building which still houses the offices of the *Western Herald* newspaper.

Above left: Jim Gordon, taken many years after his trekking experience in the Bourke district with Henry Lawson.

Above right: Donald Macdonell was a Bourke shearer, unionist and later Member of Parliament. Lawson wrote the eulogistic poem 'Donald Macdonell' in his honour in 1911.

Below: Lawson took a room at the Great Western Hotel on his arrival in Bourke in September 1892.

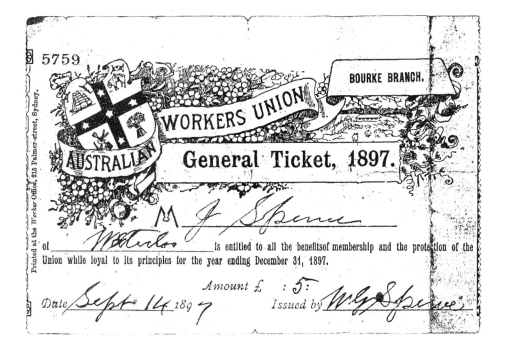

5759

BOURKE BRANCH.

AUSTRALIAN WORKERS UNION

General Ticket, 1897.

Printed at the Worker Office, 215 Palmer-street, Sydney.

M J Spence

of Waterloo is entitled to all the benefits of membership and the protection of the Union while loyal to its principles for the year ending December 31, 1897.

Date Sept 14 189 7

Amount £ : 5 :

Issued by W.G. Spence

Above: Bourke union members were issued with a ticket such as this before heading off to the local shearing sheds. The General Labourers' Union and the Amalgamated Shearers' Union later joined to become the Australian Workers' Union (A.W.U.).

Below: The punt that operated on the Darling River at Bourke. Jim Gordon later wrote, 'We crossed on the punt and tramped down the river to Toorale Station.'

Above: A bullock team rests outside the Lake Eliza Hotel, near Yantabulla on the Bourke-Hungerford Road. Lawson's poem 'Lake Eliza' was published in the *Bulletin* in December 1893.

Left: Part of the shearing board at Toorale Station, where Lawson worked as a rouseabout during November-December 1892.

Left: Remains of the shearing shed at Toorale Station, 1995.

Above: Lawson and Gordon visited the Gumbalie Hotel while trekking along the Warrego River during late 1892.

Right: Henry Lawson first stepped onto the platform at the Bourke railway station on September 21, 1892. This photograph shows several horse-drawn carriages waiting on the arrival of the train.

Right: Lawson is reputed to have lived in this small weatherboard house during his final months in Bourke, in 1893. Despite its age, the building is still habitable and boasts the original iron roof and timber front walls.

Above: The Royal Hotel at Hungerford was also the Cobb & Co. staging post.

Below: Banner of the Bourke branch of the Amalgamated Shearers' Union. Local unionist Hugh Langwell stands on the right. 'Defence not defiance' was the motto.

Also on the track were large numbers of men looking for work. Unaware of the great distances between townships and stations, hopeful workers arriving from the city were dismayed to discover that long treks were necessary for those travelling on foot. Lawson described this predicament when he wrote 'In a Dry Season', published on 5 November 1892.

> Often a member of the unemployed starts cheerfully out, with a letter from the Government Labour Bureau in his pocket, and nothing else. He has an idea that the station where he has the job will be within easy walking distance of Bourke. Perhaps he thinks there'll be a cart or buggy waiting for him. He travels for a night and a day without a bite to eat, and, on arrival, he finds that the station is eighty or a hundred miles away. Then he has to explain matters to a publican and a coach-driver. God bless the publican and the coach-driver! God forgive our social system!

Bush workers travelled mainly on foot, being too poor to buy, let alone provide feed for, a horse. Those who were fortunate enough to own a horse, or even a horse and sulky, were discouraged by station owners because of the general shortage of feed around the stations.

It was not until 1895 that the bicycle became a popular means of conveyance, and by 1900 there were hundreds of them being used on the outback tracks. The shearers expertly packed and balanced their swag and other gear on these machines, and if the going became heavy they would simply dismount and walk beside the bike, pushing it along. As time progressed, shearers were able to ride from Bourke to Wanaaring on the well-compacted camel pads in one day.

Lawson's sketch 'Carriers' aptly describes the scenes along those outback tracks. It was written in 1893 and published in the *Worker* on 24 November 1894. Later Lawson reworked and enlarged this story and it became the 'The Lost Souls' Hotel', which was published in *Children of the Bush*.

CARRIERS

Hungerford Road, February. One hundred and thirty miles of heavy sand, bordered by dry, hot scrubs. Dense cloud of hot dust. Four woolteams passing through a gate in a 'rabbit-proof' fence which crosses the road. 'Clock, clock, clock' of the wheels, rattle and clink of chains, &c., crack of whips. Bales and everything else coated with dust. Stink of old axle-grease and tarpaulins. Tyres hot enough to fry chops on; bows and chains so hot that it is a wonder they do not burn through the bullocks' hides. Water luke-warm in the blistered casks behind. Bullocks dragging along as only bullocks do. Wheels ploughing through the sand, and load lurching from side to side. Half way on a 'dry-stretch' of seventeen miles. Big tank full of good water through the scrub to the right, but a bound'ry rider is guarding it. Mulga scrub, and sparse, spiky undergrowth.

The carriers camp for dinner, and boil their billies, while the bullocks droop under their yokes in the blazing heat; one or two lie down, and the leaders drag and twist themselves round under a dead tree, under the impression that there is shade there. The carriers look like red Indians with the masks of red dust 'bound'* with sweat on their faces, but there is an unhealthy-looking whitish space round their optics, caused by wiping away the blinding dust, sweat and flies.

One man takes off his boot and sock, and empties half a pint of sand out of them, and pulls up his trouser leg. His leg is sheathed to the knee in dust and sweat; he absently scrapes it with his knife, and presently he amuses himself by moistening a strip with his fore-finger and shaving it — to see if he's still a whiteman, perhaps.

The Hungerford coach ploughs by, amid a dense cloud of dust, passengers and all.

The teams drag on again, 'like a wounded snake' that dies at sundown — if a wounded snake, that dies at sundown could be revived sufficiently next morning to drag on again till another sun goes down, and so on.

Hopeless-looking swagmen are met with during the afternoon, and one carrier — he of the sanded leg — halves his tobacco with them; his mates contribute 'bits o'' flour, tea and sugar &c.

Sundown and the bullocks about done up. The teamsters unyoke them, and drive them on to the next water — five miles — having previously sent a mate on to reconnoitre and see that the bound'ry rider is not round; otherwise to make terms with him, for it is a squatter's bore. They hurry the cattle down to the water and back in the twilight, and then under cover of darkness turn them in to a patch of scrub off the road, where a sign of grass might be seen — if you look close.

Carriers with horse teams fare the worse, perhaps, in dry seasons, when bad chaff is sold by the 'lb', and corn is worth its weight in gold.

The Carriers' Unions are being crushed, the Afghans over-run the country with their camels, rates are being cut down, and everything else is rising. Carriers have now to take provisions not only for themselves, but for the poor beggars whom they meet, and whom they cannot find it in their hearts to refuse. They are constantly had up for 'trespass', and robbed and ruined under the pretence of 'damages'; and, taking it all round, the woolteam doesn't 'rumble' as cheerfully as some bards seem to imagine.

* bind: from house painters' vocabulary. They put size in water-colour to bind it.
NB. The above sketch was written in 1893.

With such descriptions as 'blazing drought overhead and all round, burning the Darling banks to ashes ... '[53] and 'The Darling, when we had last seen it, was a narrow streak of mud between ashen banks, with a barge bogged in it ... '[54], Lawson gave the impression that he had arrived in the far-western district during a time of a severe drought. To the contrary, the summer of 1892–93 did not present the usual signs of drought, and the extremely hot conditions that Lawson experienced were normal for the area at that time of year. In his writing there was no report on the prevalence of dust storms, known locally as 'a Bourke shower' or, more generally, as a 'Darling River shower'. Neither did he mention any associated conditions such as stock dying along the stock routes or near the Public Watering Places.

Despite the ongoing union problems within the wool industry, the district actually witnessed an exceedingly high annual wool production during this time. The local newspaper, the *Western Herald*, stated on Saturday 3 December 1892 that: 'The pastoral prospects are now good, as after last month's rainfall; there is abundance of feed, stock consequently are improving daily, and good beef and mutton will soon be plentiful.' Four days later, on Wednesday 7 December 1892, a letter from a resident of Louth, printed in the same newspaper, informed the readers that: 'pastoral affairs about here bear a very promising appearance, grass everywhere in abundance. The local punt is now useless owing to the high state of the river; it is impossible to get to within 50 yards of it on the opposite side of the river, bringing traffic between Louth and Wanaaring to a standstill.'

Jim Gordon himself confirmed the true seasonal conditions of that year when he wrote: 'It had been a wet season, and, although at times we were walking through water, he [Lawson] always insisted on keeping the bag full — "in case of accidents" . . .'[55] The billabongs around Bourke were also full of water in November, evidenced when the stockman John Hallahan drowned near North Bourke.

The following rainfall figures, are taken from both official and unofficial records. 1891, 26 inches (660 mm) — twice yearly average; 1892, 9 inches (228 mm) — below average; 1893, 13 inches (330 mm) — yearly average. This gave an average of 16 inches (406 mm) a year over the three year period which was (and still is) considered to be reasonably good for the semi-arid zone of the western division of New South Wales.

What could have contributed to Lawson's perception of a dry spell over the summer of 1892–93 was that only 2 mm of rain fell in Bourke during the month of December, and none in January. During the time of his trek to Hungerford, however, a heavy shower of rain fell somewhere west of the Darling, resulting in a supply of fresh surface water. Gordon confirmed this when he admitted 'it had been a wet season, and . . . at times we were walking though water'.[56]

In 1893, 5 inches (127 mm) of rain fell in a two-day period beginning on 17 March. This rainfall saw the beginning of 'A Wet Season', the sketch that chronicled Lawson's departure from Bourke.

Water Pump

1 1

A Singer
of Wide Spaces

Christmas in Bourke, the metropolis of the great scrubs and
plains, 500 miles west, with the thermometer 100-and-something-
scarey in the shade . . . [57]

Lawson did not return to Sydney that year as he had predicted in his
letter to Arthur Parker on 24 November. Instead he spent the
Christmas of 1892 in Bourke with his union mates. Billy Wood, Bourke
unionist and friend of Lawson, wrote some thirty years later: 'On
Christmas Day, 1892, Lawson, Donald Mac., Teddy Thompson and I
had dinner at Mrs Hall's.'[58] Christine Hall was the wife of the General
Labourers' Union secretary Thomas Hicks Hall, and lunch was taken at
her home in Mitchell Street. Following lunch, the men spent a
refreshing afternoon on Wood's verandah.

After the meal, Henry, Donald and myself, came back to my house,
and, as my wife was away visiting her people, we got off everything
that we had on, except our underpants, and sat under a spray on the
verandah most of that afternoon drinking beer. It must have been

172

115 in the shade that day. The spray of river water was a great idea and kept us beautifully cool. I'm sure we all enjoyed ourselves. T. H. Hall, Teddy Thompson, 'Scotty' Anderson and Dan McDonald [sic, Donald Macdonell] came along after tea, and we all went boating up stream, and camped in a nice bend, boiled the billy, and had something to eat as well, afterwards smoking and yarning until late evening, when we drifted gently down the stream. Those were very pleasant days, and we enjoyed them to the full.[59]

It appears that Gordon and Lawson spent Christmas Day separately, as no mention is made by Wood of Jim Gordon's presence at his home or on their trip along the river. Although he records attending Christmas dinner at Billy Wood's, instead of at the Halls', Lawson was at the same event described by Wood, and very much enjoyed a non-traditional Christmas in Bourke.

We had dinner at Billy Wood's place, and a sensible Christmas dinner it was — everything cold, except the vegetables, with the hose going on the verandah in spite of the by-laws, and Billy's wife and her sister, fresh and cool-looking and jolly, instead of being hot and brown and cross like most Australian women who roast themselves over a blazing fire in a hot kitchen on a broiling day, all the morning, to cook scalding plum pudding and red-hot roasts, for no other reason than that their grandmothers used to cook hot Christmas dinners in England.

And in the afternoon we went for a row on the river, pulling easily up the anabranch and floating down with the stream under the shade of the river timber — instead of going to sleep and waking up helpless and soaked in perspiration, to find the women with headaches, as many do on Christmas Day in Australia.[60]

Lawson also wrote of this experience in 'The Ghosts of Many Christmases':

'Christmas in Bourke, the metropolis of the great pastoral scrubs and plains, 500 miles west, with the thermometer 100-and-something-scarey in the shade. The rough, careless shearers come in from the stations many dusty miles out in the scrubs to have their Christmas sprees, to drink and 'shout' and fight — and have the horrors some of them — and be run in and locked up with difficulty, within sound of a church-going bell. The Bourke Christmas is a very beery and exciting one. The hotels shut up in front on Christmas Day to satisfy the law (or out of consideration for the feelings of the sergeant in charge of the police-station), and open behind to satisfy the public, who are supposed to have made the law. Sensible cold dinners are the fashion in Bourke, I think, with the hose going, and free-and-easy costumes.'

On Boxing Day, Lawson wrote to his friend Arthur Parker in Sydney, replying to a letter he had received on his return to Bourke.

Bourke
26th December 1892

Dear Arthur,
Your welcome note came to hand after following me about a week or two. I am sorry to hear you are doing no better, but lay your ears back and fight. We just returned after working a month in a shearing shed on the Darling, and start north with my mate tomorrow. Very hot and dry and dusty up here. It would take a very long letter to tell you all the news, so I'll wait till I get money enough to come down. Your books will be at Redfern railway station, passage paid, today. Sorry to give you so much trouble. Good-bye, old chap, and a happy New Year to you, Charley.

Your just the same
Henry Lawson

Lawson's reference to Parker's note following him about 'for a week or two' probably arose from the letter being sent on to Toorale by Thomas

Hicks Hall. However, as Lawson and Gordon had already left on their trek along the Warrego, the letter had been sent back to Bourke where Lawson eventually received it. The books Lawson referred to had been lent to him by Parker in Sydney. The 'mate' that he planned to 'start north with' on the following day (27 December) appears to be Jim Gordon, although he did not say so.

Lawson did not post Arthur Parker's book, as promised, that day. In an undated letter, possibly written the following night, he apologised to his friend.

> *Dear Arthur,*
> *I didn't get your books off tonight; will send them tomorrow without fail. They will reach Redfern on Saturday morning. I posted a letter to you yesterday.*
>
> *Your tangled*
> *Henry Lawson*

Perhaps Lawson's arrival back in Bourke in late December indicates his intention to return to Sydney, as suggested by his November 24 letter to Parker which stated 'I will be down [to Sydney] at Christmas'. If this was the case, then something or someone had changed his mind. A few days later he ventured out on the track again, this time determined to reach Hungerford on the New South Wales-Queensland border.

One of the most unusual chapters in Australian history was the 1893 establishment of a group of Australians members of the New Australia Co-operative Settlement Association, as a colony in Paraguay, in South America. The proposer of the venture was William Lane, a staunch supporter of the Australian Labour Federation and involved with the formation of the Brisbane Trades and Labour Council. Recruiting offices for the movement, manned by loyal supporters, were set up in both city and country locations. In September 1892, shortly before Lawson's arrival in the town, Lane had visited Bourke, speaking in public on the merits of his proposal. In the far west, the opportunity for recruitment could not have come at a more opportune time. The area was experiencing a high rate of unemployment, caused by widespread pastoral unrest along the Darling and a general economic recession.

By late 1892, an enlistment centre had been established in Bourke and two of Lawson's union friends — Billy Wood and Thomas Hicks Hall — were actively involved. Lane returned to the town early the following year. The *Western Herald* reported on 19 April 1893: 'New Australia Movement. About 300 people assembled at Ralph's Hall on Sunday afternoon to hear Mr. Lane speak on the aims and intentions of the above movement. Secretary Hall [Thomas Hicks Hall] of the GLU took the chair.'

Lane was already well known to Henry Lawson and, as a previous editor of the Brisbane *Worker*, he had previously accepted some of Lawson's radical verse for publication. Another of Lawson's close friends, Mary Cameron — the poet later known as Dame Mary Gilmore — was a keen follower of Lane's ideals and eventually joined the colony in Paraguay. Though Lawson was approached several times as a possible recruit for the 'New Australia' settlement, on each occasion he declined. Living in continual poverty, it is doubtful whether he could have raised the cash for the passage to South America (and the return fare if the venture was not successful). In addition, a proposed regulation of the new colony was the banning of alcohol, which meant Lawson would immediately have lost interest in the whole concept. Despite his own personal lack of commitment, Lawson's sympathy was with Lane and his followers. He eventually expressed his views publicly in the poem 'Something Better', which was published in 1893 in the *New Australian*, the official publication of the New Australia movement.

It was in his capacity as a recruitment officer for Lane's movement that Ernest De Guinney met up with Henry Lawson in Bourke in 1892. A man of Russian descent, De Guinney had previously worked as a rouseabout in the Riverina district. He was sufficiently well educated to obtain some occasional journalistic work; he had contributed articles to the *Worker*, and was probably already acquainted with Lawson's work, if not the poet himself.

Lawson and De Guinney probably met through mutual acquaintances in the local union office and De Guinney was invited to accompany Lawson on his trek to Hungerford. Lawson did not mention De Guinney by name in any of his writings, alluding to him only as the 'Warrego bard' who was 'born in St Petersburg',[61] or the '"ratty" Russian Nihilist'.[62] Jim Gordon did not refer to him either, but by the same token Gordon did not mention his own presence on the trek to Hungerford, and it is only assumed that he accompanied Lawson and De Guinney. It was Billy Wood who later identified Lawson's co-trekker as De Guinney when he wrote:

> On the 29th December 1892, Lawson and a chap named De Guinney, a supposed Russian, turned nihilist, set off on foot for the 'Corner', where N. S. Wales, Queensland and South Australia meet. The partnership did not last long, and Henry soon got full up of De Guinney. I met Henry in Sydney later, and he told me that De Guinney was a griper. What he said was true for De Guinney afterwards came to Cosme colony (Paraguay) and proved to be a waster. The result of Lawson's short trip towards the 'Corner' was many sketches and some verses, one of the latter being 'Lake Eliza'.[63]

In 1931 Wood wrote a slightly different account of his association with Henry Lawson:

> 'He (Henry Lawson) was at my home on a few occasions, the last being just before he went on his tramp to 'the corner' where New South Wales, Queensland and South Australia meet . . . From 'the corner' he went down the river Darling in time for shearing and had a job as a wool-roller at Toorale shed. He remained there until 'cut out' in October (1893). He spent more than a year out back and gleaned a lot of material which he published in prose and verse.'[64]

At times Wood's memory did not serve him well and his recollections, written over thirty years later, are not completely reliable. Lawson did not spend 'more than a year out back', and his wool-rolling job at Toorale had finished before his outback treks. In addition, Hungerford is nowhere near 'the corner where New South Wales, Queensland and South Australia meet'. Notwithstanding the inaccuracies, the letters left by Wood are essential in piecing together Lawson's days in Bourke. And while neither Gordon nor De Guinney left a record of their actual trek to Hungerford, Lawson later chronicled that journey through his poems and stories.

As the second letter to Arthur Parker showed, the poet was still in Bourke on 27 December, confirming Wood's claim that Lawson departed two days later. Leaving Bourke for the second time, Lawson, De Guinney and Gordon made their way to North Bourke, about four miles north of the main town. Here they crossed the Darling via the bridge that spanned the river. Officially opened in 1883, the North Bourke bridge was the first to be built across the Darling in any location. In constant use by the wool wagons and travelling stock, it possessed a central platform that could be raised to allow steamers to pass through. The only other way of crossing the river was a small punt near the Bourke township. Although many western poets composed poems about the Darling River, N. Turnbull of Cunnamulla was the only person who ever wrote of the bridge itself in the *Western Herald* of 31 May 1922:

THE BOURKE BRIDGE

Stretched across the Darling River,
Linking up the south and north,
Bravely you are watching over
Helping all who journey forth;
Whirling depths of water flowing,
Underneath your stalwart beams,
While the Summer sun is glowing,
And the churning water gleams.

Mark those frantic Paroo cattle,
Wildly 'rining' in the dust,
While the cursing stockmen battle,

Break the surging 'ring' they must.
'Whoa there, bullocks!' Now they're crushing,
As they tread upon the plank,
Forging o'er your timbers rushing
As they strike the other bank.

Now the heated mob is over,
Here's the Cunnamulla coach.
How the lifting dust wreaths hover,
Round about your North approach.
Closely watch the trusty horses,
Swing the gallant coach along,
(Quickly cover up remorses)
Hear the passengers in song.
Hardy hoofs and wheels a'clatter,
Rushing o'er your ringing planks,
While a joyous rhythmic patter
Echoes 'tween the timbered banks.
What's that distant sullen rumbling?
Ah! A dusty bullock team —
Twenty hornies straining, stumbling,
As they pull towards the stream.

See the giant whip unfurling.
Watch the bridle leader squirm.
Ah! that deadly lash a'whirling,
Makes a fiery beast a worm;
Now the heavy load is swaying,
Groaning weirdly o'er the floor,
Soon the green-hide whip is flaying
On the dusty road once more.

Here's the lonely swagman trudging
From some God-forsaken lair,

Clearly all the world begrudging,
Racked with aching dull despair.
Now the sultry day is ended,
Lights are gleaming in the town,
And the traffic all suspended,
Peaceful night has settled down.

After crossing the North Bourke bridge, the three men tramped across Walkden's Plain, which in those days was also known as Wild Turkey Plain. The countryside in this first part of the journey was familiar to Lawson and Gordon, as it was the same route that had brought them back to Bourke several days before. The landscape mainly consisted of elevated red soil, where mulga and gidgee grew, and sandy stretches interspersed by alluvial flats, claypans and cane-grass swamps. The sandhills, as on the previous trip, proved arduous. This particular section of their trek could have been on Lawson's mind when he penned the first two verses of 'Says You' (sometimes referred to as 'Sez You') probably later during that same year, 1893.

SAYS YOU

When the heavy sand is yielding backward from your
*   blistered feet,*
And across the distant timber you can see the flowing
*   heat;*
When your head is hot and aching, and the shadeless
*   plain is wide,*
And it's fifteen miles to water in the scrub the other
*   side —*
Don't give up, don't be down-hearted, to a man's
*   strong heart be true!*
Take the air in through your nostrils, set your lips and
*   see it through —*
For it can't go on forever, and — 'I'll have my day!'
*   says you.*

When you're camping in the mulga, and the rain is
   falling slow,
While you nurse your rheumatism 'neath a patch of
   calico,
Short of tucker or tobacco, short of sugar or of tea,
And the scrubs are dark and dismal, and the plains are
   like the sea;
Don't give up and be down-hearted — to the soul of
   man be true!
Grin, if you've a mate to grin for! Grin and joke, and
   don't look blue;
For it can't go on for ever, and — 'I'll rise some day,'
   says you.

During the first stage of their trek, the men were able to replenish their water supplies at Fords Bridge Tank and Sutherland's Lake (or the hotel that bore the same name). They probably skirted Kelly's Camp Bore, the scene of the earlier incident with the dead snake in the drinking water. From this point onward, the men were on unfamiliar territory. The next village was Fords Bridge, and it was here that the trekkers are reported to have welcomed in the new year of 1893. A few celebratory drinks were undoubtedly consumed at the Salmon Ford Hotel, which was situated between the Warrego River and the bywash (anabranch) on the western side. Here they would have been welcomed by the hotel licensee Richard Green, a former mayor of Bourke, who ran the hotel from 1891 until 1896.

As Lawson wrote in 'Ghosts of Many Christmases', which was published in *Children of the Bush* in 1902:

New Year — on the Warrego River, outback (an alleged river with a sickly stream that looked like bad milk). We spent most of that night hunting around in the dark and feeling on the ground for camel and horse droppings with which to build fires and make smoke round our camp to keep off the mosquitoes. The mosquitoes started at sunset and left off at daybreak, when the flies got to work again.

Although the Warrego was given the official title of 'river', it varied from a chain of stagnating waterholes during a dry season, to a broad, shallow stream after heavy rain. In later years Lawson commented on the Warrego:

> I watched a mate of mine sit down in a camp on the parched Warrego — which was a dusty gutter with a streak of water like dirty milk — and write about 'the broad, shining Darling'. The Darling, when we had last seen it, was a narrow streak of mud between ashen banks, with a barge bogged in it. Two weeks later this mate was sitting in a dusty depression in the surface, which he alleged was a channel of a river called the Paroo, writing an ode to 'the rippling Warrego'.[65]

Lawson himself used poetic licence when he referred to the Darling as a 'narrow streak of mud between two ashen banks', as the river in this period was never low.

During these years, vast numbers of men moved through inland Australia, trekking from station to station, following the faint, wind-blown tracks. These men were not curious visitors such as Lawson himself; they were commonly known as swagmen, and were refugees from the cities and country towns, jobless victims of the great Depression of the 1890s. Often in a debilitated state of health, they drifted along seeking any kind of stock work, dependent on an accommodating cook or station boss for food. Some were inevitably found dead by the roadside. Lawson's poem 'The Swagman and His Mate', which was published in the *Town and Country Journal* in 1896, tells of these men, their struggles, and their 'memories of Hope'.

THE SWAGMAN AND HIS MATE

From north to south throughout the year
The shearing seasons run,
The Queensland stations start to shear
When Maoriland has done;
But labour's cheap and runs are wide,

And some the track must tread
From New Year's Day till Christmastide
And never get a shed!
North, west, and south — south, west, and north —
They lead and follow Fate —
The stoutest hearts that venture forth —
The swagman and his mate.

A restless, homeless class they are
Who tramp in border land.
They take their rest 'neath moon and star —
Their bed the desert sand,
On sunset tracks they ride and tramp,
Till speech has almost died,
And still they drift from camp to camp
In silence side by side.
They think and dream, as all men do;
Perchance their dreams are great —
Each other's thoughts are sacred to
The swagman and his mate.

With scrubs beneath the stifling skies
Unstirred by heaven's breath;
Beyond the Darling Timber lies
The land of living death!
A land that wrong-born poets brave
Till dulled minds cease to grope,
A land where all things perish, save
The memories of Hope.
When daylight's fingers point out back
(And seem to hesitate)
The far faint dust cloud marks their track —
The swagman and his mate.

And one who followed through the scrub
And out across the plain,
And only in a bitter mood
Would seek those tracks again;
Can only write what he has seen —
Can only give his hand —
And greet those mates in words that mean
'I know', 'I understand'.
I hope they'll find the squatter 'white',
The cook and shearers 'straight',
When they have reached the shed to-night —
The swagman and his mate.

Undoubtedly, during that summer of 1892–93, Lawson encountered many such men along the track, either walking into the sunset or out of it. And it was probably these men he had in mind when he wrote 'Stragglers', which was published in the *Bulletin* on 27 May 1893. While the term 'stragglers' usually refers to the sheep that have been missed during the annual shearing muster, Lawson painted these itinerant men, and not the sheep, as the ones left behind. They were, he noted, the victims of a harsh society still largely controlled by English banks.

STRAGGLERS

An oblong hut, walled with blue-grey hardwood slabs, adzed at the ends and set horizontally between the round sapling studs; high roof of the eternal galvanised iron. A big rubbish-heap lies about a yard to the right of the door, which opens from the middle of one of the side walls; it might be the front or the back wall — there is nothing to fix it. Two rows of rough bunks run round three sides of the interior; and a fireplace occupies one end — the kitchen end. Sleeping, eating, gambling, and cooking accommodation for thirty men in about eighteen by forty feet.

The rouseabouts and shearers use the hut in common during shearing. Down the centre of the place runs a table made of stakes driven into the ground, with cross-pieces supporting a top of half round slabs set with the flat sides up, and affording a few level places for soup plates; on each side are crooked, unbarked poles laid in short forks, to serve as seats. The poles are worn smoothest opposite the level places on the table. The floor is littered with rubbish — old wool-bales, newspapers, boots, worn-out shearing pants, rough bedding, etc., raked out of the bunks in an impatient search for missing articles — signs of a glad and eager departure with cheques when the shed last cut out.

To the west is a dam, holding back a broad, shallow sheet of grey water, with dead trees standing in it.

Further up along this water is a brush shearing shed, a rough framework of poles with a brush roof. This kind of shed has the advantage of being cooler than iron. It is not rain-proof, but shearers do not work in rainy weather; shearing even slightly damp sheep is considered the surest and quickest way to get the worst kind of rheumatism. The floor is covered with rubbish from the roof, and here and there lies a rusty pair of shears. A couple of dry tar-pots hang by nails in the posts. The 'board' is very uneven and must be bad for sweeping. The pens are formed by round, crooked stakes driven into the ground in irregular lines, and the whole business reminds us of the 'cubby-house' style of architecture of our childhood.

Opposite stands the wool-shed, built entirely of galvanised-iron; a blinding object to start out of the scrub on a blazing, hot day. God forgive the man who invented galvanised iron, and the greed which introduced it into Australia; you could not get worse roofing material for a hot country.

The wool-washing, soap-boiling, and wool-pressing arrangements are further up the dam. 'Government House' is a mile away, and is nothing better than a bush hut: this station belongs to a company. And the company belongs to a bank. And the banks belong to England, mostly.

Mulga scrub all round, and, in between, patches of reddish sand where the grass ought to be.

It is New Year's Eve. Half-a-dozen travellers are camping in the hut, having a spell. They want it, for there are twenty miles of dry lignum plain between here and the Government bore to the east; and about eighteen miles of heavy, sandy, cleared road north-west to the next water in that direction. With one exception, the men do not seem too hard-up; at least, not as that condition is understood by the swagmen of these times. The least lucky one of the lot had three weeks' work in a shed last season, and there might probably be five pounds amongst the whole crowd. They are all shearers, or at least they say they are. Some might only be 'rousers'.

These men have a kind of stock hope of getting a few stragglers to shear somewhere; but their main objective is to live till next shearing. In order to do this they must tramp for tucker, and trust to the regulation — and partly mythical — pint of flour, and bit of meat, or tea and sugar, and to the goodness of cooks and storekeepers and boundary riders. You can only depend on getting tucker *once* at one place; then you must tramp on to the next. If you cannot get it once you must go short; but there is a lot of energy in an empty stomach. If you get an extra supply you may camp for a day and have a spell. To live you must walk. To cease walking is to die.

The Exception is an outcast amongst bush outcasts, and looks better fitted for Sydney Domain. He lies on the bottom of a galvanised iron case, with a piece of blue blanket for a pillow. He is dressed in a blue cotton jumper, a pair of very old and ragged tweed trousers, and one boot and one slipper. He found the slipper in the last shed, and the boot in the rubbish-heap here. When his own boots gave out he walked 150 miles with his feet roughly sewn up in pieces of sacking from an old wool-bale. No sign of a patch, or an attempt at mending anywhere about his clothes, and that is a bad sign; when a swagman leaves off mending or patching his garments, his case is about hopeless. The Exception's swag consists of the aforesaid piece of blanket rolled up and tied with pieces of rag. He has no water-bag; carries his water in a billy; and how he manages without a bag is known only to himself. He has read every scrap of print within reach, and now lies on his side, with his face to the wall and one arm thrown up over his head; the jumper is twisted back and leaves his skin bare from hip to arm-pit. His lower face is brutal, his eyes small and shifty, and ugly straight lines run across his low forehead. He says very little, but scowls most of the time — poor devil. He might be, or at least *seem*, a totally different man under more favourable conditions. He is probably a free labourer.

A very sick jackaroo lies in one of the bunks. A sandy sawney-looking* Bourke native takes a great interest in this wreck; watches his every movement as though he never saw a sick man before. The men lie about in the bunks, or the shade of the hut, and rest, and read all the soiled and mutilated scraps of literature they can rake out of the rubbish, and sleep, and wake up swimming in perspiration, and growl about the heat.

It *is* hot, and the two shearers' cats — a black and a white one — sit in one of the upper bunks with their little red tongues out, panting like dogs. These cats live well during shearing, and take their chances the rest of the year — just as shed rouseabouts have to do. They seem glad to see the traveller come; he makes things more homelike. They curl and sidle affectionately around the table-legs, and the legs of the men, and purr, and carry their masts up, and regard the cooking with feline interest and approval, and look as cheerful as cats can — and as contented. God knows how many tired, dusty, and sockless ankles they rub against in their time.

Now and then a man takes his tucker-bags and goes down to the station for a bit of flour, or meat, or tea, or sugar, choosing the time when the manager is likely to be out on the run. The cook here is a 'good cook', from a traveller's point of view; too good to keep his place long.

Occasionally someone gets some water in an old kerosene tin and washes a shirt or a pair of trousers, and a pair or two of socks — or foot rags (Prince Alfreds, they call them). That is, he soaks some of the stiffness out of these articles.

Three times a day the black billies and cloudy nose-bags are placed on the table. The men eat in a casual kind of way, as though it were only a custom of theirs, a matter of form — a habit which could be left off if it were worthwhile.

The Exception is heard to remark to no one in particular that he'll give all he has for a square meal.

'An' ye'd get it cheap, begod!' says a big Irish shearer. 'Come and have dinner with us; there's plenty there.'

But the Exception only eats a few mouthfuls, and his appetite is gone; his stomach has become contracted, perhaps.

The Wreck cannot eat at all, and seems internally disturbed by the sight of others eating.

One of the men is a cook, and this morning he volunteered good-naturedly to bake bread for the rest. His mates amuse themselves by chiaking him.

'I've heard he's a dirty and slow cook,' says one, addressing Eternity.

'Ah!' says the cook, 'you'll be glad to come to me for a pint of flour when I'm cooking and you're on the track, some day.'

Sunset. Some of the men sit at the end of the hut to get the full benefit of a breeze which comes from the west. A great bank of rain clouds is rising in that direction, but no one says he thinks it will rain; neither does anybody think we're going to have some rain. None but the greenest jackaroo would venture that risky and foolish observation. Out here, it can look more like rain without raining, and continue to do so for a longer time, than in most other places.

The Wreck went down to the station this afternoon to get some medicine and bush medical advice. The Bourke sawney helped him to do up his swag; he did it with an awed look and manner, as though he thought it a great distinction to be allowed to touch the belongings of such a curiosity. It was afterwards generally agreed that it was a good idea for the Wreck to go to the station; he would get some physic and a bit of tucker to take him on. 'For they'll give tucker to a sick man sooner than to a chap what's all right.'

The Exception is rooting about in the rubbish for the other blucher boot.

The men get a little more sociable, and 'feel' each other to find out who's 'union', and talk about water, and exchange hints as to good tucker-tracks, and discuss the strike, and curse the squatter (which is all they have got to curse), and growl about union leaders, and tell lies against each other sociably. There are tally lies; and lies about getting tucker by trickery; and long-tramp-with-heavy-swag-and-no-water lies; and lies about getting the best of squatters and bosses-over-the-board; and droving, fighting, racing, gambling and drinking lies. Lies *ad libitum*; and every true Australian bushman must try his best to tell a bigger out back lie than the last bush-liar.

Pat is not quite easy in his mind. He found an old pair of pants in the scrub this morning, and cannot decide whether they are better than his own, or, rather, whether his own are worse — if that's possible. He does not want to increase the weight of his swag unnecessarily by taking both pairs. He reckons that the pants were thrown away when the shed cut out last, but then they might have been lying out exposed to the weather for a longer period. It is rather an important question, for it is very annoying, after you've mended and patched an old pair of pants, to find, when a day or two further on the track, that they are more rotten than the pair you left behind.

There is some growling about the water here, and one of the men makes a billy of tea. The water is better cooked. Pint-pots and sugar-bags are groped out and brought to the kitchen hut, and each man fills his pannikin; the Irishman keeps a thumb on the edge of his, so as to know when the pot is full, for it is very dark and there is no more firewood. You soon know this way, especially if you are in the habit of pressing lighted tobacco down into your pipe with the top of your thumb. The old slush-lamps are all burnt out.

Each man feels for the mouth of his sugar bag with one hand while he keeps the bearings of his pot with the other.

The Irishman has lost his match-box, and feels for it all over the table without success. He stoops down with his hands on his knees, gets the table-top on a level with the flicker of firelight, and 'moons' the object, as it were.

Time to turn in. It is very dark inside and bright moonlight without; and every crack seems like a ghost peering in.

Some of the men will roll up their swags on the morrow and depart; and some will take another day's spell. It is all according to the tucker.

* *sawney*: simpleton

After a few days rest at Fords Bridge, Lawson, De Guinney and Gordon were again negotiating the sandy country on the Hungerford track. Between the Warrego River and Cuttaburra Creek they passed two flowing artesian bores. The first was a Government Watering Place at Kerribree Creek, where the watercourse was naturally dry except in times of wet weather. However a local station-owner and former Bourke MP, William Davis, had diverted artesian water from a large bore on his property into the dry creek bed. (The bore on Davis's property was the first deep bore to be privately drilled in Australia.) The second watering place was Youngerina Bore, with a flow rate of over half a million gallons (2,270,000 litres) per day.

After another 12 miles (20 km) the trekkers came to the Lake Eliza Hotel, operated by Arthur Attwood. When full, nearby Lake Eliza was a popular stop-over for the teamsters, drovers and travelling public. Expecting 'green and shady banks' and 'pleasant waters', the disappointment Lawson experienced when he found the lake dry, as it usually was during summer, probably sent him to seek the hotel bar. Luckily Lawson found humour in the situation and his indignation eventually gave voice to a poem that captured the mood of the day. 'Lake Eliza' was published in the *Bulletin* on 16 December 1893.

LAKE ELIZA

The sand was heavy on our feet,
A Christmas sky was o'er us,*
And half a mile through dust and heat

Lake 'Liza lay before us.
'You'll have a long and heavy tramp' —
So said the last adviser —
'You can't do better than to camp
To-night at Lake Eliza.'

We quite forgot our aching shanks,
A cheerful spirit caught us;
We thought of green and shady banks,
We thought of pleasant waters.
'Neath sky as niggard of its rain
As of his gold the miser,
By mulga scrub and lignum plain
We'd tramp, to Lake Eliza.

A patch of grey discoloured sand,
A fringe of tufty grasses,
A lonely pub in mulga scrub
Is all the stranger passes.
He'd pass the Lake a dozen times
And yet be none the wiser;
I hope that I shall never be
As dry as Lake Eliza.

No patch of green nor water seen
To cheer the weary plodder;
The grass is tough as fencing-wire,
And just as good for fodder.
And when I see it mentioned in
Some local Advertiser,
'Twill make me laugh, or make me grin —
The name of Lake Eliza.

* *Christmas sky*: Poetic licence, as it was about two weeks after Christmas when
Lawson visited Lake Eliza.

While Lawson, Gordon and De Guinney trekked towards the border town of Hungerford, it is possible that wandering job-seekers joined them along the way. In the years immediately following Lawson's death, many letters and articles were published in newspapers by people claiming association with the poet. The following article appeared in *Aussie* on 15 December 1926. The writer, W. J. Bournes, claimed to have been Lawson's travelling companion in the vicinity of Lake Eliza.

It was in '93 that I first met him, in the library of the A.W.U. office at Bourke (N.S.W.). Other men were there reading the papers, but he alone attracted me. I did not know his name, and I found myself fascinated by his large brown eyes sparkling as they penetrated gradually right through me and into my secret heart. He spoke to me and I told him I was 'waltzing Matilda' on the far western tracks. We became mates, and to me his only name was 'Long Harry'. That was enough, for his kindly solicitude, his advice and his humanitarian reflections made me feel that I wanted to be with him all the time; but after several days in his company he had 'to be going'.

I was a youth and 'Long Harry' regarded me as a lonely lad, and though I had been invited to his heart he could not take me with him.

I met him again, this time with our blueys up on the Hungerford track, making west. That night we camped at Mother Nosey's Spring, and started out again in the morning for Yantabulla. As the distance was not more than eleven miles we carried our water-bags only half full.

Soon the temperature climbed to 115 deg. in the shade, and, half roasted, after going three miles we decided to rest in the shade of a friendly bloodwood until the cool of evening.

'Long Harry' questioned me about my boyhood, and I began to wonder if he was a sleuth after somebody who was 'wanted'.

I could not induce him to speak about himself, but no suspicions could take root in me when I looked into his big brown eyes.

Gradually our water-bags were emptied, and we took the track again, facing a wind that seemed to blow from the Seven Furnaces of

192

Hell. We were anxious for our own welfare now, as eight thirsty miles lay before us, and the sun was at such an angle that our faces smarted under its piercing glow.

Rounding a bend in the track we met another swagman. He squatted on his swag as we approached, and, seeing our water-bags were dry, invited us to 'have a wet' from his full one, remarking on the heat being 'a fair cow'.

'Where are you making camp tonight?' he asked.

'Yantabulla,' my mate replied.

He said we'd have a pretty sultry tramp and advised us to camp at Lake Eliza, only half a mile distant through the mulga and close to a pub.

We had never heard of the lake, much less the pub, and the news cheered us considerably. In my mind's eye I saw the shady banks of the lake and already in imagination I felt myself taking a header into the cool waters; but when we reached the place there was no water. The bed of the lake was as dry as the Sands of Time.

We camped on the sandhill a short distance from the pub, which depended on shallow wells for its water supply.

After breakfast next morning 'Long Harry' sat writing for a while, and did not seem to be in any mood for conversation. By-and-by, in silence, he left the camp for a few minutes and, during his absence, a small whirlwind scattered his sheets of paper towards me. I gathered them up and on one sheet I read these lines:

LAKE ELIZA
(Commonly pronounced Eliser)
The sand was heavy on our feet,
A Xmas sky was o'er us;
A half a mile through mulga scrub
Lake Eliser lay before us.

'You'll have a pretty sultry tramp.'
So said our last adviser;

'You can't do better than to camp
To-night at Lake Eliser.'

We sat to rest our aching shanks
A cheerful spirit caught us;
We thought of green and shady banks,
We thought of pleasant waters —

I had read thus far when 'Long Harry' returned. My thoughts, although I had not expressed them, were exactly described, and I wondered if telepathy had played some part between us. Often he had anticipated a question I intended asking by himself putting the same question to me.

That evening we strolled up to the pub and before we left we had been engaged by Mr Alex. Preston, of Reid and Preston to start work in a few days time in the Oomoobah woolshed.

Two days later 'Long Harry' rolled his swag and told me that he had decided to push on to Hungerford, on the Queensland border.

Upon that, I, too, started to roll my swag, but he persuaded me to stay and tackle the job at the shed.

We shook hands and sadly I watched him pass from sight round a bend in the track. I felt at that moment — well, it doesn't matter now what I felt like.

An hour later Alex. Preston came to me and said that I could start work in the morning.

'Where's Lawson?' he asked. 'Is he down at the pub?'

'Lawson?' I replied. 'I don't know anyone by the name of Lawson!'

'Oh, yes you do,' said Mr Preston; 'I mean your mate.'

' 'Long Harry' was my mate,' I said, 'but he's gone on towards Hungerford.'

'That's Henry Lawson, the poet,' said Mr Preston.

I don't know that I would have been any happier if I had known he was 'the poet'. To love him as a mate was enough for me.

W. J. Bournes' letter, written over thirty years after the events, contains many inaccuracies, as well as being rather sentimental. He claims to have met Lawson in the 'library of the AWU office in Bourke' in 1893. However by this time Lawson was already on his way to Hungerford, and certainly not frequenting the union library. Bournes makes no mention of either Gordon or De Guinney being present at Lake Eliza, portraying Lawson instead as a lone traveller. Also, his reference to Lawson carrying his water bag 'only half full' differs from Gordon's insistence that the poet was extremely careful about travelling with adequate water supplies. Lastly, the precise location, and even the existence of, the 'Oomoobah' woolshed remains a mystery.

As Lawson trekked further north, the scenery became drier, more contrasting, desolate. However, the adverse conditions he encountered along the track dictated the theme of much of his writing. He observed in detail this new world of isolation. Now his descriptions, which he had previously overstated, did not require exaggeration; the exaggeration already lay in the surrounding landscape. So the 'old year' of 1892 went 'and the new returned' as Lawson took stock of what he saw around him, and wrote about it. Published in the *Bulletin* on 30 September 1893, he presented his poem 'Out Back' as a summary of this kind of existence.

OUT BACK

The old year went, and the new returned, in the
  withering weeks of drought;
The cheque was spent that the shearer earned, and the
  sheds were all cut out;
The publican's words were short and few, and the
  publican's looks were black —
And the time had come, as the shearer knew, to carry
  his swag Out Back.

For time means tucker, and tramp you must, where
  the scrubs and plains are wide,

With seldom a track that a man can trust, or a
    mountain peak to guide;
All day long in the dust and heat — when summer
    is on the track —
With stinted stomachs and blistered feet, they
    carry their swags Out Back.

He tramped away from the shanty there, when the
    days were long and hot,
With never a soul to know or care if he died on the
    track or not.
The poor of the city have friends in woe, no matter
    how much they lack,
But only God and the swagmen know how a poor man
    fares Out Back.

He begged his way on the parched Paroo and the
    Warrego tracks once more,
And lived like a dog, as the swagmen do, till the
    Western stations shore;
But men were many, and sheds were full, for work in
    the town was slack —
The traveller never got hands in wool, though he
    tramped for a year Out Back.

In stifling noons when his back was wrung by its load,
    and the air seemed dead,
And the water warmed in the bag that hung to his
    aching arm like lead,
Or in times of flood, when the plains were seas, and
    the scrubs were cold and black,
He ploughed in mud to his trembling knees, and paid
    for his sins Out Back.

He blamed himself in the year 'Too Late' for the wreck
    of his strong young life,
And no one dreamed but a shearing mate 'twas the
    fault of his faithless wife;
There are times when the wrongs of your kindred
    come, and treacherous tongues attack —
When a man is better away from home, and dead to
    the world, Out Back.

And dirty and careless and old he wore, as his lamp of
    hope grew dim;
He tramped for years, till the swag he bore seemed
    part of himself to him.
As a bullock drags in the sandy ruts, he followed the
    dreary track,
With never a thought but to reach the huts when the
    sun went down Out Back.

It chanced one day, when the north wind blew in his
    face like a furnace-breath,
He left the track for a tank he knew — 'twas a shorter
    cut to death;
For the bed of the tank was hard and dry, and crossed
    with many a crack,
And O it's a terrible thing to die of thirst in the scrub
    Out Back.

A drover came, but the fringe of law was eastward
    many a mile;
He never reported the thing he saw, for it was not
    worth his while.
The tanks are full and the grass is high in the mulga off
    the track,
Where the bleaching bones of a white man lie by his
    mouldering swag Out Back.

For time means tucker, and tramp if they must,
    where the plains and scrubs are wide,
With seldom a track that a man can trust, or a
    mountain peak to guide;
All day long in the flies and heat the men of the
    outside track
With stinted stomachs and blistered feet must
    carry their swags Out Back.

Nightfall came as a welcome respite to the heat of the day. After a meagre meal, the men rolled out their swags and lay wearily down, the hardness of the ground underneath a sober reminder of the comparative life of ease in town. While lying on his thin swag, Lawson's eyes were drawn up towards the blackness pinpricked by myriad stars. 'The Western Stars' was published in the *Freeman's Journal* on 23 December 1893. A short poem of two verses, it shows that despite the bleakness of the bush, Lawson saw also a stark underlying beauty that came to him in sudden, surprising snatches.

THE WESTERN STARS

On my blankets I was lyin',
Too tired to lift my head,
An' the long hot day was dyin',
An' I wished that I was dead.

From the West the gold was driven.
I watched the death of day,
An' the distant stars in Heaven
Seemed to draw my heart away.

After leaving Lake Eliza, Lawson, Gordon and De Guinney passed through Yantabulla. An embryo village, close to Cuttaburra Creek, it consisted of a few houses and a hotel that bore the same name. From there they probably skirted Kilberoo Tank, which would certainly have been dry, but obtained precious water from Kenmere and Brindingabba bores.

The next watering hole was Warroo Spring where, in the early 1860s, John Costello, the brother-in-law of Patrick Durack, lived for a time while on his way north with a mob of cattle to establish Thylungra station in south-west Queensland. In the early part of the twentieth century, following the widespread tapping of the artesian basin and the subsequent reduction in its pressure, these springs ceased to flow.

By the time of their arrival at Waroo Springs, the three men were only a short distance from the Queensland border after spending over two weeks on the track. We can only imagine the physical agony as they marched along in the peak of summer. 'Knocked Up', which was published by the *Bulletin* later that year, sums up the wanderer's exhaustion as he wonders how he can ever go on.

KNOCKED UP

I'm lyin' on the barren ground that's baked and
    cracked with drought,
And dunno if my legs or back or heart is most wore
    out;
I've got no spirits left to rise and smooth me achin'
    brow —
I'm too knocked up to light a fire and bile* the billy
    now.
Oh it's trampin', trampin', tra-a-mpin', in flies an'
    dust an' heat,
Oh it's trampin', trampin', tra-a-mpin' through
    mud and slush 'n sleet;
It's tramp an' tramp for tucker — one everlastin'
    strife,
An' wearin' out yer boots an' heart in the wastin'
    of yer life.

They whine o' lost an' wasted lives in idleness and
    crime —
I've wasted mine for twenty years, and grafted all the
    time
And never drunk the stuff I earned, nor gambled when
    I shore —
But somehow when yer on the track yer life seems
    wasted more.

A long dry stretch of thirty miles I've tramped this
    broilin' day,
All for the off-chance of a job a hundred miles away;
There's twenty hungry beggars wild for any job this
    year,
An' fifty might be at the shed while I am lyin' here.

The sinews in my legs seem drawn, red-hot — 'n
    that's the truth;
I seem to weigh a ton, and ache like one tremendous
    tooth;
I'm stung between my shoulder blades — my blessed
    back seems broke;
I'm too knocked out to eat a bite — I'm too knocked
    up to smoke.

The blessed rain is comin' too — there's oceans in the
    sky,
An' I suppose I must get up and rig the blessed fly;
The heat is bad, the water's bad, the flies a crimson
    curse,
The grub is bad, mosquitoes damned — but
    rheumatism's worse.

I wonder why poor blokes like me will stick so fast ter
    breath,

Though Shakespeare says it is the fear of somethin'
    after death;
But though Eternity be cursed with God's almighty
    curse —
What ever that same somethin' is I swear it can't be
    worse.

For it's trampin', trampin', tra-a-mpin', thro' hell
    across the plain,
And it's trampin', trampin' tra-a-mpin', through
    slush 'n mud 'n rain —
A livin' worse than any dog — without a home 'n
    wife,
A-wearin' out yer heart 'n soul in the wastin' of
    yer life.

* *bile*: boil

Finally, after tramping for over two weeks and enduring all the
hardships found on that long and dusty track, Lawson, Gordon and De
Guinney reached their destination: the village of Hungerford, perched
on the New South Wales–Queensland border, close to the Paroo River.

Old Kettle

CHAPTER 12

The Heart of the Swag

Travelling with the swag in Australia is variously and picturesquely described as 'humping bluey', 'walking Matilda', 'humping Matilda', 'humping your drum', 'being on the wallaby', 'jabbing trotters', and 'tea and sugar burglaring', but most travelling shearers now call themselves trav'lers and say simply 'on the track', or 'carrying swag'.[66]

Also known as a 'shiralee', the swag was the hallmark of the men who trudged the outback tracks. Usually containing no more than a pair of thin blankets tightly rolled to minimal size, it consisted of a sheet of canvas or calico held together with a pair of leather straps or light rope. On this unrolled swag, the weary traveller rested his head during the day under a gum tree, anxious to escape the relentless rays of the sun. At night he lay beside a fire, rolled in its blankets. In many cases the swag amounted to his home. And as he tramped, he carried beside him all his worldly possessions: photographs, a few faded letters, a lock of hair, memories of sweethearts or loved ones from long ago.

Lawson exercised a strict code of discipline in respect to his swag while on the Hungerford track. Gordon elaborated on this when he wrote:

> Henry was at times inclined to be what to-day would be termed 'fussy'. For instance, I was in some ways a bit of a sloven in regard to rolling and carrying the swag and kit. I'd use a piece of rope or a strap to sling it over my shoulder. This used to annoy him; it wasn't the right way. The towel, its ends tied to the binding-straps, should be used. Another thing was the billy. Mine used to bump my leg and soil the brown moleskin trousers — washed nearly white: it was before the day of the dungaree. His billy had a kind of calico sheath pulled stocking-wise over it when we were on the tramp. And again we'd argue about the water-bag. It had been a wet season, and although at times we were walking though water he always insisted on keeping the bag full — 'in case of accidents,' he said. And be it said there was wisdom in his side of the argument. [67]

Lawson wrote a number of works reflecting the crucial importance of the swag, which he knew well. 'The Heart of the Swag' was published in *The Skyline Riders and Other Verses* in 1910.

THE HEART OF THE SWAG

Oh, the track through the scrub groweth ever more
    dreary,
And lower and lower his grey head doth bow;
For the swagman is old and the swagman is weary —
He's been tramping for over a century now.
He tramps in a worn-out old 'side spring' and
    'blucher',
His hat is a ruin, his coat is a rag,
And he carries forever, far into the future,
The key of his life in the core of his swag.

There are old-fashioned portraits of girls who are
    grannies,
There are tresses of dark hair whose owners are grey;
There are faded old letters from Marys and Annies,
And Toms, Dicks and Harrys, dead many a day.
There are broken-heart secrets and bitter-heart
    reasons —
They are sewn in a canvas or calico bag,
And wrapped up in oilskin through dark rainy seasons,
And he carries them safe in the core of his swag.

There are letters that should have been burnt in the
    past time,
For he reads them alone, and a devil it brings;
There were farewells that should have been said for the
    last time,
For, for ever and ever the love for her springs.
But he keeps them all precious, and keeps them in
    order,
And no matter to man how his footsteps may drag,
There's a friend who will find, when he crosses the
    Border,
That the Heart of the Man's in the Heart of his Swag.

'Enter Mitchell' was originally named 'That Swag' and was published in the *Bulletin* on 15 December 1894. Lawson reworked it for inclusion in *While the Billy Boils* to enlarge the Mitchell Series. This humorous sketch tells of a swagman and his dog arriving at the Redfern Station.

ENTER MITCHELL

The Western train had just arrived at Redfern railway station with a lot of ordinary passengers and one swagman.

He was short, and stout, and bow-legged, and freckled, and sandy. He had red hair and small, twinkling, grey eyes, and — what often goes with such things — the expression of a born comedian. He was dressed in a ragged, well-washed print shirt, an old black waist-coat with a calico back, a pair of cloudy moleskins patched at the knees and held up by a plaited greenhide belt buckled loosely around his hips, a pair of well-worn, fuzzy blucher boots, and a soft felt hat, green with age, and with no brim worth mentioning, and no crown to speak of. He swung a swag on to the platform, shouldered it, pulled out a billy and a water-bag, and then went to a dog-box in the brake van.

Five minutes later he appeared on the edge of the cab platform, with an anxious-looking cattle-dog crouching against his legs, and one end of the chain in his hand. He eased down the swag against a post, turned his face to the city, tilted his hat forward, and scratched the well-developed back of his head with a little finger. He seemed undecided what track to take.

'Cab, sir!'

The swagman turned slowly and regarded cabby with a quiet grin.

'Now, do I look as if I want a cab?'

'Well, why not? No harm, anyway — I thought you might want a cab.'

Swaggy scratched his head, reflectively.

'Well,' he said, 'you're the first man that has thought so these ten years. What do I want with a cab?'

'To go where you're going, of course.'

'Do I look knocked up?'

'I didn't say you did.'

'And I didn't say you said I did . . . Now, I've been on the track this five years. I've tramped two thousan' miles since last Chris'mas, and I don't see why I can't tramp the last mile. Do you think my old dog wants a cab?'

The dog shivered and whimpered; he seemed to want to get away from the crowd.

'But then, you see, you ain't going to carry that swag through the streets, Are you?' asked the cabman.

'Why not? Who'll stop me? There ain't no law agin it, I b'lieve?'

'But then, you see, it don't look well, you know.'

'Ah! I thought we'd get to it at last.'

The traveller up-ended his bluey against his knee, gave it an affectionate pat, and then straightened himself up and looked fixedly at the cabman.

'Now look here!' he said, sternly and impressively, 'can you see anything wrong with that old swag o' mine?'

It was a stout, dumpy swag, with a red blanket outside, patched with blue, and the edge of a blue blanket showing in the inner rings at the end. The swag might have been newer; it might have been cleaner; it might have been hooped with decent straps, instead of bits of clothes-line and greenhide — but otherwise there was nothing the matter with it, as swags go.

'I've humped that old swag for years,' continued the bushman; 'I've carried that old swag thousands of miles — as that old dog knows — an' no one ever bothered about the look of it, or of me, or of my old dog, neither; and do you think I'm going to be ashamed of that old swag for a cabby or anyone else? Do you think I'm going to study anybody's feelings? No one ever studied mine! I'm in two minds to summon you for using insulting language towards me!'

He lifted the swag by the twisted towel which served for a shoulder-strap, swung it into the cab, got in himself, and hauled the dog after him.

'You can drive me somewhere where I can leave my swag and dog while I get some decent clothes to see a tailor in,' he said to the cabman. 'My old dog ain't used to cabs, you see.'

Then he added, reflectively: 'I drove a cab myself, once, for five years in Sydney.'

'The Romance of the Swag' was written in London and was published in *Children of the Bush*, which was first released in London in 1902 and later in Sydney in 1907. This sketch shows little of Lawson's earlier contempt for the bush. Instead, it could easily have been written in a fit of homesickness while longing for the heat and dryness of the Australian countryside.

THE ROMANCE OF THE SWAG

The Australian swag fashion is the easiest way in the world of carrying a load. I ought to know something about carrying loads; I've carried babies, which are the heaviest and most awkward and heart-breaking loads in this world for a boy or man to carry, I fancy. God remember mothers who slave about the housework (and do sometimes a man's work in addition in the Bush) with a heavy, squalling kid on one arm! I've humped logs on the Selection, 'burning off', with loads of fencing posts and rails and palings out of steep, rugged gullies (and was happier then, perhaps); I've carried a shovel, crowbar, heavy 'rammer', a dozen insulators on an average (strung round my shoulders with raw flax) — to say nothing of soldering kit, tucker bag, billy and climbing spurs — all day on a telegraph line in rough country in New Zealand, and in places where a man had to manage his load with one hand and help himself climb with the other; and I've helped hump and drag telegraph poles up cliffs and sidings where the horses couldn't go. I've carried a portmanteau on the hot dusty roads in green old Jackeroo days. Ask any actor who's been stranded and had to count railway sleepers from one town to another! he'll tell you what sort of an awkward load a portmanteau is, especially if there's a broken-hearted man underneath it. I've tried knapsack fashion — one of the least healthy and most likely to give a man sores; I've carried my belongings in a three-bushel sack slung over my shoulder — blankets, tucker, spare boots and poetry all lumped together. I tried carrying a load on my head, and got a crick in my neck and spine for days. I've carried a load on my mind that should have been shared by editors and publishers. I've helped hump luggage and furniture up to, and down from, a top flat in London. And I've carried swag for months outback in Australia — and it was life, in spite of its 'squalidness' and meanness and wretchedness and hardship, and in spite of the fact

207

that the world would have regarded us as 'tramps' — and a free life amongst *men* from all the world!

The Australian swag was born of Australia and no other land — of the Great Lone Land of magnificent distances and bright heat; the land of Self-reliance, and Never-give-in, and Help-your-mate. The grave of many of the world's tragedies and comedies — royal and otherwise. The land where a man out of employment might shoulder his swag in Adelaide and take the track, and years later walk into a hut on the Gulf, or never be heard of anymore, or a body be found in the Bush and buried by the mounted police, or never found and never buried — what does it matter?

The land I love above all others — not because it was kind to me, but because I was born on Australian soil, and because of the foreign father who died at his work in the ranks of Australian pioneers, and because of many things. Australia! my country! her very name is music to me. God bless Australia! for the sake of the great hearts of the heart of her! God keep her clear of the old-world shams and social lies and mockery, and callous commercialism, and sordid shame! and Heaven send that, if ever in my time her sons are called upon to fight for her young life and honour, I die with the first rank of them and be buried in Australian ground.

But this will probably be called false, forced, or 'maudlin sentiment' here in England, where the mawkish sentiment of the music halls, and the popular applause it receives, is enough to make a healthy man sick, and is only equalled by music-hall vulgarity. So I'll get on.

In the old digging days the knapsack, or straps-across-the-chest fashion, was tried, but the load pressed on a man's chest and impeded his breathing, and a man needs to have his bellows free on long tracks in hot, stirless weather. Then the 'horse-collar', or rolled military overcoat style — swag over one shoulder and under the other arm — was tried, but it was found to be too hot for the Australian climate, and was discarded along with Wellington boots and leggings. Until recently, Australian city artists and editors —

who knew as much about the Bush as Downing Street knows about the British colonies in general — seemed to think the horse-collar was still in existence; and some artists gave the swagman a stick, as if he were a tramp of civilisation with an eye on the backyard and a fear of the dog. English artists, by the way, seem firmly convinced that the Australian Bushman is born in Wellington boots with a polish on 'em you could shave yourself by.

The swag is usually composed of a tent 'fly' or strip of calico (a cover for the swag and a shelter in bad weather — in New Zealand it is oilcloth or waterproof twill), a couple of blankets, blue by custom and preference, as that colour shows the dirt less than any other (hence the name 'bluey' for swag), and the core is composed of spare clothing and small personal effects. To make or 'roll up' your swag: lay the fly or strip of calico on the ground, blueys on top of it; across one end, with eighteen inches or so to spare, lay your spare trousers, shirt, etc., folded, light boots tied together by the laces toe to heel, books, bundle of old letters, portraits — or whatever little nick-nacks you have or care to carry, bag of needles, thread, pen and ink, spare patches for your pants, bootlaces, etc. Lay or arrange the pile so that it will roll evenly with the swag (some pack the lot in an old pillowslip or canvas bag), take a fold over of blanket and calico the whole length on each side, so as to reduce the width of the swag to, say, three feet, throw the spare end, with an inward fold, over the little pile of belongings, and then roll the whole to the other end, using your knees and judgement to make the swag tight, compact and artistic; when within eighteen inches of the loose end take an inward fold in that, and bring it up against the body of the swag. There is a strong suggestion of a roley-poley in a rag about the business, only the ends of the swag are folded in, in rings, and not tied. Fasten the swag with three or four straps, according to judgement and the supply of straps. To the top strap, for the swag is carried (and eased down in shanty bars and against walls or verandah posts when not on the track) in a more or less vertical position — to the top strap, and lowest, or lowest but one, fasten the ends of the shoulder strap (usually a towel is preferred as being softer to the shoulder), your coat being carried outside the swag at the back, under the straps. To the top strap fasten the string of the nose-bag, a calico bag about the size of a pillowslip, containing the tea, sugar and flour bags, bread, meat, baking powder, salt etc., and brought, when the swag is carried from the left shoulder, over the right onto the chest, and so balancing the swag behind. But a swagman can throw a heavy swag in a nearly vertical position against his spine, slung from one shoulder only and without any balance, and carry it as easily as you might wear your overcoat. Some Bushmen arrange their belongings so neatly and conveniently, with swag straps in a sort of harness, that they can roll up the swag in about a minute, and unbuckle it and throw it out as easily as a roll of wall-paper, and there's the bed ready on the ground with the wardrobe for a pillow. The swag is always used for a seat on the track; it is a soft seat, so trousers last a long time. And the dust being mostly soft and silky on the long tracks outback, boots last marvellously. Fifteen miles a day is the average with the swag, but you must travel according to the water: if the next bore or tank is five miles on, and the next twenty beyond, you camp at the five-mile water to-night and do the twenty the next day. But if it's thirty miles you have to do it . . .

And there you have the Australian swag. Men from all the world have carried it — lords and low-class Chinamen, saints and world martyrs, and felons, thieves and murderers, educated gentlemen and boors who couldn't sign their mark, gentlemen who fought for Poland and convicts who fought the world, women and more than one woman disguised as a man. The Australian swag has held its core letters and papers in all languages, the honour of great houses, and more than one national secret, papers that would send well-known and highly-respected men to jail, and proofs of the innocence of men going mad in prisons, life tragedies and comedies, fortunes and papers that secured titles and fortunes, and the last pence of lost fortunes, life secrets, portraits of mothers and dead loves, pictures of fair women, heartbreaking old letters written long ago by vanished hands, and the pencilled manuscript of more than one book which will be famous yet.

The weight of the swag varies from the light rouseabout's swag, containing one blanket and a clean shirt, to the 'royal Alfred', with tent and all complete, and weighing part of a ton. Some old sundowners have a mania for gathering, from selectors' and shearers' huts, dust heaps etc., heart-breaking loads of rubbish which can never be of any possible use to them or anyone else. Here is an inventory of the contents of the swag of an old tramp who was found dead on the track, lying on his face in the sand, with his swag on top of him, and his arms stretched straight out as if he were embracing the Mother Earth, or had made, with his last movement, the Sign of the Cross to the blazing heavens.

Rotten old tent in rags. Filthy blue blanket, patched with squares of red and calico. Half of 'white blanket', nearly black now, patched with pieces of various material and sewn to half of red blanket. Three-bushel sack slit open. Pieces of sacking. Part of a woman's skirt. Two rotten old pairs of moleskin trousers. One leg of a pair of trousers. Back of a shirt. Half a waistcoat. Two tweed coats, green, old and rotting, and patched with calico, blanket etc. Large bundle of assorted rags for patches, all rotten. Leaky billy can, containing fishing line, papers, suet, needles and cotton, etc., etc. Jam tins, medicine bottles, corks on strings, to hang on his hat to keep the flies off (a sign of madness in the Bush, for the corks would madden a sane man sooner than the flies could). Three boots of different sizes, all belonging to the right foot, and a left slipper. Coffee pot, without handle or spout, and quart-pot full of rubbish — broken knives and forks, with the handles burnt off, spoons, etc., etc., picked up on rubbish heaps; and many rusty nails, to be used as buttons, I suppose.

Broken saw blade, hammer, broken crockery, old pannikins, small rusty frying-pan without a handle, children's old shoes, many bits of old boot leather and greenhide, part of yellow-back novel, mutilated English dictionary, grammar and arithmetic book, a ready reckoner, a cookery book, a bulgy Anglo-foreign dictionary, part of a Shakespeare, book in French and book in German, and a book on etiquette and courtship. A heavy pair of blucher boots, with uppers parched and cracked, and soles so patched (patch over patch) with leather, boot protectors, hoop iron and hob nails that they were about two inches thick, and the boots weighed over five pounds. (If you don't believe me go into the Melbourne Museum, where, in a glass case in a place of honour, you will see a similar, perhaps the same, pair of bluchers labelled 'An Example of Colonial Industry'). And in the core of the swag was a sugar bag tied tightly with a whip-lash, and containing another old skirt, rolled very tight and fastened with many turns of a length of clothesline, which last, I suppose, he carried to hang himself with if he felt that way. The skirt was rolled round a packet of old portraits and almost undecipherable letters — one from a woman who had evidently been a sensible woman and a widow, and who stated in the letter that she did not intend to get married again as she had enough to do already, slavin' her fingernails off to keep a family, without having a second husband to keep. And her answer was 'final for good and all', and it wasn't no use comin' 'bungfoodlin' round her again. If he did she'd set Satan onto him. 'Satan' was a dog, I suppose.

The letter was addressed to 'Dear Bill', as were others. There were no envelopes. The letters were addressed from no place in particular, so there weren't any means of identifying the dead man. The police buried him under a gum, and a young trooper cut on the tree the words:

SACRED TO THE MEMORY OF
BILL,
WHO DIED.

CHAPTER 13

Hungerford

> Hungerford consists of two houses and a humpy in New South
> Wales, and five houses in Queensland. Characteristically enough,
> both pubs are in Queensland. We got a glass of sour yeast at one and
> paid sixpence for it — we had asked for English ale.[68]

After carrying their swags for almost three weeks, the sight of sunlight
glinting on corrugated iron roofs must have been a welcome sight for
Lawson, Gordon and De Guinney when they arrived in Hungerford on
or about 16 January 1893. Although food was available from roadside
inns, the men had existed mainly on a diet of on-the-track-made cakes
and salted mutton, the latter adding to their summer thirsts. Lawson
claimed that the meat came from generous station owners along the
way, however there were few stations near the Hungerford road in
those days so the offerings were probably few and far-between.

A letter from Aunt Emma awaited Lawson at the local post office.
Whether he had written to tell her of his plans, or her letter had been
forwarded by one of his Bourke union mates is unclear. On Lawson's
own admission in 'Hungerford', he only stayed one day in the village;
long enough to down 'a glass of sour yeast' or two, and to pen a reply to
Aunt Emma's letter (on 16 January 1893).

Dear Aunt,

I found your letter in the Post Office of this God-Forgotten town. I carried my swag nearly two hundred miles since I last wrote to you, and I am now camped on the Queensland side of the border — a beaten man. I start back tomorrow — 140 miles by the direct road — and expect to reach Bourke in nine days. My mate goes on to Thargomindah. No work and very little to eat; we lived mostly on Johnny cakes and cadged a bit of meat here and there at miserable stations. Have been three days without sugar. Once in Bourke I'll find the means of getting back to Sydney — never to face the bush again. I got an offer to go over and edit a New Zealand paper and wrote to say that I doubted my ability to edit but would take a place on the staff. They seemed anxious to get me, and asked me to state my own terms. Simpson is negotiating with 'em. You can have no idea of the horrors of the country out here. Men tramp and beg and live like dogs. It is two months since I slept in what you can call a bed. We walk as far as we can — according to the water — and then lie down and roll ourselves in our blankets. The flies start at daylight and we fight them all day till dark — then mosquitoes start. We carry water in bags. Got bushed on a lignum plain Sunday before last and found the track at four o'clock in the afternoon — then tramped for four hours without water and reached a government dam. My mate drank nearly all night. But it would take a year to tell you all about my wanderings in the wilderness.

It would not be so bad if it was shearing season — then, at least we'd be sure of tucker. But the experience will help me to live in the city for the next year or so. So much for myself.

I'm real glad to hear that you are still at North Shore (you may expect me there within the next six months — as soon as I can get a few decent clothes). Sorry Don is dead.

I'm writing on an old tin and my legs ache too much to let me sit any longer. I've always tried to write cheerful letters so you'll excuse this one. Will tell you all about it when I get down.

And now for a lonely walk of 140 miles. Will write from Bourke.

Your affectionate nephew,
Henry Lawson

P.S. I'm going off the track to try and get a few weeks' work on a
Warrego station. Will write from there if successful.

The letter raises an important question. Who was Lawson's 'mate' who intended travelling on to Thargomindah, which was situated approximately 90 road miles (145 km) north-west of Hungerford on the Bulloo River? Gordon later says of the end of his trek with Lawson 'we landed back in Bourke, broke', indicating that he accompanied the poet back to the 'metropolis of the great scrubs', so it could be assumed that Lawson was referring to De Guinney when he wrote these words.

In Aunt Emma's letter, Lawson only refers to one mate accompanying him on his journey to Hungerford. His closing words, 'and now for a lonely walk of 140 miles', imply that he intended to travel back to Bourke alone. Yet in the poem 'The Paroo' he mentions his 'mate — a native of the land — . . . a bushman he, and clever', a description that appears to be of Gordon. Jim Gordon's later claim that he accompanied Lawson back to Bourke is also supported by Lawson's 'Baldy Thompson', in which he suggests, by the use of 'we', that he had company on his trip.

Although the accounts are contradictory in nature, Lawson's admitted habit of shuffling personalities, descriptions and the chronology or sequence of events to suit the rhyming or mood of his writings suggests that Gordon's version of events should be considered as a more reliable source of information.

Like Lawson, De Guinney took note of the scenery and events along the way, later using his outback experience to compose a short story titled 'Somebody's Victim'. It was published in the *Worker* on 2 December 1893.

SOMEBODY'S VICTIM

Scene — Bank of the Upper Paroo, plain stretching for miles back; on the plain a flock of travelling sheep, running for all the green patches of grass, and overtaking a swagman with a dog. They are surrounding him now, and suddenly he drops his swag on the ground and sings out:

'Here, Bluey! Go for 'em! Away there!'

Dog starts excitedly barking and running about, and in a few minutes rounds all the sheep in one close mob. Seeing this, the two drovers gallop up to the man.

'What the — are you doing that for? Can't you leave the blankety sheep alone?' says one of them.

'Why, is that your sheep?' innocently asks the traveller. 'I thought they was squatters' sheep, and I don't give no squatters' sheep no chance or mercy. But if it's yours I'm sorry for disturbing 'em. Where are you takin' 'em?'

Drover tells him, and also that that day's camp will be about two miles further on, and that he'd better come and stop there for the night.

* * *

After supper I went to have a chat with the enemy of the squatters' sheep. He was a well-built, middle-aged man, with restless eyes and close-cropped hair. His dog sat alongside of him.

'It's not a bad dog you've got!' I said.

'No, not too bad! He cost me two thousand pounds.'

'What? Two thousand pounds! You don't say so! But what made you set him on to our sheep?'

'Well, I'll tell you. I don't like the squatters' sheep. One of the squatters on the Darling done me out of ten thousand pounds. I came up from Sydney at the time of the strike to work in the shed, and they promised me heaps of money for coming up, but when I stopped there a few weeks they sacked me, and never gave me anything for my work. And then the scabs on the steamer treated me shamefully. You know, I took my passage on the steamer up to

216

Bourke, and when the crew found that I came from Rumbumbo
Station they wouldn't give me any rest at all. Why, they put a rope
round me and threw me overboard, and towed me, I believe, nearly a
mile before they pulled me up on deck again. I was going to shoot
every one of them but I didn't have any firearms. Oh, the wretches!
Oh, the scoundrels!'

And here his eyes became more restless than ever, with a
strange glare in them. I knew then that he was what they call in the
bush 'a bit gone,' and I tried to calm him. He seemed to be sane
enough on anything but money matters, and that must have been his
loose screw in the brain. Presently he started again —

'I've been travelling now for months and months, waiting for
that ten thousand pounds, but I never got it yet. Hold on, though,
when I get it I'll go back again to Sydney, and then I'd like to see
anybody asking me to come up and help the squatters, and the —
now won't give me even a bit of tucker. I've been living now for the
last six days on Johnnycakes, and I am tired of it. Have you got any
tobacco on you?'

I gave him some. The camp fire was going out, the night air was
getting cold, and I turned in. In the morning I couldn't find him. He
had wandered away across the plain, looking for the squatters' sheep.
There are dozens like him in the bush, mostly from Whitely King's*
office.

* *Whitely King*: chairman of the Pastoralists' Union which brought non-union labour
to the shearing sheds of the north-west during the shearers' strikes of the 1890s

Though Hungerford was officially situated in the colony of Queensland, a
southward expansion of the village, before the official 1880 survey named
the 29th parallel of latitude as the official border between New South
Wales and Queensland, meant that the one section lay in Queensland
while the other lay in New South Wales. It was along this new border
that a rabbit-proof fence was subsequently built, effectively dividing the
town and resulting in tiresome legal and jurisdiction problems.

Hungerford was an important border crossing location, as was
Barringun to the east. The village boasted a post office, customs office,

police station, school and store. The two pubs, one known as the Royal Hotel, were located on the Queensland side of the border because of legal requirements. Lawson lost no time in jotting down his impressions of the village. The resulting 'Hungerford' was published in the *Bulletin* on 16 December 1893, and later in *While the Billy Boils*.

HUNGERFORD

One of the hungriest cleared roads in New South Wales runs to within a couple of miles of Hungerford, and stops there; then you strike through the scrub to the town. There is no distant prospect of Hungerford — you don't see the town till you are quite close to it, and then two or three white-washed galvanised-iron roofs start out of the mulga.

They say that a past Ministry commenced to clear the road from Bourke, under the impression that Hungerford was an important place, and went on, with the blindness peculiar to Governments, till they got within two miles of the town. Then they ran short of rum and rations, and sent a man on to get them, and make enquiries. The member never came back, and two more were sent on to find him — or Hungerford. Three days later the two returned in an exhausted condition, and submitted a motion of want-of-confidence, which was lost. Then the whole House went on and was lost also. Strange to relate, that Government was never missed.

However, we found Hungerford and camped there for a day. The town is right on the Queensland border, and an interprovincial rabbit-proof fence — with rabbits on both sides of it — runs across the main street.

This fence is a standing joke with Australian rabbits — about the only joke they have out there, except the memory of Pasteur and poison and inoculation. It is amusing to go a little way out of town about sunset, and watch them crack Noah's Ark rabbit jokes about that fence, and burrow under and play leap-frog over till they get tired. One old buck rabbit sat up and nearly laughed his ears off at a joke of his own about that fence. He laughed so much that he couldn't get away when I reached for him. I could hardly eat him for laughing. I never saw a rabbit laugh before; but I've seen a 'possum do it.

Hungerford consists of two houses and a humpy in New South Wales, and five houses in Queensland. Characteristically enough, both the pubs are in Queensland. We got a glass of sour yeast at one and paid sixpence for it — we had asked for English ale.

The post office is in New South Wales, and the police barracks in Bananaland. The police cannot do anything if there is a row going on across the street in New South Wales, except to send to Brisbane and have an extradition warrant applied for; and they don't do much if there's a row in Queensland. Most of the rows are across the border, where the pubs are.

At least, I believe that's how it is, though the man who told me might have been a liar. Another man said he was a liar, but then *he* might have been a liar himself — a third person said he was one. I heard that there was a fight over it, but the man who told me about the fight might not have been telling the truth.

One part of the town swears at Brisbane when things go wrong, and the other part curses Sydney.

The country looks as though a great ash-heap had been spread out there, and mulga scrub and firewood planted — and neglected. The country looks just as bad for a hundred miles around Hungerford, and beyond that it gets worse — a blasted, barren wilderness that doesn't even howl. If it howled it would be a relief.

I believe that Burke and Wills found Hungerford, and it's a pity that they did; but, if I ever stand by the graves of the men who first travelled through this country, when there were neither roads nor stations, nor tanks, nor bores, nor pubs, I'll — I'll take my hat off. There were brave men in the land in those days.

It is said that the explorers gave the district its name chiefly because of the hunger they found there, which has remained there ever since. I don't know where the 'ford' comes in — there's nothing to ford, except in flood-time. Hungerthirst would have been better.

The town is supposed to be situated on the banks of a river called the Paroo, but we saw no water there, except what passed for it in a tank. The goats and sheep and dogs and the rest of the population drink there. It is dangerous to take too much of that water in a raw state.

Except in flood-time you couldn't find the bed of the river without the aid of a spirit level and a long straight-edge. There is a Custom-house against the fence on the northern side. A pound of tea often costs six shillings on that side, and you can get a common lead pencil for fourpence at the rival store across the street in the mother province. Also, a small loaf of sour bread sells for a shilling at the humpy aforementioned. Only about sixty percent of the sugar will melt.

We saw one of the storekeepers give a deadbeat swagman five shillings' worth of rations to take him on into Queensland. The storekeepers often do this, and put it down on the loss side of their books. I hope the recording angel listens, and puts it down on the right side of his book.

We camped on the Queensland side of the fence, and after tea had a yarn with an old man who was minding a mixed flock of goats and sheep; and we asked him if he thought Queensland was better than New South Wales, or the other way about.

He scratched the back of his head, and thought awhile, and hesitated like a stranger who is going to do you a favour at some personal inconvenience.

At last, with the bored air of a man who has gone through the same performance too often before, he stepped deliberately up to the fence and spat over it into New South Wales. After which he got leisurely through and spat back on Queensland.

'That's what I think of the blanky colonies!' he said.

He gave us time to become sufficiently impressed; then he said:

'And if I was at the Victorian and South Australian border I'd do the same thing.'

He let that soak into our minds, and added: 'And the same with West Australia — and — and Tasmania.' Then he went away.

The last would have been a long spit — and he forgot Maoriland.

We heard afterwards that his name was Clancy, and he had that day been offered a job droving at 'twenty-five shillings a week and find your own horse'. Also find your own horse-feed and tobacco and soap and other luxuries, at station prices. Moreover, if you lost your own horse you would have to find another, and if that died or went astray you would have to find a third — or forfeit your pay and return on foot. The boss drover agreed to provide flour and mutton — when such things were procurable.

Consequently Clancy's unfavourable opinion of the colonies.

My mate and I sat down on our swags against the fence to talk things over. One of us was very deaf. Presently a black-tracker went past and looked at us, and returned to the pub. Then a trooper in Queensland uniform came along and asked us what the trouble was about, and where we came from and were going, and where we camped. We said we were discussing private business, and he explained that he thought it was a row, and came over to see us. Then he left us, and later on we saw him sitting with the rest of the population on a bench under the hotel verandah. Next morning we rolled up our swags and left Hungerford to the North-West.

As shown by the derogatory tone of his sketch, Lawson wasn't impressed with Hungerford. The village had been named in 1875, not in respect of the apparent 'hunger' of the town, as Lawson suggested, but after Thomas Hungerford (later Sir Thomas), a Queensland pastoralist who had previously travelled cattle through that district on his way to southern markets. Although Lawson believed that Burke and Wills had founded Hungerford, this was not so; in fact the pair did not travel within a hundred miles of the site and the village was not established until about fifteen years after the two explorers perished.

'Crawlalong', which was published in the *Bulletin* on 4 February 1893, could also have been created with Hungerford in mind.

CRAWLALONG

The 'TOWNSHIP' of Crawlalong lies 'out back'. It is so often mentioned in stock reports that city people regard it as being quite an important place. The traveller, on first arriving there, will most likely ask the coach-driver how much further it is to Crawlalong; and the driver will answer, with a twinkle in his eye:

'This is it!'

The principal buildings are the 'Carriers' Arms', the blacksmith's shop, the 'Commercial Stores', and a weatherboard box, roofed with galvanised iron, and called a 'cottage'. The main street is that portion of the Government road extending from the blacksmith's shop to the pub — about fifty yards. The smithy is a slab shed with a flat, bark roof and kerosene-tin flue. The pub. is a low, weatherboard building with a very low verandah round two sides, and a door in the corner. The verandah slouches down over the door and windows like the hat of a common back-lane variety of larrikin. The bar is low, dark, dingy, and altogether evil-looking. The sinister doors and windows look furtively out from under the verandah — like the eyes of the aforesaid larrikin scowling under his hat-brim.

The water supply of Crawlalong is invisible. The town's average temperature is Sheol in the shade. Visible population: two men going in to have a drink, and a drunkard lying bare-headed in the blazing heat by the dusty roadside. Trade: A bullock-team and a hawker's waggonette standing outside the 'Carriers' Arms'. Politics: freetrade and Protection. Religion: liquor and horse-racing. Church: the 'Carriers' Arms'. Principal imports: beer, rum, brandy, whisky, gin, flour, tea and sugar. Exports: dead drunkards — as far as the cemetery. Products: jim-jams.* Chief industry: 'lambing down'. Principal occupation of population when not dead-drunk: fighting three luke-warm rounds fearfully, and shaking hands afterwards with great enthusiasm.

The town is supported by a few old shearers who come there regularly to be shorn. The government is communistic to a certain extent, and 'liberty prevails', but the law of the land is represented

222

by two mounted troopers who visit the place about once a year, and borrow — in the Queen's name — a horse and dray and pick and shovel from the local blacksmith, and bury the remains of any dead bushmen that may be lying around.

* *jim-jams*: alcohol-induced delusions

It was at Hungerford that Lawson came across a wide, shallow depression in the local topography that was the dry creek-bed of the Paroo River. However it wasn't 'a week from Christmas-time', as Lawson claimed, but mid-January, and it is unlikely that Lawson saw the Paroo River at any other location except at Hungerford itself. The poem 'The Paroo River' was first published in 1893, then later in *Verses Popular and Humorous*.

THE PAROO RIVER

It was a week from Christmas-time,
As near as I remember,
And half a year since in the rear,
We'd left the Darling Timber.
The track was hot and more than drear;
The long day seemed forever;
But now we knew that we were near
Our camp — the Paroo River.

With blighted eyes and blistered feet,
With stomachs out of order,
Half mad with flies and dust and heat
We'd crossed the Queensland Border.
I longed to hear a stream go by
And see the circles quiver;
I longed to lay me down and die
That night on Paroo River.

'Tis said the land out West is grand —
I do not care who says it,

It isn't even decent scrub,
Nor yet an honest desert;
It's plagued with flies and broiling hot,
A curse is on it ever;
I really think that God forgot
The country round that river.

My mate — a native of the land —
In fiery speech and vulgar,
Condemned the flies and cursed the sand,
And doubly damned the mulga.
He peered ahead, he peered about —
A bushman he*, and clever —
'Now mind you keep a sharp look-out;
We must be near the river.'
The 'nose bags' heavy on each chest
(God bless one kindly squatter!)
With grateful weight our hearts they pressed —
We only wanted water.
The sun was setting (in the west)
In colour like a liver —
We'd fondly hoped to camp and rest
That night on Paroo River.

A cloud was on my mate's broad brow,
And once I heard him mutter:
'I'd like to see the Darling now,
God bless the Grand Old Gutter!'
And now and then he stopped and said
In tones that made me shiver —
'It cannot well be on ahead —
I think we've crossed the river.'

But soon we saw a strip of ground
That crossed the track we followed,

224

No barer than the surface round,
But just a little hollowed.
His brows assumed a thoughtful frown —
This speech he did deliver:
'I wonder if we'd best go down
Or up the blessed river?'

'But where,' said I, ' 's the blooming stream?'
And he replied, 'We're at it!'
I stood awhile as in a dream,
'Great Scott,' I cried, 'is that it?
Why, that is some old bridle track!'
He chuckled 'Well, I never!
It's nearly time you came out-back —
This is the Paroo River!'

No place to camp — no spot of damp —
No moisture to be seen there;
If e'er there was it left no sign
That it had ever been there.
But ere the morn, with heart and soul
We'd cause to thank the Giver —
We found a muddy water-hole
Some ten miles down the river.

* *bushman*: probably refers to Jim Gordon

If we believe verbatim Lawson's letter to Aunt Emma, stating that he would begin his return journey to Bourke the following day, he filled his water bag, slung his swag on his back and headed towards the Darling and the 'metropolis of the great scrubs' on 17 January 1893.

Probably with his mate Jim Gordon, he travelled back over the same route taken just days previously: past Warroo Springs, Brindingabba Bore, Kenmere Bore, the village of Yantabulla, Lake Eliza and Youngerina Bore. In his letter to Aunt Emma he had mentioned that he planned to go 'off the track to try and get a few weeks' work on a Warrego station' and that he would write to her while there. It is not known what Warrego station Lawson was referring to, unless he inadvertently believed that Kerribree Station lay on the Warrego River instead of Kerribree Creek, and no letter to his aunt from that part of the countryside has survived.

The Kerribree run, west of the village of Fords Bridge, was owned by William Walter Davis, an active pastoralist–businessman and local ex-member of Parliament. In 1886 he became the first pastoralist in Australia to successfully drill for a proper source of flowing artesian water on a private basis.

On reaching Kerribree homestead, Lawson and Gordon stopped and asked for a supply of food to assist them on their way to Bourke. If Lawson had not yet met Davis, he already knew the grazier by reputation. In fact, Lawson had referred to him in his first Bourke-written poem, 'Our Members Present and Future', when he wrote 'An' Davis had to stand aside for such a man as that!' Assuming that Davis knew the identity of his guest and had read his favourable mention in Lawson's poem, a refusal of food for the poet and his friend would have been unthinkable. Being a generous man, he gave the travellers as much food as they could carry and a pound note, as Lawson's letter to his Aunt Emma later confirmed.

Davis was usually (if irreverently) referred to by those who knew and worked for him as 'Baldy Davis'. He is generally believed to be the model for the remarkable debater, curmudgeon and philanthropist Baldy Thompson, the main character in Lawson's story by the same name which was published the *Worker* on 13 October 1894 and later in *When the Billy Boils*. In it Lawson referred to his Kerribree benefactor as 'a squatter of the old order' who 'when he wasn't cursing the banks and government . . . cursed the country'. Some years later William Davis re-entered the political arena and, all told, he represented the electorate of Bourke for fifteen years.

BALDY THOMPSON

Rough, squarish face, curly auburn wig, bushy grey eyebrows and moustache, and grizzly stubble — eyes that reminded one of Dampier the actor. He was a squatter of the old order — new-chum, swagman, drover, shearer, super, pioneer, cocky, squatter, and finally bank victim. He had been through it all, and knew all about it.

He had been in Parliament, and wanted to go again; but the men mistrusted him as Thompson, M.P., though they swore by him as old Baldy Thompson the squatter. His hobby was politics, and his politics were badly boxed. When he wasn't cursing the banks and government he cursed the country. He cursed the Labour leaders at intervals, and seemed to think he could run the Unions better than they could. Also, he seemed to think he could run Parliament better than any Premier. He was generally voted a hard case, which term is mostly used in a kindly sense out back.

He was always grumbling about the country. If a shearer or rouseabout was good at argument, and a bit of a politician, he hadn't to slave much at Thompson's shed, for Baldy would argue with him all day and pay for it.

'I can't put on any more men,' he'd say to travellers who were after 'stragglers'. 'I can't put on a lot of men to make big cheques when there's no money in the bank to pay 'em — and I've got all I can do to get tucker for the family. I shore nothing but burrs and grass-seed last season, and it didn't pay carriage. I'm just sending away a flock of sheep now, and I won't make threepence a head on 'em. I had twenty thousand in the bank season before last, and now I can't count on one. I'll have to roll up my swag and go on the track myself next.'

'All right, Baldy,' they'd say, 'git out your blooming swag and come along with us, old man; we'll stick to you and see you through.'

'I swear I'd show you round first,' he'd reply. 'Go up to the store and get what rations you want. You can camp in the huts to-night, and I'll see you in the morning.'

But most likely he'd find his way over after tea, and sit on his heels in the cool outside the hut, and argue with the swagman about Unionism and politics. And he'd argue all night if he met his match.

The track by Baldy Thompson's was reckoned as a good tucker track, especially when a dissolution of Parliament was threatened. Then the guileless traveller would casually let Baldy know that he'd got his name on the electoral list, and show some interest in Baldy's political opinions, and oppose them at first, and finally agree with them and see a lot in them — be led around to Baldy's way of thinking, in fact; and ultimately depart, rejoicing, with a full nose-bag, and a quiet grin for his mate.

There are many camp-fire yarns about old Baldy Thompson.

One New Year the shearers — shearing stragglers — roused him in the dead of night and told him that the shed was on fire. He came out in his shirt and without his wig. He sacked them all there and then, but of course they went to work as usual the next morning. There is something sad and pathetic about that old practical joke — as indeed there is with all bush jokes. There seems a quiet sort of sadness always running through out back humour — whether alleged or otherwise.

There's the usual yarn about a jackaroo mistaking Thompson for a brother rouser, and asking him whether old Baldy was about anywhere, and Baldy said:

'Why, are you looking for a job?'

'Yes, do you think I stand any show? What sort of a boss is Baldy?'

'You'd tramp from here to Adelaide,' said Baldy, 'and north to the Gulf country, and couldn't find a worse. He's the meanest squatter in Australia. The damned old crawler! I grafted like a nigger to him for over fifty years' — Baldy was over sixty — 'and now the old skunk won't even pay me the last two cheques he owes me — says the bank has got everything he had — that's an old cry of his, the damned old sneak; seems to expect me to go short to keep his wife and family and relations in comfort, and by God I've done it for the last thirty or forty years, and I might go on the track tomorrow

228

worse off than the meanest old whaler that ever humped bluey. Don't you have anything to do with Scabby Thompson, or you'll be sorry for it. Better tramp to hell than take a job from him.'

'Well, I think I'll move on. Would I stand any show for some tucker?'

'Him! He wouldn't give a dog a crust, and like as not he'd get you run in for trespass if he caught you camping on the run. But come along to the store and I'll give you enough tucker to carry you on.'

He patronised literature and arts, too, though in an awkward, furtive way. We remember how we once turned up at the station hard up and short of tucker, and how we entertained Baldy with some of his own ideas as ours — having been posted beforehand by our mate — and how he told us to get some rations and camp in the hut and see him in the morning.

And we saw him in the morning, had another yarn with him, agreed and sympathised with him some more, were convinced on one or two questions which we had failed to see at first, cursed things in chorus with him, and casually mentioned that we expected soon to get some work on a political paper.

And at last he went inside and brought out a sovereign.

'Wrap this in a piece of paper and put it in your pocket, and don't lose it,' he said.

But we learnt afterwards that the best way to get along with Baldy, and secure his good will, was to disagree with him on every possible point.

After leaving Kerribree, the greater part of the return journey had passed. Fords Bridge, Sutherland's Lake, Fords Bridge Tank and Walkdens Bore: these were familiar and welcome sights that heralded Lawson's ever-increasing proximity to Bourke. During this section of their journey, Lawson and Gordon met up with Ebenezer Davis, one of William's sons, who was escorting a mob of Kerribree sheep along the Travelling Stock Route bound for Bourke. After introducing themselves, the two travellers were invited to share a drovers'-style meal with young Davis and his assistants. This fact was often related in later years by one of Ebenezer's sons, William (Wilkie) Davis, who learned it from his father as a young lad.

It appears that Lawson did not deviate from the main track on his return journey, which took three weeks, and did not obtain any work along the way. Gordon summed up their days together when he wrote:

> We were together four or five months at that time, wool rolling here, picking up there, and tramping a good deal. And then we landed back in Bourke, broke, where my friends discovered me and consigned me, as a 'colonial experience', to a very far-back station under a spirit-breaking dog of a manager. It was hell, or nearly so, for me. [69]

Assuming that Gordon had first met Henry Lawson during early November the previous year, by the time of their return to Bourke in early February 1893 they had known each other for a little over three months, making Gordon's claim of 'four or five months' slightly exaggerated.

Old Milk Pail

CHAPTER 14

When the Army Prays for Watty

... the Army does no good in outback Australia — except from a business point of view. It is simply there to collect funds for hungry headquarters. The Bushmen are much too intelligent for the Army ... [70]

Henry Lawson had been back in Bourke long enough to find himself a painting job when he penned a brief letter to his Aunt Emma on 6 February. Two days earlier, 'Crawlalong', the second piece of prose written since his arrival in Bourke, had been published in the *Bulletin*.

Bourke.
6th February 1893.

Dear Aunt,
I got back again all right, and am at work painting. Will no doubt be able to get down your way in a few weeks. It's hot as hell here —
too hot to think or write. Bulletin hunting me up for copy, but they

must wait till I get down. I have some work to do for a local paper here, the Western Herald, and so I'll be able to get together a pound or two and some clothes. A squatter who knew me gave me as much tucker as I could carry, when I was coming down, and a pound to help me along*. Squatters are not all bad. My boots were worn out and I was in rags when I arrived here — you should have seen the hat I wore. I find that I've tramped more than 300 miles since I left here last. That's all I ever intend to do with a swag. It's too hot to write more. Send some news by return.

Your affectionate nephew,
Henry Lawson
* William Davis

Lawson did not get down Aunt Emma's way in a few weeks. Nor did he follow through with his promise of working for the *Western Herald*. A careful scrutiny of copies of that newspaper reveals no sign of any additional work being published there.

Up to his return from Hungerford around 6 February 1893, Lawson's movements can be approximately accounted for. From early February onwards, until his return to Sydney around June of the same year, however, his movements are hazy. We know from his letter to Aunt Emma that Lawson was busy painting. This was reinforced in 'Send Round the Hat', where he wrote: 'The shearing season was over in that district, but I got a job of house painting, which was my trade, at the Great Western Hotel (a two-storey brick place), and I stayed in Bourke for a couple of months.' Later in the same story, Lawson refers to being 'on a plank, painting the ceiling of the bar of the Great Western Hotel'. The job was taking longer than expected owing to the practice of the 'chaps handing up long beers' and chiacking him about 'putting on the paint wrong side out'.

In his spare time Lawson was writing hard for the *Bulletin* and other newspapers, evidenced by the large quantity of verse and prose published later during that same year. Other Bourke-inspired stories and verse published in the *Bulletin* during Lawson's last few months in Bourke included 'Mitchell: A Character Sketch' (15 April), 'On the Edge of a Plain' (6 May), 'Mitchell Doesn't Believe in the Sack' (13 May), 'Stragglers' (27 May), 'Rats' (3 June) and 'Great Doings at Ganterbullingabbaree', which was later added to and renamed 'Two Sundowners'.

Lawson walked the streets, frequenting the bars of local pubs such as the Carriers' Arms, gathering experiences for his stories and poems. The union offices in Mitchell Street were also a favourite haunt where the poet renewed old acquaintances and strengthened his ties with the union officials he had previously become friendly with. His outback experiences reinforced any socialistic bond that had existed between him and the union movement. As Billy Wood later recorded, 'Lawson often visited the offices of the ASU and the GLU and met many old stalwarts there, Donald Macdonell, A. Andrews, Scotty Anderson, Mick O'Brien, Con Barry, Jack Boreham, Tom Hurdis and many others.'[71] Lawson, too, had now worked in a shearing shed and had walked many miles of the great outback ostensibly looking for work. Now he could count himself among the ranks of the oppressed pastoral workers; finally, he was one of them.

Lawson's living arrangements at this time are vague. Probably because of a lack of money, he was reported for a time to be sleeping under a skillion at the rear of the union office, and also in the local park. In 'That Pretty Girl in the Army', a lengthy story which was published in *Children of the Bush* in 1902 and is reprinted in full later in this chapter, Lawson wrote: 'The free portion of the male population were in the habit of taking their blankets and sleeping out in 'The Park' or town square, in hot weather . . . I camped in a corner of the park that night.' Later in the same story he mentioned: 'we walked together towards the Union Office, where I had a camp in the skillion room at the back'.

According to local legend, Lawson eventually took up residence in a cottage in Mitchell Street, about a hundred yards west of the Carriers' Arms Hotel, on the opposite side of the road. The cottage is still standing and habitable today, albeit disguised by the addition of fibro cladding and roof renovations. Close inspection of the front of the building reveals the original weatherboards.

Immediately to the west of Lawson's Mitchell Street cottage were four shops owned by Cobb & Co., though leased to other businesses. At the rear of these shops was the Cobb & Co. depot and coach stables. Besides the Carriers' Arms, there were also two other pubs within a few hundred yards: the two-storeyed Caledonian known at various times as The Pride of Erin and The Golden Stairs, and the Shakespeare Hotel where the first New South Wales branch of the Amalgamated Shearers' Union was formed in 1886.

Across the road from Lawson's cottage stood a horse bazaar and general store, owned by brothers William and Sam Doughty, where every Saturday morning horses were offered for auction to the general public. Privately owned mounts were cared for in adjoining stables, and horses and buggies were hired out for local use.

With Lawson living in close proximity to three hotels, the Cobb & Co. yards and the horse bazaar, the odours of beer and horses and molasses undoubtedly predominated. It was in this busy, boisterous neighbourhood that Lawson reportedly spent his final months in Bourke.

The Carriers' Arms Hotel, which is still in use today, is situated on the corner of Mitchell and Wilson Streets, several blocks away from the busier western section of the town. Judging by its architectural design, the brick single-storeyed hotel was probably built about the mid–1870s. For a time it doubled as a booking agency for the Cobb and Co. coach service. The original Cobb & Co. sign, which was painted on the hotel's exterior red brick wall, remained until the building was damaged by fire. A facsimile has since been substituted.

In 1892–93 the licensee was Watson Braithwaite, known affectionately by his friends as 'Watty'. He had taken over the proprietorship of the Carriers' Arms Hotel shortly before Lawson's arrival in Bourke. Previously he had held the licence of the Warrego Inn at Enngonia, a village 60 miles (100 km) to the north of Bourke.

He was also associated with the Teamsters' Union and had a close alliance with the Bourke union scene in general.

Watty Braithwaite was a 'stout, contented, good-natured' man.[72] Because of his stature Lawson referred to him as 'Watty Broadweight', or, more familiarly, 'Watty Bothways'.[73] Similarly, Mrs Braithwaite is referred to as 'Mrs Bothways . . . as fat as Watty, and very much like him in the face, but she was emotional and sympathetic'.[74]

When neither painting nor writing, the focus of Lawson's spare hours became Watty Braithwaite's Carriers' Arms Hotel. The owner of the pub, as well as the social life of the patrons who breasted the bar, provided Lawson with ongoing material for his writing. He often used the hotel itself and sometimes, in an attempt to disguise its identity, he referred to it as The Shearer' Arms. One Bourke local, W. H. Barnett, claimed in his memoirs that the hotel should have been named the Drovers' Arms, on account of the large numbers of drovers who patronised the premises.

John Hawley, Bourke painting contractor and Lawson's one-time employer, provided an insight to the poem that resulted from the Salvation Army's regular gatherings at the pub:

> He [Lawson] frequently came round to my quarters at the Shakespeare Hotel, Sturt Street [sic, actually Mitchell Street], and we used to go for a walk in the quiet part of the river town, past Wattie Braithwaite's hotel, Wattie, sitting in an armchair in the side doorway and the Salvation Army holding its usual meeting a few yards from him. This gave rise to the poem 'When the Army Prays for Watty'.[75]

Spiritually, the residents of Bourke were well provided for to by St Ignatius, the Roman Catholic church which had been opened in 1874, and St Andrew's Presbyterian church which had been built after the 1890 flood. The Salvation Army had probably been operating in the town since the early 1880s. Founded by William Booth, a Methodist minister, in London in 1865, it was an international religious and charitable organisation run along military lines. The general members were known as the corps, commanded by an officer ranging in rank from lieutenant to brigadier. This officer was responsible to a divisional headquarters.

The antics of the 'Army', as Lawson preferred to call it, gave Lawson much material for his writing. On Saturday evenings during the summer months, Mitchell Street came alive with the music from three brass bands. The Town Band and the Cobb & Co. Band took up varying positions outside other hotels such as the Jolly Wagoner, Telegraph, Gladstone, Royal and Tattersall hotels, which were situated in the main commercial part of town and therefore had the greatest number of passers-by. However the Salvation Army Band favoured the quieter neighbourhood at the eastern end of Mitchell Street, near the Carriers' Arms Hotel. During these occasions, they engaged in their regular drum-beating activities while Watty Braithwaite sat in a wicker chair on the footpath outside the Mitchell Street entrance to his pub.

Billy Wood wrote in 1926: 'Henry used greatly to enjoy watching 'Watty' Braithwaite, sitting in his chair in front of the Carriers' Arms, while the 'Army' was holding forth in front. 'Watty' used to look cherubic.' [76]

Despite his partial deafness, Lawson could hear the Salvation Army men and women as they lectured on the evils of mankind while testifying to their own spiritual awareness. Loud and long they prayed in an effort to save not only the soul of the often-dozing licensee, but the souls of those men who still breasted the bar within. 'When the Army Prays for Watty' was published in the *Bulletin* on 13 May 1893.

WHEN THE ARMY PRAYS FOR WATTY

*When the kindly hours of darkness, save for light of
    moon and star,
Hide the picture on the signboard over Doughty's
    Horse Bazaar;
When the last rose-tint is fading on the distant mulga
    scrub,
Then the Army prays for Watty at the entrance of his
    pub.*

Now I often sit at Watty's when the night is very near,
With a head that's full of jingle, and the fumes of
    bottled beer;
For I always have a fancy that, if I am over there
When the Army prays for Watty, I'm included in the
    prayer.

Watty lounges in his arm-chair, in its old accustomed
    place,
With a fatherly expression on his round and passive
    face;
And his arms are clasped before him in a calm,
    contented way,
And he nods his head and dozes when he hears the
    Army pray.

And I wonder does he ponder on the distant years and
    dim,
Or his chances over yonder when the Army prays for
    him?
Has he not a fear connected with the warm place
    down below,
Where, according to good Christians, all the publicans
    should go?

But his features give no token of a feeling in his breast,
Save of peace that is unbroken and a conscience well
    at rest;
And we guzzle as we guzzled long before the Army
    came,
And the loafers wait for 'shouters', and — they get
    there just the same.

It would take a lot of praying, lots of thumping on the
    drum —

To prepare our sinful, straying, erring souls for
   Kingdom Come;
But I love my fellow sinners, and I hope, upon the
   whole,
That the Army gets a hearing when it prays for
   Watty's soul.

The presence of the Salvation Army in small towns such as Bourke obviously captured Lawson's imagination, and he wrote of them again in 'Booth's Drum', which was written much later in 1915 for *My Army, Oh My Army*.

BOOTH'S DRUM
[excerpt]

Somewhere in the early eighties they had banged the
   drum to Bourke,
Where the job of fighting Satan was white-hot and
   dusty work.
Oh, the Local Lass was withered in the heat that bakes
   and glares,
And we sent her food and firewood, but took small
   need of her prayers.
We were blasphemous and beery, we were free from
   Creed or care —
Till they sent their prettiest Lassies — and they broke
   our centre there.
So that, moderately sober, we could stand to hear them
   sing —
And we'd chaff their Testifiers, and throw quids into
   the ring.
(Never less than bobs or 'dollars' — sometimes quids
   into the ring.)

Lawson, however, wasn't finished with the 'Army'. The scenes outside the Carriers' Arms Hotel stayed in his mind for years, eventually voicing themselves in the lengthy 'That Pretty Girl in the Army'. For the characters, he drew on his Bourke union mates — Tom Hall, Billy Wood, Donald Macdonell, the mythical One-eyed Bogan and Barcoo-Rot, local shearers such as Bob Brothers, Jack Boreham and John Merrick, not to mention the indomitable Watty and his hotel.

THAT PRETTY GIRL IN THE ARMY

The Salvation Army does good business in some of the outback towns of the great pastoral wastes of Australia. There's the thoughtless, careless generosity of the Bushman, whose pockets don't go far enough down his trousers (that's what's the matter with him), and who contributes to anything that comes along, without troubling to ask questions, like long Bob Brothers of Bourke, who, chancing to be 'a Protestant by rights', unwittingly subscribed towards the erection of a new Catholic church, and, being chaffed for his mistake said:

'Ah, well, I don't suppose it'll matter a hang in the end, any way it goes. I ain't got nothink agenst Roming Carflicks.'

There's the shearer, fresh with his cheque from a cut-out shed, gloriously drunk and happy, in love with all the world, and ready to subscribe to any creed and shout for all hands — including Old Nick if he happened to come along. There's the shearer, half drunk and inclined to be nasty, who has got the wrong end of all things with a tight grip, and who flings a shilling in the face of outback conventionality (as he thinks) by chucking a bob into the Salvation Army ring. Then he glares round to see if he can catch anybody winking behind his back. There's the cynical joker, a queer mixture, who contributes generously and tempts the reformed boozer afterwards. There's the severe-faced old station hand — in clean shirt and neckerchief and white moleskins — in for his annual or semi-annual spree, who contributes on principle, and then drinks religiously until his cheque is gone and the horrors are come. There's the shearer, feeling mighty bad after a spree, and in danger of seeing things when he tries to go to sleep. He has dropped ten or twenty pounds over bar counters and at cards, and he now 'chucks' a repentant shilling into the ring, with a very private and rather vague sort of feeling that something might come of it. There's the stout, contented, good-natured publican, who tips the Army as if it were a barrel-organ. And there are others and other reasons — black sheep and ne'er-do-wells — and faint echoes of other times in Salvation Army tunes.

Bourke, the metropolis of the Great Scrubs, on the banks of the Darling River, about 500 miles from Sydney, was suffering from a long drought when I was there in '92; and the heat may or may not have been another cause contributing to the success, from a business point of view, of the Bourke garrison. There was much beer boozing — and, besides, it was vaguely understood (as most things are vaguely understood out there in the drought-haze) that the place the Army came to save us from was hotter than Bourke. We didn't hanker to go to a hotter place than Bourke. But that year there was an extraordinary reason for the Army's great financial success there.

She was a little girl, nineteen or twenty, I should judge, the prettiest girl I ever saw in the Army, and one of the prettiest I've ever seen out of it. She had the features of an angel, but her expression was wonderfully human, sweet and sympathetic. Her big grey eyes were sad with sympathy for sufferers and sinners, and her poke bonnet was full of bunchy, red-gold hair. Her first appearance was somewhat dramatic — perhaps the Army arranged it so.

The Army used to pray, and thump the drum, and sing, and take up collections every evening outside Watty Bothway's hotel, the 'Carriers' Arms'. They performed longer and more often outside Watty's than any other pub in town — perhaps because Watty was considered the most hopeless publican and his customers the hardest crowd of boozers in Bourke. The band generally began to play about dusk. Watty would lean back comfortably in a basket easy-chair on his wide verandah, and clasp his hands, in a calm, contented way, while the Army banged the drum and got steam up, and whilst, perhaps, there was a barney going on in the bar, or a bloodthirsty fight in the backyard. On such occasions there was something like an indulgent or fatherly expression on his fat and usually emotionless face. And by-and-by he'd move his head gently and doze. The banging and the singing seemed to soothe him, and the praying, which was often very personal, never seemed to disturb him in the least.

Well, it was about dusk one day; it had been a terrible day, a hundred and something startling in the shade, but there came a breeze after sunset. There had been several dozen of buckets of water thrown on the verandah floor and the ground outside. Watty was seated in his accustomed place when the Army arrived. There was no barney in the bar because there was a fight in the backyard, and that claimed the attention of all the customers.

The Army prayed for Watty and his clients; then a reformed drunkard started to testify against publicans and all their works. Watty settled himself comfortably, folded his hands, and leaned back and dozed.

The fight was over, and the chaps began to drop round to the bar. The man who was saved waved his arms, and danced round and howled.

'Ye-es!' he shouted hoarsely. 'The publicans, and boozers, and gamblers, and sinners may think that Bourke is hot, but hell is a thousand times hotter! I can tell you —'

'Oh, Lord!' said Mitchell, the shearer, and he threw a penny into the ring.

'Ye-es! I tell you that hell is a million times hotter than Bourke! I tell you —'

'Oh, look here,' said a voice from the background, 'that won't wash. Why, don't you know that when the Bourke people die they send back for their blankets?'

The saved brother glared round.

'I hear a freethinker speaking, my friends —' he said. Then, with sudden inspiration and renewed energy, 'I hear the voice of a freethinker. Show me the face of a freethinker,' he yelled, glaring round like a hunted, hungry man. 'Show me the face of a freethinker, and I'll tell you what he is.'

Watty hitched himself into a more comfortable position and clasped his hands on his knee and closed his eyes again.

'Ya-a-s!' shrieked the brand. 'I tell you, my friends, I can tell a freethinker by his face. Show me the face of a —'

At this point there was an interruption. One-eyed, or Wall-eyed, Bogan — who had a broken nose, and the best side of whose face was reckoned the ugliest and most sinister — One-eyed Bogan thrust his face forward from the ring of darkness into the torchlight of salvation. He had got the worst of a drawn battle; his nose and mouth were bleeding, and his good eye was damaged.

'Look at my face!' he snarled, with dangerous earnestness. 'Look at my face! That's the face of a freethinker, and I don't care who knows it. Now! what have you got to say against my face, "Man-without-a-Shirt?"'

The brother drew back. He had been known in the North-West in his sinful days as 'Man-without-a-Shirt', *alias* 'Shirty', or 'The Dirty Man', and was flabbergasted at being recognised in speech. Also, he had been in a shearing shed and in a shanty orgy with One-eyed Bogan, and knew the man.

Now most of the chaps respected the Army, and, indeed, anything that looked like religion, but the Bogan's face, as representing freethought, was a bit too sudden for them. There were sounds on the opposite side of the ring as from men being smitten repeatedly and rapidly below the belt, and long Tom Hall and one or two of the others got away into the darkness in the background, where Tom rolled helplessly on the grass and sobbed.

It struck me that Bogan's face was more the result of free speech than anything else.

The Army was about to pray when the Pretty Girl stepped forward, her eyes shining with indignation and enthusiasm. She had arrived by the evening train, and had been standing shrinkingly behind an Army lass of fifty Australian summers, who was about six feet high, flat and broad, and had a square face, and a mouth like a joint in boiler plates.

The Pretty Girl stamped her pretty foot on the gravel, and her eyes flashed in the torchlight.

'You ought to be ashamed of yourselves,' she said. 'Great big men like you to be going on the way you are. If you were ignorant or poor, as I've seen people, there might be some excuse for you. Haven't you got any mothers, or sisters, or wives to think of? What sort of a life is this you lead? Drinking, and gambling, and fighting, and swearing your lives away! Do you ever think of God and the time when you were children? Why don't you make homes? Look at that man's face!' (she pointed suddenly at Bogan, who collapsed and sidled behind his mates out of the light). 'Look at that man's face! Is it a face of a Christian? And you help and encourage him to fight. You're worse than he is. Oh, it's brutal. It's — it's wicked. Great big men like you, you ought to be ashamed of yourselves.'

Long Bob Brothers — about six-foot-four — the longest and most innocent there, shrunk down by the wall and got his inquiring face out of the light. The Pretty Girl fluttered on for a few moments longer, greatly excited, and then stepped back, seemingly much upset, and was taken under the wing of the woman with the boiler-plate mouth.

It was a surprise, and very sudden. Bogan slipped round to the backyard, and was seen bathing his battered features at the pump. The rest wore the expression of men who knew that something unusual has happened, but don't know what, and are waiting vacantly for developments — except Tom Hall, who had recovered and returned. He stood looking over the head of the ring of Bushmen, and apparently taking the same critical interest in the girl as he would a fight — his expression was such as a journalist might wear who is getting exciting copy.

The Army had it all their own way for the rest of the evening, and made a good collection. The Pretty Girl stood smiling round with shining eyes as the bobs and tanners dropped in, and then, being shoved forward by the flat woman, she thanked us sweetly, and said we were good fellows, and that she was sorry for some things she'd said to us. Then she retired, fluttering and very much flushed, and hid herself behind the hard woman — who, by the way, had an excrescence on her upper lip which might have stood for a rivet.

Presently the Pretty Girl came from behind the big woman and stood watching things with glistening eyes. Some of the chaps on the opposite side of the ring moved a little to one side and were all careful not to meet her eye — not to be caught looking at her — lest she should be embarrassed. Watty had roused himself a little at the sound of the strange voice in the Army (and such a clear, sweet voice, too!) and had a look; then he settled back peacefully again, but it was noticed that he didn't snore that evening.

And when the Army prayed, the Pretty Girl knelt down with the rest on the gravel. One or two tall Bushmen bowed their heads as if they had to, and One-eyed Bogan, with the blood washed from his face, stood with his hat off, glaring round to see if he could catch anyone sniggering.

Mitchell, the shearer, said afterwards that the whole business made him feel for the moment like he felt sometimes in the days when he used to feel things.

The town discussed the Pretty Girl in the Army that night and for many days thereafter, but no one could find out who she was or where she belonged to — except that she came from Sydney last. She kept her secret, if she had one, very close — or else the other S.A. women were not to be pumped. She lived in skillion-rooms at the back of the big weather-board Salvation Army barracks with two other 'lassies', who did washing and sewing and nursing, and went shabby, and half starved themselves and were baked in the heat, like scores of women in the Bush, and even as hundreds of women, suffering from religious mania, slave and stint in the city slums, and neglect their homes, husbands and children — for the glory of Booth.

The Pretty Girl was referred to as Sister Hannah by the Army people, and came somehow to be known by sinners as 'Miss Captain'. I don't know whether that was her real name or what rank she held in the Army, if indeed she held any.

She sold *War Crys*, and the circulation doubled in a day. One-eyed Bogan, being bailed up unexpectedly, gave her 'half a caser' for a *Cry*, and ran away without the paper or the change. Jack Mitchell bought a *Cry* for the first time in his life, and read it. He said he found some of the articles intensely realistic, and many of the statements were very interesting. He said he read one or two things in the *Cry* that he didn't know before. Tom Hall, taken unawares, bought three *Crys* from the Pretty Girl, and blushed to find it fame.

Little Billy Woods, the Labourers' Union Secretary — who had a poetic temperament and more than the average Bushman's reverence for higher things — Little Billy Woods told me in a burst of confidence that he generally had two feelings, one after the other, after encountering that girl. One was that unfathomable, far-away feeling of loneliness and longing, that comes at odd times to the best of married men, with the best of wives and children — as Billy had. The other feeling, which came later on, and was a reaction in fact, was the feeling of a man who thinks he's been twisted round a woman's little finger for the benefit of somebody else. Billy said that he couldn't help being reminded by the shy, sweet smile and the shy, sweet 'thank you' of the Pretty Girl in the Army, of the shy, sweet smile and the shy, sweet gratitude of a Sydney private barmaid, who had once roped him in, in the days before he was married. Then he'd reckon that the Army lassie had been sent outback to Bourke as a business speculation.

Tom Hall was inclined to reckon so too — but that was after he'd been chaffed for a month about the three *War Crys*.

The Pretty Girl was discussed from psychological points of view; not forgetting the sex problem. Donald Macdonald — shearer, union leader and labour delegate to other colonies on occasion — Donald Macdonald said that whenever he saw a circle of plain or ugly, dried-up women or girls round a shepherd, evangelist or a Salvation Army drum, he'd say 'sexually starved!' They were hungry for love. Religious mania was sexual passion dammed out of its course. Therefore he held that morbidly religious girls were the most easily seduced.

But this couldn't apply to Pretty Girl in the Army. Mitchell reckoned that she'd either had a great sorrow — a lot of trouble or a disappointment in love (the 'or' is Mitchell's); but they couldn't see how a girl like her could possibly be disappointed in love — unless the chap died or got into jail for life. Donald decided that her soul had been starved somehow.

Mitchell suggested that it might be only a craving for notoriety, the same thing that makes women and girls go amongst lepers, and out to the battlefield, and nurse ugly pieces of men back to life again; the same thing that makes some women and girls swear ropes around men's necks. The Pretty Girl might be the daughter of well-to-do people — even aristocrats, said Mitchell — she was pretty enough and spoke well enough. 'Every woman's a barmaid at heart,' as the *Bulletin* puts it, said Mitchell.

But not even one of the haggard women at Bourke ever breathed a suspicion of scandal against her. They said she was too good and too pretty to be where she was. You see it was not as in an old settled town where hags blacken God's word with their tongues. Bourke was just a little camping town in a big land, where free, good-hearted democratic Australians, and the best of black sheep from the old world were constantly passing through; where husbands were often obliged to be away from home for twelve months, and the storekeepers had to trust the people, and mates trusted each other, and the folks were broad-minded. The mind's eye had a wide range.

After her maiden speech the Pretty Girl seldom spoke, except to return thanks for collections — and she never testified. She had a sweet voice and used to sing.

Now, if I were writing pure fiction, and were not cursed with an obstinate inclination to write the truth, I might say that, after the advent of the Pretty Girl, the morals of Bourke improved suddenly and wonderfully. That One-eyed Bogan left off gambling and drinking and fighting and swearing, and put on a red coat and testified and fought the devil only; that Mitchell dropped his mask of cynicism; that Donald Macdonald ate no longer of the tree of knowledge and ceased to worry himself with psychological problems, and was happy; and that Tom Hall was no longer a scoffer. That no one sneaked round through the scrub after dusk to certain necessary establishments in weatherboard cottages on the outskirts of the town; and that the broad-minded and obliging ladies thereof became Salvation Army lassies.

But none of these things happened. Drunks quieted down or got out of the way if they could when the Pretty Girl appeared on the scene, fights and games of 'headin' 'em' were adjourned, and weak, ordinary language was used for the time being, and that was about all.

Nevertheless, most of the chaps were in love with that Pretty Girl in the Army — all those who didn't *worship* her privately. Long Bob Brothers hovered around in hopes, they said, that she'd meet with an accident — get run over by a horse or something — and he'd have to carry her in; he scared the women at the Barracks by dropping firewood over the fence after dark. Barcoo-Rot, the meanest man in the back country, was seen to drop a threepenny bit into the ring, and a rumour was industriously circulated (by Tom Hall) to the effect that One-eyed Bogan intended to shave and join the Army disguised as a lassie.

Handsome Jake Boreham (*alias* Bore-'em), a sentimental shearer from New Zealand, who had read Bret Harte, made an elaborate attempt for the Pretty Girl, by pretending to be going to the dogs headlong, with an idea of first winning her sorrowful interest and sympathy, and then making an apparently hard struggle to straighten up for her sake. He related his experience with the cheerful and refreshing absence of reserve which was characteristic of him, and is of most Bushmen.

'I'd had a few drinks,' he said, 'and was having a spell under a gum tree by the river, when I saw the Pretty Girl and another Army woman coming down along the bank. It was a blazing hot day. I thought of Sandy and the Schoolmistress in Bret Harte, and I thought it would be a good idea to stretch out in the sun and pretend to be helpless; so I threw my hat on the ground and lay down, with my head in the blazing heat, in the most graceful position I could get at, and I tried to put a look of pained regret on my face as if I was dreaming of my lost boyhood and me mother. I thought, perhaps, the Girl would pity me, and I felt sure she'd stoop and pick up my hat and put it gently over my poor troubled head. Then I was going to become conscious for a moment, and look hopelessly round, and into her eyes, and then start and look sorrowful and ashamed, and stagger to my feet, taking off my hat like the Silver King does to the audience when he makes his first appearance drunk on the stage; and then I was going to reel off, trying to walk as straight as I could. And next day I was going to clean up my teeth and nails and put on a white shirt, and start to be a new man henceforth.

'Well, as I lay there with my eyes shut, I heard the footsteps come closer up and stop, and heard 'em whisper, and I thought I heard the Pretty Girl say "Poor fellow!" or something that sounded like that; and just then I got a God-almighty poke in the ribs with an umbrella — at least I suppose it was aimed for my ribs; but women are bad shots, and the point of the umbrella caught me in the side, just between the bottom rib and the hip bone, and I sat up with a click, like the blade of a pocket-knife.

'The other lassie was the big square-faced woman. The Pretty Girl looked rather more frightened and disgusted than sentimental, but she had plenty of pluck, and soon pulled herself together. She said I ought to be ashamed of myself, a great, big man like me, lying there in the dust like a drunken tramp — an eyesore and a disgrace to all the world. She told me to go to my camp, wherever that was, and sleep myself sober. The square-jawed woman said I looked like a fool sitting there. I did feel ashamed, and I reckon I did look like a fool — a man generally does in a fix like that. I felt like one, anyway. I got up and walked away, and it hurt me so much that I went over to West Bourke and went to the dogs properly for a fortnight, and lost twenty quid on a game of draughts against a blind-fold player. Now both those women had umbrellas, but I'm not sure to this day which of 'em it was that gave me the poke. It wouldn't have mattered much anyway. I haven't borrowed one of Bret Harte's books since.'

Jake reflected a while.

'The worst of it was,' he said ruefully, 'that I wasn't sure that the girl or the woman didn't see through me, and that worried me a bit. You never can tell how much a woman suspects, and that's the worst of 'em. I found that out after I got married.'

The Pretty Girl in the Army grew pale and thin and bigger-eyed. The women said it was a shame, and that she ought to be sent home to her friends, wherever they were. She was laid up for two or three days, and some of the women cooked delicacies and handed 'em over the barracks fence, and offered to come in and nurse her; but the square woman took washing home and nursed the girl herself.

The Pretty Girl still sold *War Crys* and took up collections, but in a tired, listless, half shame-faced way. It was plain that she was tired of the Army, and growing ashamed of the Salvationists. Perhaps she had come to see things too plainly.

You see, the Army does no good in outback Australia — except from a business point of view. It is simply there to collect funds for hungry headquarters. The Bushmen are much too intelligent for the Army. There was no poverty in Bourke — as it is understood in the city; there was plenty of food; and camping out and roughing it come natural to the Bushmen. In cases of sickness, accident, widows or orphans, the chaps sent round the hat, without banging a drum or testifying, and that was all right. If a chap was hard up he borrowed a couple of quid from his mate. If a strange family arrived without a penny, someone had to fix 'em up, and the storekeepers helped them till the man got work. For the rest, we work out our own salvation, or damnation — as the case is — in the Bush, with no one to help us, except a mate, perhaps. The Army can't help us, but a fellow-sinner can, sometimes, who has been through it all himself. The Army is only a drag on the progress of Democracy, because it attracts many who would otherwise be aggressive Democrats — and for other reasons.

Besides, if we all reformed the Army would get deuced little from us for its city missions.

The Pretty Girl went to service for a while with the Stock Inspector's wife, who could get nothing out of her concerning herself or her friends. She still slept at the barracks, stuck to the Army, and attended its meetings.

It was Christmas morning, and there was peace in Bourke and goodwill towards all men. There hadn't been a fight since yesterday evening, and that had only been a friendly one, to settle an argument concerning the past ownership, and, at the same time, to decide as to the future possession of a dog.

It had been a hot, close night, and it ended in a suffocating sunrise. The free portion of the male population were in the habit of taking their blankets and sleeping out in 'the Park', or town square, in hot weather; the wives and daughters of the town slept, or tried to sleep, with bedroom windows and doors open, while husbands lay outside on the verandahs. I camped in a corner of the park that night, and the sun woke me.

As I sat up I caught sight of a swagman coming along the white, dusty road from the direction of the bridge, where the cleared road ran across west and on, a hundred and thirty miles, through the barren, broiling mulga scrubs, to Hungerford, on the border of Sheol. I knew that swagman's walk. It was John Merrick (Jack Moonlight), one time Shearers' Union Secretary at Coonamble, and generally 'Rep' (Shearers' Representative) in any shed where he sheared. He was a 'better-class shearer', one of those quiet, thoughtful men of whom there are generally two or three in the roughest of rough sheds, who have great influence, and give the shed a good name from a Union point of view. Not quiet with the resentful or snobbish reserve of the educated Englishman, but with a sad or subdued sort of quietness that has force in it — as if they fully realised that their intelligence is much higher than the average, that they have suffered more real trouble and heartbreak than the majority of their mates, and that their mates couldn't possibly understand them if they spoke as they felt and couldn't see things as they do — yet men who understand and are intensely sympathetic in their loneliness and sensitive reserve.

I had worked in a shed with Jack Moonlight, and had met him in Sydney, and to be mates with a Bushman for a few weeks is to know him well — anyway, I found it so. He had taken a trip to Sydney the Christmas before last, and when he came back there was something wanting. He became more silent, he drank more, and sometimes alone, and took to smoking heavily. He dropped his mates, took little or no interest in Union matters, and travelled alone, and at night.

The Australian Bushman is born with a mate who sticks to him through life — like a mole. They may be hundreds of miles apart sometimes, and separated for years, yet they are mates for life. A Bushman may have many mates in his roving, but there is always one *his* mate, 'my mate'; and it is common to hear a Bushman — who is, in every way, a true mate to the man he happens to be travelling with, speak of *his mate's mate* — 'Jack's mate' — who might be in Klondyke or South Africa. A Bushman has always a mate to comfort him and argue with him, and work and tramp and drink with him, and lend him quids when he's hard up, and call him a b— fool, and fight him sometimes; to abuse him to his face and defend his name behind his back; to bear false witness and perjure his soul for his sake; to lie to the girl for him if he's single, and to his wife if he's married; to secure a 'pen' for him at a shed where he isn't

251

on the spot, or, if the mate is away in New Zealand or South Africa, to write and tell him if it's any good coming over this way. And each would take the word of the other against all the world, and each believes that the other is the straightest chap that ever lived — 'a white man!' And next best of your old mate is the man you're tramping, riding, working or drinking with.

About the first thing the cook asks you when you come along to a shearers' hut is, 'Where's your mate?' I travelled alone for a while at one time, and it seemed to me sometimes, by the tone of the enquiry concerning the whereabouts of my mate, that the Bush had an idea that I might have done away with him and that the thing ought to be looked into.

When a man drops mateship altogether and takes to 'hatting' in the Bush, it's a step towards a convenient tree and a couple of saddle-straps buckled together.

I had an idea that I, in a measure, took the place of Jack Moonlight's mate about this time.

' 'Ullo, Jack!' I hailed as he reached the corner of the park.

'Good morning, Harry!' said Jack, as if he'd seen me last yesterday evening instead of three months ago. 'How are you getting on?'

We walked together towards the Union Office, where I had a camp in the skillion room at the back. Jack was silent. But there's no place in the world where a man's silence is respected so much (within reasonable bounds) as in the Australian Bush, where every man has a past more or less sad, and every man a ghost — perhaps from other lands that we know nothing of, and speaking in a foreign tongue. They say in the Bush, 'Oh, Jack's only thinking!' And they let him think. Generally you want to think as much as your mate; and when you've been together some time it's quite natural to travel all day without exchanging a word. In the morning Jim says, 'Well, I think I made a bargain with that horse, Bill,' and some time later in the afternoon, say twenty miles further on, it occurs to Bill to 'rejoin', 'Well, I reckon the blank as sold it to you had yer proper!'

I like a good thinking mate, and I believe that thinking in

company is a lot more healthy and more comfortable, as well as less risky, than thinking alone.

On the way to the Union Office Jack and I passed the Royal Hotel, and caught a glimpse through the open door of a bedroom off the verandah, of the landlord's fresh, fair, young Sydney girl-wife, sleeping prettily behind the mosquito net, like a sleeping beauty, while the boss lay on a mattress outside on the verandah, across the open door. (He wasn't necessary for publication, but an evidence of good faith.)

I glanced at Jack for a grin, but didn't get one. He wore the pained expression of a man who is suddenly hit hard with the thought of something that might have been.

I boiled the billy and fried a pound of steak.

'Been travelling all night, Jack?' I asked.

'Yes,' said Jack. 'I camped at Emus yesterday.'

He didn't eat. I began to reckon he was brooding too much for his health. He was much thinner than when I saw him last, and pretty haggard, and he had something of the hopeless, haggard look that I'd seen in Tom Hall's eyes after the last big shearing strike, when Tom had worked day and night to hold his mates up all through the hard, bitter struggle, and the battle was lost.

'Look here, Jack!' I said at last. 'What's up?'

'Nothing's up, Harry,' said Jack. 'What made you think so?'

'Have you got yourself into any fix?' I asked. 'What's the Hungerford track been doing to you?'

'No, Harry,' he said, 'I'm all right. How are you?' And he pulled some string and papers and a roll of dusty pound notes from his pocket and threw them on the bunk.

I was hard up just then, so I took a note and the billy to go to the Royal and get some beer. I thought the beer might loosen up his mind a bit.

'Better take a couple of quid,' said Jack. 'You look as if you want some new shirts and things.' But a pound was enough for me, and I think he had reason to be glad of that later on, as it turned out.

'Anything new in Bourke?' asked Jack as we drank the beer.

'No,' I said, 'not a thing — except there's a pretty girl in the Salvation Army.'

'And it's about time,' growled Jack.

'Now, look here, Jack,' I said presently, 'what's come over you lately at all? I might be able to help you. It's not a bit of use telling me that there's nothing the matter. When a man takes to brooding and travelling alone it's a bad sign, and it will end in a leaning tree and a bit of clothes-line as likely as not. Tell me what the trouble is. Tell us all about it. There's a ghost, isn't there?'

'Well, I suppose so,' said Jack. 'We've all got our ghosts for that matter. But never you mind, Harry; I'm all right. I don't go interfering with your ghosts, and I don't see what call you've got to come haunting mine. Why, it's as bad as kicking a man's dog.' And he gave the ghost of a grin.

'Tell me, Jack,' I said, 'is it a woman?'

'Yes,' said Jack, 'it's a woman. Now, are you satisfied?'

'Is it a girl?' I asked.

'Yes,' he said.

So there was no more to be said. I'd thought it might have been a lot worse than a girl. I'd thought he might have got married somewhere, some time, and made a mess of it.

We had dinner at Billy Woods' place, and a sensible Christmas dinner it was — everything cold, except the vegetables, with the hose going on the verandah in spite of the bye-laws, and Billy's wife and sister, fresh and cool-looking and jolly, instead of being hot and brown and cross like most Australian women who roast themselves over a blazing fire in a hot kitchen on a broiling day, all the morning, to cook scalding plum puddings and red-hot roasts, for no other reason than that their grandmothers used to cook hot Christmas dinners in England.

And in the afternoon we went for a row on the river, pulling easily up the anabranch and floating down with the stream under the shade of the river timber — instead of going to sleep and waking up helpless and soaked in perspiration, to find the women with headaches, as many do on Christmas Day in Australia.

Mrs Woods tried to draw Jack out, but it was no use, and in the evening he commenced drinking, and that made Billy uneasy. 'I'm afraid Jack's on the wrong track,' he said.

After tea most of us collected about Watty's verandah. Most things that happened in Bourke happened at Watty's pub, or near it.

If a horse bolted with a buggy or cart, he was generally stopped outside Watty's, which seemed to suggest, as Mitchell said, that most of the heroes drank at Watty's — also that the pluckiest men were found amongst the hardest drinkers. (But sometimes the horse fetched up against Watty's sign and the lamp-post — which was a stout one of 'iron-bark' — and smashed the trap.) Then Watty's was the 'Carriers' Arms', a Union pub; and Australian teamsters are mostly hard cases: while there was something in Watty's beer which made men argue fluently, and the best fights came off in his backyard. Watty's dogs were the most quarrelsome in town, and there was a dog-fight there every other evening, followed as often as not by a man-fight. If a Bushman's horse ran away with him the chances were that he'd be thrown on to Watty's verandah, if he wasn't pitched into the bar; and victims of accidents, and sick, hard-up shearers, were generally carried to Watty's pub, as being the most convenient and comfortable for them. Mitchell denied that it was generosity or good nature on Watty's part, he said it was all business — advertisement. Watty knew what he was doing. He was very deep, was Watty. Mitchell further hinted that if he was sick *he* wouldn't be carried to Watty's, for Watty knew what a thirsty business a funeral was. Tom Hall reckoned that Watty bribed the Army on the quiet.

I was sitting on a stool along the verandah wall with Donald Macdonald, Bob Brothers (the Giraffe) and Mitchell, and one or two others, and Jack Moonlight sat on the floor with his back to the wall and his hat well down over his eyes. The Army came along at the usual time, but we didn't see the Pretty Girl at first — she was a bit late. Mitchell said he liked to be at Watty's when the Army prayed and the Pretty Girl was there; he had no objection to being prayed for by a girl like that, though he reckoned that nothing short of a real angel could save him now. He said his old grandmother used to pray for him every night of her life and three times on Sunday, with Christmas day extra when Christmas day didn't fall on a Sunday; but Mitchell reckoned that the old lady couldn't have had much influence because he became more sinful every year, and went deeper in ways of darkness, until finally he embarked on a career of crime.

The Army prayed, and then a thin, 'ratty' little woman bobbed up in the ring; she'd gone mad on religion as women do on women's rights and hundreds of other things. She was so skinny in the face, her jaws so prominent, and her mouth so wide, that when she opened it to speak it was like a ventriloquist's dummy and you could almost see the cracks open down under her ears.

'They say I'm cracked!' she screamed in a shrill, cracked voice. 'But I'm not cracked — I'm only cracked on the Lord Jesus Christ! That's all I'm cracked on —' And just then the Amen man of the Army — the Army groaner we called him, who was always putting both feet in it — just then he blundered forward, rolled up his eyes, threw his hands up and down as if he were bouncing two balls, and said with deep feeling:

'Thank the Lord she's got a crack in the right place!'

Tom Hall doubled up, and most of the other sinners seemed to think there was something very funny about it. And the Army, too, seemed struck with an idea that there was something wrong somewhere, for they started a hymn.

A big American negro, who'd been a night watchman in Sydney, stepped into the ring and waved his arms and kept time, and as he got excited he moved his hands up and down rapidly, as if he was hauling down a rope in a great hurry through a pulley block above, and he kept saying 'Come down, Lord!' all through the hymn, like a bass accompaniment, 'Come down, Lord; Come down, Lord; Come down, Lord; Come down, Lord!' and the quicker he said it the faster he hauled. He was as good as a drum. And, when the hymn was over, he started to testify.

'My Frens!' he said, 'I was once black as der coals in der mined! I was once as black as der ink in der ocean of sin! But now — thank an' bless the Lord! — I am whiter dan der dribben snow!'

Tom Hall sat down on the edge of the verandah and leaned his head against a post and cried. He had contributed a bob this evening, and he was getting his money's worth.

Then the Pretty Girl arrived and was pushed forward into the ring. She looked thinner and whiter than I'd ever seen her, and there was a feverish brightness in her eyes that I didn't like.

'Men!' she said, 'this is Christmas Day —' I didn't hear any more for, at the sound of her voice, Jack Moonlight jumped up as if he'd sat on a baby. He started forward, stared at her for a moment as though he couldn't believe his eyes, and then said 'Hannah!' short and sharp. She started as if she was shot, gave him a wild look, and stumbled forward; the next moment he had her in his arms and was steering for the private parlour.

I heard Mrs Bothways calling for water and smelling salts; she was as fat as Watty, and very much like him in the face, but she was emotional and sympathetic. Then presently I heard, through the open window, the Pretty Girl say to Jack, 'Oh, Jack, Jack! Why did you go away and leave me like that? It was cruel!'

'But you told me to go, Hannah,' said Jack.

'That — that didn't make any difference. Why didn't you write?' she sobbed.

'Because you never wrote to me, Hannah,' he said.

'That — that was no excuse,' she said. 'It was so k-k-k-cruel of you, Jack —'

Mrs Bothways pulled down the window. A newcomer asked Watty what the trouble was, and he said that the Army girl had found her chap, or husband, or long-lost brother or something, but the missus was looking after the business; then he dozed again.

And then we adjourned to the Royal and took the Army with us.

'That's the way of it,' said Donald Macdonald. 'With a woman it's love or religion; with a man it's love or the devil.'

'Or with a man,' said Mitchell presently, 'it's love and the devil both, sometimes, Donald.'

I looked at Mitchell hard, but for all his face expressed he might only have said, 'I think it's going to rain.'

Original Section, Hospital — Bourke, NSW

CHAPTER 15

Send Round the Hat

Now this is the creed from the Book of the Bush —
Should be simple and plain to a dunce:
If a man's in a hole you must pass round the hat —
Were he gaol-bird or gentleman once.[77]

Much of Lawson's writing over the next few years was inspired by his time in Bourke, and he drew heavily on local Bourke identities as characters in his work. As confirmed in 'That Pretty Girl in the Army', John (Jack) Merrick was the model for 'Jack Moonlight', and unionists such as Thomas Hicks Hall, Donald Macdonell and Billy Wood featured regularly in Lawson's stories. One-eyed Bogan, Box-o'-Tricks and Barcoo-Rot were probably composites of the rough western men he met in the shearing sheds west of the Darling. Though many of Lawson's stories appear to have been written after his return trip from Hungerford, some had possibly been conceived at Toorale shearing shed or along the outback tracks. The work completed after his departure from Bourke suggests the lasting impressions, be they good or bad, he retained of the town and its region.

One of Lawson's best known stories is 'Send Round the Hat' which was written in England in 1901. It was first published in *Children of the Bush* in 1902 and later in *Send Round the Hat*, the book of the same name published in Sydney in 1907.

The story is set in Bourke and centres around an individual named the 'Giraffe'. Lawson admits to basing this character on local shearer 'Bob Brothers, and his bush names, 'Long-un', 'The Giraffe', 'Send Round the Hat', 'Chuck-in-a-bob' and 'Ginger Ale'. Lawson also confirmed this when he wrote: 'Bob Brothers, also called 'The Giraffe' in 'Send Round the Hat', was a west o' Bourke shearer in the early nineties, and a native of Victoria or South Australia . . . '[78]

Billy Wood traced some of the lives of these characters:

Of those mentioned in Lawson's *Send Round the Hat*, Donald Macdonell, Teddy Thompson, as well as Henry himself, are gone. T. Hicks Hall is in Western Australia, and I think, if alive, Jack Boreham is in New Zealand. Boreham was a champion at draughts, playing the game. Most of the other characters in Henry's book are, I think, composites.[79]

The story is concerned with the socio-economic culture of that era. In times of hardship, money was collected from the sympathetic public (passing round of the hat) to help the less privileged who were victims of unemployment or bad luck. It is interesting to note Lawson has included himself in the story, not in the first person but as 'a deaf Jackaroo who was staying at the shanty and was something like me'.

SEND ROUND THE HAT

Now this is the creed from the Book of the Bush —
Should be simple and plain to a dunce:
'If a man's in a hole you must pass round the hat —
Were he gaol-bird or gentleman once.'

'Is it any harm to wake yer?'

It was about nine o'clock in the morning, and, though it was a

Sunday morning, it was no harm to wake me; but the shearer had mistaken me for a deaf Jackaroo, who was staying at the shanty and was something like me, and had good-naturedly shouted almost at the top of his voice, and he woke the whole shanty. Anyway he woke three or four others who were sleeping on beds and stretchers, and one on a shakedown on the floor, in the same room. It had been a wet night, and the shanty was full of shearers from Big Billabong Shed which had cut-out the day before. My room mates had been drinking and gambling overnight, and they swore luridly at the intruder for disturbing them.

He was six-foot-three or thereabout. He was loosely built, bony, sandy-complexioned and grey eyed. He wore a good-humoured grin at most times, as I noticed later on; he was of a type of Bushman that I always liked — the sort that seemed to get more good-natured the longer they grow, yet are hard-knuckled and would accommodate a man who wanted to fight, or thrash a bully in a good-natured way. The sort that liked to carry somebody's baby round, and cut wood, carry water and do little things for overworked married Bushwomen. He wore a saddle-tweed sac suit two sizes too small for him, and his face, neck, great hands and bony wrists were covered with sun blotches and freckles.

'I hope I ain't disturbing yer,' he shouted, as he bent over my bunk, 'but there's a cove —'

'You needn't shout!' I interrupted. 'I'm not deaf.'

'Oh — I beg your pardon!' he shouted. 'I didn't know I was yellin'. I thought you was the deaf feller.'

'Oh, that's all right,' I said. 'What's the trouble?'

'Wait till them other chaps is done swearin' and I'll tell yer,' he said. He spoke with a quiet, good-natured drawl, with something of the nasal twang, but tone and drawl distinctly Australian — altogether apart from that of the Americans.

'Oh, spit it out for Christ's sake, Long-un!' yelled One-eyed Bogan, who had been the worst swearer in a rough shed, and he fell back on his bunk as if his previous remarks had exhausted him.

'It's that there sick Jackaroo that was pickin'-up at Big Billabong,' said the Giraffe. 'He had to knock off the first week, an' he's been here ever since. They're sendin' him away to the hospital in Sydney by the speeshall train. They're just goin' to take him up in the wagonette to the railway station, an' I thought I might as well go round with the hat an' get him a few bob. He's got a missus and kids in Sydney.'

'Yer always goin' round with yer gory hat!' growled Bogan. 'Yer'd blanky well take it round in hell!'

'That's what he's doing, Bogan,' muttered 'Gentleman-Once', on the shakedown, with his face to the wall.

The hat was a genuine 'cabbage tree', one of the sort that 'lasts a lifetime', it was well coloured, almost black in fact with weather and age, and it had a new strap around the base of the crown. I looked into it and saw a dirty pound note and some silver. I dropped in half a crown, which was more than I could spare, for I had only been a green hand at Big Billabong.

'Thank yer!' he said. 'Now then, you fellers!'

'I wish you'd keep your hat on your head, and your money in your pockets and your sympathy somewhere else,' growled Jack Moonlight as he raised himself painfully on his elbow and felt under his pillow for two half-crowns. 'Here,' he said, 'here's two half-casers. Chuck 'em in and let me sleep for God's sake!'

'Gentleman-Once', the gambler, rolled round on his shakedown, bringing his good-looking, dissipated face from the wall. He had turned in in his clothes and, with considerable exertion he shoved his hand down into the pocket of his trousers, which were a tight fit. He brought up a roll of pound notes and could find no silver.

'Here,' he said to the Giraffe, 'I might as well lay a quid. I'll chance it anyhow. Chuck it in.'

'You've got rats this mornin', Gentleman-Once,' growled the Bogan. 'It ain't a blanky horse race.'

'P'r'aps I have,' said Gentleman-Once, and he turned to the wall again with his head on his arm.

'Now, Bogan, yer might as well chuck in somethin',' said the Giraffe.

'What's the matter with the — Jackaroo?' asked the Bogan, tugging his trousers from under the mattress.

Moonlight said something in a low tone.

'The — he has!' said Bogan. 'Well, I pity the —! Here, I'll chuck in half a — quid!' and he dropped half a sovereign into the hat.

The fourth man, who was known to his face as 'Barcoo-Rot', and behind his back as 'the Mean Man', had been drinking all night, and not even Bogan's stump-splitting adjectives could rouse him. So Bogan got out of bed, and calling on us (as blanky female cattle) to witness what he was about to do, he rolled the drunkard over, prospected his pockets till he made up five shillings (or a 'caser' in Bush language), and 'chucked' them into the hat.

And Barcoo-Rot is probably unconscious to this day that he was ever connected with an act of charity.

The Giraffe struck the deaf Jackaroo in the next room. I heard the chaps cursing 'Long-un' for waking them, and 'Deaf-un' for being, as they thought at first, the indirect cause of the disturbance. I heard the Giraffe and his hat being condemned in other rooms and cursed along the verandah where more shearers were sleeping; and after a while I turned out.

The Giraffe was carefully fixing a mattress and pillows on the floor of the wagonette, and presently a man, who looked like a corpse, was carried out and lifted into the trap.

As the wagonette started, the shanty keeper — a fat, soulless-looking man — put his hand in his pocket and dropped a quid into the hat which was still going round, in the hands of the Giraffe's mate, little Teddy Thompson, who was as far below medium height as the Giraffe was above it.

The Giraffe took the horse's head and led him along the most level part of the road towards the railway station, and two or three chaps went along to help get the sick man into the train.

The shearing season was over in that district, but I got a job of house painting, which was my trade, at the Great Western Hotel (a two-storey brick place), and I stayed in Bourke for a couple of months.

The Giraffe was a Victorian native from Bendigo. He was well known in Bourke and to many shearers who came through the great dry scrubs from hundreds of miles round. He was stakeholder, drunkard's banker, peacemaker where possible, referee or second to oblige the chaps when a fight was on, big brother or uncle to most of the children in town, final court of appeal when the youngsters had a dispute over a footrace at the school picnic, referee at their fights, and he was the stranger's friend.

'The feller as knows can battle around for himself,' he'd say. 'But I always like to do what I can for a hard-up stranger cove. I was a green hand jackaroo once meself, and I know what it is.'

'You're always bothering about other people, Giraffe,' said Tom Hall, the Shearers' Union Secretary, who was only a couple of inches shorter than the Giraffe. 'There's nothing in it, you can take it from me — I ought to know.'

'Well, what's a feller to do?' said the Giraffe. 'I'm only hangin' round here till shearin' starts agen, an' a cove might as well be doin' something. Besides, it ain't as if I was like a cove that had old people or a wife and kids to look after. I ain't got no responsibilities. A feller can't be doin' nothin'. Besides, I like to lend a helpin' hand when I can.'

'Well, all I've got to say,' said Tom, most of whose screw went in borrowed quids, etc. 'All I've got to say is that you'll get no thanks, and you might blanky well starve in the end.'

'There ain't no fear of me starvin' so long as I've got me hands about me; an' I ain't a cove as wants thanks,' said the Giraffe.

He was always helping someone or something. Now it was a bit of a 'darnce' that we was gettin' up for the girls; again it was Mrs Smith, the woman whose husban' was drowned in the flood in the

Bogan River lars' Crismas, or that there poor woman down by the Billabong — her husban' cleared out and left her with a lot o' kids. Or Bill Something, the bullocky, who was run over by his own wagon, while he was drunk, and got his leg broke.

Toward the end of his spree One-eyed Bogan broke loose and smashed nearly all the windows of the Carriers' Arms, and next morning he was fined heavily at the police court. About dinner time I encountered the Giraffe and his hat, with two half-crowns in it for a start.

'I'm sorry to trouble yer,' he said, 'but One-eyed Bogan carn't pay his fine, an' I thought we might fix it up for him. He ain't half a bad sort of feller when he ain't drinkin'. It's only when he gets too much booze in him.'

After shearing the hat usually started round with the Giraffe's own dirty crumpled pound note in the bottom of it as a send-off, later on it was half a sovereign, and so on down to half a crown and a shilling, as he got short of stuff; till in the end he would borrow a 'few bob' — which he always repaid after next shearing — 'just to start the thing goin'.'

There were several yarns about him and his hat. 'Twas said that the hat had belonged to his father, whom he resembled in every respect, and it had been going round for so many years that the crown was worn as thin as paper by the quids, half-quids, casers, half-casers, bobs and tanners or sprats — to say nothing of the scrums — that had been chucked into it in its time and shaken up.

They say that when a new governor visited Bourke the Giraffe happened to be standing on the platform close to the exit, grinning good-humouredly, and the local toady nudged him urgently and said in an awful whisper, 'Take off your hat! Why don't you take off your hat?'

'Why?' drawled the Giraffe, 'he ain't hard up, is he?' And they fondly cherish an anecdote to the effect that, when the One-Man-One-Vote Bill was passed (or Payment of Members, or when the first Labour Party went in — I forget on which occasion they said it was) the Giraffe was carried away by the general enthusiasm, got a few beers in him, 'chucked' a quid into his hat, and sent it round. The boys contributed by force of habit, and contributed largely, because of the victory and the beer. And when the hat came back to the Giraffe, he stood holding it in front of him with both hands and stared blankly into it for a while. Then it dawned on him.

'Blowed if I haven't bin an' gone an' took up a bloomin' collection for meself!' he said.

He was almost a teetotaller, but he stood his shout in reason. He mostly drank ginger beer.

'I ain't a feller that boozes, but I ain't got nothin' agen chaps enjoyin' themselves, so long as they don't go too far.'

It was common for a man on the spree to say to him:

'Here! Here's five quid. Look after it for me, Giraffe, will yer, till I git off the booze.'

His real name was Bob Brothers, and his Bush names, 'Long-'un', 'The Giraffe', 'Send-round-the-hat', 'Chuck-in-a-bob', and 'Ginger-ale'.

Some years before, camels and Afghan drivers had been imported to the Bourke district; the camels did very well in the dry country, they went right across country and carried everything from sardines to flooring boards. And the teamsters loved the Afghans nearly as much as Sydney furniture makers love the cheap Chinese in the same line. They loved 'em even as union shearers on strike love blacklegs brought up-country to take their places.

Now the Giraffe was a good, straight unionist, but in cases of sickness or trouble he was as apt to forget his unionism, as all Bushmen are, at all times (and for all time), to forget their creed. So, one evening, the Giraffe blundered into the 'Carriers' Arms' — of all places in the world — when it was full of teamsters; he had his hat in his hand and some small silver and coppers in it.

'I say, you fellers, there's a poor, sick Afghan in the camp down there along the —'

A big, brawny bullock driver took him firmly by the shoulders, or, rather, by the elbows, and ran him out before any damage was done. The Giraffe took it as he took most things, good-humouredly; but, about dusk, he was seen slipping down towards the Afghan camp with a billy of soup.

'I believe,' remarked Tom Hall, 'that when the Giraffe goes to heaven — and he's the only one of us, as far as I can see, that has the ghost of a show — I believe that when he goes to heaven, the first thing he'll do will be to take his infernal hat round amongst the angels — getting up a collection for this damned world that he left behind.'

'Well, I don't think there's so much to his credit, after all,' said Jack Mitchell, shearer. 'You see, the Giraffe is ambitious; he likes public life, and that accounts for him shoving himself forward with his collections. As for bothering about people in trouble, that's only common curiosity; he's one of those chaps that are always shoving their noses into other people's troubles. And, as for looking after sick men — why! There's nothing the Giraffe likes better than pottering around a sick man, and watching him and studying him. He's awfully interested in sick men, and they're pretty scarce out here. I tell you there's nothing he likes better — except, maybe, it's pottering round a corpse. I believe he'd ride forty miles to help and sympathise and potter around a funeral. The fact of the matter is that the Giraffe is only enjoying himself with other people's troubles — that's all it is. It's only vulgar curiosity and selfishness. I set it down to his ignorance; the way he was brought up.'

A few days after the Afghan incident the Giraffe and his hat had a run of luck. A German, one of a party who were building a new wooden bridge over the Big Billabong, was helping unload some girders from a truck at the railway station, when a big log slipped on the skids and his leg was smashed badly. They carried him to the Carriers' Arms, which was the nearest hotel, and into a bedroom behind the bar, and sent for the doctor. The Giraffe was in evidence as usual.

'It vas not that at all,' said German Charlie, when they asked him if he was in much pain. 'It vas not that at all. I don't cares a damn for der bain; but dis is der tird year — und I vas going home dis year — after der gontract — und der contract yoost commence!'

That was the burden of his song all through, between his groans.

There were a good few chaps sitting quietly about the bar and verandah when the doctor arrived. The Giraffe was sitting at the end of the counter, on which he had laid his hat while he wiped his face, neck and forehead with a big speckled 'sweat-rag'. It was a very hot day.

The doctor, a good-hearted young Australian, was heard saying something. Then German Charlie, in a voice that rung with pain:

'Make that leg right, doctor — quick! Dis is der tird pluddy year — und I must go home!'

The doctor asked him if he was in great pain.

'Neffer mind der pluddy bain, doctor! Neffer mind der pluddy bain! Dot vas nossing. Make dat leg well quick, doctor. Dis vas der last gontract, and I vas going home dis year.' Then the words jerked out of him by physical agony: 'Der girl vas vaiting dree year, und — by Got! I must go home.'

The publican — Watty Braithwaite, known as 'Watty Broadweight', or, more familiarly, 'Watty Bothways' — turned over the Giraffe's hat in a tired, bored sort of way, dropped a quid into it, and nodded resignedly at the Giraffe.

The Giraffe caught up the hint and the hat with alacrity. The hat went all round town, so to speak; and, as soon as his leg was firm enough not to come loose on the road, German Charlie went home.

It was well known that I contributed to the *Sydney Bulletin* and several other papers. The Giraffe's bump of reverence was very large, and swelled especially for sick men and poets. He treated me with much more respect than is due from a Bushman to a man, and with an odd sort of extra gentleness I sometimes fancied. But one day he rather surprised me.

'I'm sorry to trouble yer,' he said in a shamefaced way. 'I don't know as you go in for sportin', but One-eyed Bogan and Barcoo-Rot is goin' to have a bit of a scrap down the Billybong this evenin', an' —'

'A bit of a what?' I asked.

'A bit of fight to a finish,' he said apologetically. 'An' the chaps is tryin' to fix up a fiver to put some life into the thing. There's bad blood between One-eyed Bogan and Barcoo-Rot, an' it won't do them any harm to have it out.'

It was a great fight, I remember. There must have been a couple of score blood-soaked handkerchiefs (or 'sweat-rags') buried in a hole on the field of battle, and the Giraffe was busy the rest of the evening helping to patch up the principals. Later on he took up a small collection for the loser, who happened to be Barcoo-Rot in spite of the advantage of an eye.

The Salvation Army lassie, who went round with the *War Cry*, nearly always sold the Giraffe three copies.

A new-chum parson, who wanted a subscription to build or enlarge a chapel, or something, sought the assistance of the Giraffe's influence with his mates.

'Well,' said the Giraffe, 'I ain't a churchgoer meself. I ain't what you might call a religious cove, but I'll be glad to do what I can to help yer. I don't suppose I can do much. I ain't been to church since I was a kiddy.'

The parson was shocked, but later on he learned to appreciate the Giraffe and his mates, and to love Australia for the Bushman's sake, and it was he who told me the above anecdote.

The Giraffe helped fix some stalls for a Catholic church bazaar, and some of the chaps chaffed him about it in the union office.

'You'll be taking up a collection for a Joss-House down in the Chinamen's camp next,' said Tom Hall in conclusion.

'Well, I ain't got nothin' agen the Roming Carflics,' said the Giraffe. 'An' Father O'Donovan's a very decent sort of cove. He stuck up for the unions all right in the strike anyway.' ("He wouldn't be Irish if he wasn't,' someone commented.) 'I carried swags once for six months with a feller that was a Carflick, an' he was a very straight feller. And a girl I knowed turned Carflick to marry a chap that had got her into trouble, an' she was always jes' the same to me after as she was before. Besides, I like to help everything that's goin' on.'

Tom Hall and one or two others went out hurriedly to have a drink. But we all loved the Giraffe.

He was very innocent and very humorous, especially when he meant to be most serious and philosophical.

'Some of them Bush girls is regular tomboys,' he said to me solemnly one day. 'Some of them is too cheeky altogether. I remember once I was stoppin' at a place — they was sort of relations o' mine — an' they put me to sleep in a room off the verander, where there was a glass door an' no blinds. An' the first mornin' the girls — they was sort o' cousins o' mine — they come gigglin' and foolin' round outside the door on the verander, an' kep' me in bed till nearly ten o'clock. I had to put me trowsis on under the bedclothes in the end. But I got back on 'em the next night,' he reflected.

'How did you do that, Bob?' I asked.

'Why, I went to bed in me trowsis!'

One day I was on a plank, painting the ceiling of the bar of the Great Western Hotel. I was anxious to get the job finished. The work had been kept back most of the day by chaps handing up long beers to me, and drawing my attention to the alleged fact that I was putting on the paint wrong side out. I was slapping it on over the last few boards when:

'I'm very sorry to trouble yer; I always seem to be troublin' yer; but there's that there woman and them girls —'

I looked down — about the first time I had looked down on him — and there was the Giraffe, with his hat brim up on the plank and two half-crowns in it.

'Oh, that's all right, Bob,' I said, and I dropped in half a crown.

There were shearers in the bar, and presently there was some barracking. It appeared that that there woman and them girls were strange women, in the local as well as the Biblical sense of the word, who had come from Sydney at the end of the shearing season, and had taken a cottage on the edge of the scrub on the outskirts of the town. There had been trouble this week in connection with a row at their establishment, and they had been fined, warned off by the police, and turned out by their landlord.

'This is a bit too red hot, Giraffe,' said one of the shearers. 'Them —s has made enough out of us coves. They've got plenty of stuff, don't you fret. Let 'em go to —! I'm blanked if I give a sprat.'

'They ain't got their fares to Sydney,' said the Giraffe. 'An', what's more, the little 'un is sick, an' two of them has kids in Sydney.'

'How the — do you know?'

'Why, one of 'em come to me an' told me all about it.'

There was an involuntary guffaw.

'Look here, Bob,' said Billy Woods, the Rouseabouts' Secretary, kindly. 'Don't you make a fool of yourself. You'll have all the chaps laughing at you. Those girls are only working you for all you're worth. I suppose one of 'em came crying and whining to you. Don't you bother about them. You don't know them; they can pump water at a moment's notice. You haven't had any experience with women yet, Bob.'

'She didn't come whinin' and cryin' to me,' said the Giraffe, dropping his twanging drawl a little. 'She looked me straight in the face an' told me all about it.'

'I say, Giraffe,' said Box-o'-Tricks, 'what have you been doin'? You've bin down there on the nod. I'm surprised at yer, Giraffe.'

'An' he pretends to be so gory soft an' innocent too,' growled the Bogan. 'We know all about you, Giraffe.'

'Look here, Giraffe,' said Mitchell the shearer. 'I'd never have thought it of you. We all thought you were the only virgin youth west of the river; I always thought you were a moral young man. You mustn't think that because your conscience is pricking you everyone else's is.'

'I ain't had anything to do with them,' said the Giraffe, drawling again. 'I ain't a cove that goes in for that sort of thing. But other chaps has, and I think they might as well help 'em out of their fix.'

271

'They're a rotten crowd,' said Billy Woods. 'You don't know them, Bob. Don't bother about them — they're not worth it. Put your money in your pocket. You'll find a better use for it before next shearing.'

'Better shout, Giraffe,' said Box-o'-Tricks.

Now in spite of the Giraffe's softness he was the hardest man in Bourke to move when he'd decided on what he thought was 'the fair thing to do'. Another peculiarity of his was that on occasion, such for instance as 'sayin' a few words' at a strike meeting, he would straighten himself, drop the twang, and rope in his drawl, so to speak.

'Well, look here, you chaps,' he said now. 'I don't know anything about them women. I s'pose they're bad, but I don't suppose they're worse than men has made them. All I know is that there's four women turned out, without any stuff, and every woman in Bourke, an' the police, an' the law agen them. An' the fact that they is women is agenst 'em most of all. You don't expect 'em to hump their swags to Sydney! Why, only I ain't got the stuff I wouldn't trouble yer. I'd pay their fares meself. Look,' he said, lowering his voice, 'there they are now, an' one of the girls is cryin'. Don't let 'em see yer lookin'.'

I dropped softly from the plank and peeped out with the rest.

They stood by the fence on the opposite side of the street, a bit up towards the railway station, with their portmanteaux and bundles at their feet. One girl leant with her arms on the fence rail and her face buried in them, another was trying to comfort her. The third girl and the woman stood facing our way. The woman was good-looking; she had a hard face, but it might have been made hard. The third girl seemed half defiant, half inclined to cry. Presently she went to the other side of the girl who was crying on the fence and put her arm around her shoulder. The woman suddenly turned her back on us and stood looking away over the paddocks.

The hat went round. Billy Woods was first, then Box-o'-Tricks, and then Mitchell.

Billy contributed with eloquent silence. 'I was only jokin', Giraffe,' said Box-o'-Tricks, dredging his pockets for a couple of shillings. It was some time after the shearing, and most of the chaps were hard up.

'Ah, well,' sighed Mitchell. 'There's no help for it. If the Giraffe would take up a collection to import some decent girls to this God-forgotten hole there might be some sense in it . . . It's bad enough for the Giraffe to undermine our religious prejudices, and tempt us to take a morbid interest in sick chows and Afghans, and blacklegs and widows; but when he starts mixing us up with strange women it's time to buck.' And he prospected his pockets and contributed two shillings, some odd pennies, and a pinch of tobacco dust.

'I don't mind helping the girls, but I'm damned if I'll give a penny to help the old —' said Tom Hall.

'Well, she was a girl once herself,' drawled the Giraffe.

The Giraffe went round to the other pubs and to the union offices, and when he returned he seemed satisfied with the plate, but troubled about something else.

'I don't know what to do for them for to-night,' he said. 'None of the pubs or boardin'-houses will hear of them, an' there ain't no empty houses, an' the women is all agen 'em.'

'Not all,' said Alice, the big, handsome barmaid from Sydney. 'Come here, Bob.' She gave the Giraffe half a sovereign and a look for which some of us would have paid him ten pounds — had we had the money, and had the look been transferable.

'Wait a minute, Bob,' she said, and she went in to speak to the landlord.

'There's an empty bedroom at the end of the store in the yard,' she said when she came back. 'They can camp there for to-night if they behave themselves. You'd better tell 'em, Bob.'

'Thank yer, Alice,' said the Giraffe.

Next day, after work, the Giraffe and I drifted together and down by the river in the cool of the evening, and sat on the edge of the steep, drought-parched bank.

'I heard you saw your lady friends off this morning, Bob,' I said, and was sorry I said it, even before he answered.

'Oh, they ain't no friends of mine,' he said. 'Only four poor devils of women. I thought they mightn't like to stand waitin' with the crowd on the platform, so I jest offered to get their tickets an' told 'em to wait round at the back of the station till the bell rung . . . An' what do yer think they did, Harry?' he went on, with an exasperatingly unintelligent grin. 'Why, they wanted to kiss me.'

'Did they?'

'Yes. An' they would have done it, too, if I hadn't been so long . . . Why, I'm blessed if they didn't kiss me hands.'

'You don't say so.'

'God's truth. Somehow I didn't like to go on the platform with them after that; besides they was cryin', and I can't stand women cryin'. But some of the chaps put them into an empty carriage.' He thought for a moment then:

'There's some terrible good-hearted fellers in the world,' he reflected.

I thought so too.

'Bob,' I said, 'you're a single man. Why don't you get married and settle down?'

'Well,' he said, 'I ain't got no wife an' kids, that's a fact. But it ain't my fault.'

He may have been right about the wife. But I thought of the look that Alice had given him, and:

'Girls seem to like me right enough,' he said, 'but it don't go no further than that. The trouble is that I'm so long, and I always seem to get shook after little girls. At least there was one girl in Bendigo that I was properly gone on.'

'And wouldn't she have you?'

'Well, it seems not.'

'Did you ask her?'

'Oh, yes, I asked her right enough.'

'Well, and what did she say?'

274

'She said it would be redicilus for her to be seen trottin' alongside of a chimbly like me.'

'Perhaps she didn't mean that. There are any amount of little women who like tall men.'

'I thought of that too — afterwards. P'r'aps she didn't mean it that way. I s'pose the fact of the matter was that she didn't cotton on to me, and she wanted to let me down easy. She didn't want to hurt me feelin's, if yer understand — she was a very good-hearted little girl. There's some terrible tall fellers where I come from, and I know two as married little girls.'

He seemed a hopeless case.

'Sometimes,' he said, 'sometimes I wish that I wasn't so blessed long.'

'There's that there deaf Jackaroo,' he reflected presently. 'He's something in the same fix about girls as I am. He's too deaf and I'm too long.'

'How do you make that out?' I asked. 'He's got three girls, to my knowledge, and, as for being deaf, why he gasses more than any other man in the town, and knows more of what's going on than old Mother Brindle the washerwoman.'

'Well, look at that now!' said the Giraffe, slowly. 'Who'd have thought it? He never told me he had three girls, an' as for hearin' news, I always tell him anything that's goin' on that I think he doesn't catch. He told me his trouble was that whenever he went out with a girl people could hear what they were sayin' — at least they could hear what she was sayin' to him, an' draw their own conclusions, he said. He said he went out one night with a girl, and some of the chaps foxed 'em an' heard her sayin' "don't" to him, an' put it all round town.'

'What did she say "don't" for?' I asked.

'He didn't tell me that, but I s'pose he was kissin' her or huggin' her or something.'

'Bob,' I said presently, 'didn't you try the little girl in Bendigo a second time?'

'No,' he said. 'What was the use. She was a good little girl, and I wasn't goin' to go botherin' her. I ain't the sort of cove that goes hangin' round where he isn't wanted. But somehow I couldn't stay about Bendigo after she gave me the hint, so I thought I'd come over an' have a knock round on this side for a year or two.'

'And you never wrote to her?'

'No. What was the use of goin' pesterin' her with letters? I know what trouble letters give me when I have to answer one. She'd have only had to tell me the straight truth in a letter an' it wouldn't have done me any good. But I've pretty well got over it by this time.'

A few days later I went to Sydney. The Giraffe was the last I shook hands with from the carriage window, and he slipped something in a piece of newspaper into my hand.

'I hope yer won't be offended,' he drawled, 'but some of the chaps thought you mightn't be too flush of stuff — you've been shoutin' a good deal; so they put a quid or two together. They thought it might help yer to have a bit of a fly round in Sydney.'

I was back in Bourke before next shearing. On the evening of my arrival I ran against the Giraffe; he seemed strangely shaken over something, but he kept his hat on his head.

'Would yer mind takin' a stroll as fur as the Billerbong?' he said. 'I got something I'd like to tell yer.'

His big, brown, sun-burnt hands trembled and shook as he took a letter from his pocket and opened it.

'I've just got a letter,' he said. 'A letter from that little girl in Bendigo. It seems it was all a mistake. I'd like you to read it. Somehow I feel as if I want to talk to a feller, and I'd rather talk to you than any of them other chaps.'

It was a good letter, from a big-hearted little girl. She had been breaking her heart for the big ass all these months. It seemed that he had left Bendigo without saying good-bye to her. 'Somehow I couldn't bring meself to it,' he said, when I taxed him with it. She had never been able to get his address until last week; then she got it from a Bourke man who had gone South. She called him 'an awful long fool', which he was, without the slightest doubt, and she implored him to write, and come back to her.

'And will you go back, Bob?' I asked.

'My oath! I'd take the train termorrer only I ain't got the stuff. But I've got a stand in Big Billerbong shed an' I'll soon knock a few quid together. I'll go back as soon as ever shearin's over. I'm goin' to write away to her to-night.'

The Giraffe was the 'ringer' of Big Billabong shed that season. His tallies averaged 120 a day. He only sent his hat round once during the shearing, and it was noticed that he hesitated at first and only contributed half a crown. But then it was a case of a man being taken from the shed by the police for wife desertion.

'It's always that way,' commented Mitchell. 'Those soft, good-hearted fellows always end by getting hard and selfish. The world makes 'em so. It's the thought of the soft fools they've been that finds out sooner or later and makes 'em repent. Like as not the Giraffe will be the meanest man outback before he's done.'

When Big Billabong cut out, and we got back to Bourke with our dusty swags and dirty cheques, I spoke to Tom Hall:

'Look here, Tom,' I said. 'That long fool, Giraffe, has been breaking his heart for a little girl in Bendigo ever since he's been outback, and she's been breaking her heart for him, and the ass didn't know it till he got a letter from her just before Big Billabong started. He's going tomorrow morning.'

That evening Tom stole the Giraffe's hat. 'I s'pose it'll turn up in the mornin',' said the Giraffe. 'I don't mind a lark,' he added, 'but it does seem a bit red hot for the chaps to collar a cove's hat and a feller goin' away for good, p'r'aps, in the mornin'.'

Mitchell started the thing going with a quid.

'It's worth it,' he said, 'to get rid of him. We'll have some peace now. There won't be so many accidents or women in trouble when the Giraffe and his blessed hat are gone. Anyway, he's an eyesore in the town, and he's getting on my nerves for one. . . . Come on, you sinners! Chuck 'em in; we're only taking quids and half-quids.'

About daylight next morning Tom Hall slipped into the Giraffe's room at the 'Carriers' Arms'. The Giraffe was sleeping peacefully. Tom put the hat on a chair by his side. The collection had been a record one, and, besides the packet of money in the crown of the hat, there was a silver-mounted pipe with case — the best that could be bought in Bourke, a gold brooch, and several trifles — besides an ugly valentine of a long man in his shirt walking the room with a twin on each arm.

Tom was about to shake the Giraffe by the shoulder, when he noticed a great foot, with about half a yard of big-boned ankle and shank, sticking out at the bottom of the bed. The temptation was too great. Tom took up the hair-brush, and, with the back of it, he gave a smart rap on the point of an in-growing toe-nail, and slithered.

We heard the Giraffe swearing good-naturedly for a while, and then there was a pregnant silence. He was staring at the hat we supposed.

We were all up at the station to see him off. It was rather a long wait. The Giraffe edged me up to the other end of the platform.

He seemed overcome.

'There's — there's some terrible good-hearted fellers in this world,' he said. 'You mustn't forget 'em, Harry, when you make a big name writin'. I'm — well, I'm blessed if I don't feel as if I was jist goin' to blubber!'

I was glad he didn't. The Giraffe blubbering would have been a spectacle. I steered him back to his friends.

'Ain't you going to kiss me, Bob?' said the Great Western's big, handsome barmaid, as the bell rang.

'Well, I don't mind kissin' you, Alice,' he said, wiping his mouth. 'But I'm goin' to be married, yer know.' And he kissed her fair on the mouth.

'There's nothin' like gettin' into practice,' he said, grinning round.

We thought he was improving wonderfully; but at the last moment something troubled him.

'Look here, you chaps,' he said hesitatingly, with his hand in his pocket. 'I don't know what I'm going to do with all this stuff. There's that there poor washerwoman that scalded her legs liftin' the boiler of clothes off the fire,'

We shoved him into the carriage. He hung — about half of him — out the window, wildly waving his hat, till the train disappeared in the scrub.

And, as I sit here writing by lamplight at mid-day, in the midst of a great city of shallow social sham, of hopeless, squalid poverty, of ignorant selfishness, cultured or brutish, and of noble and heroic endeavour frowned down or callously neglected, I am almost aware of a burst of sunshine in the room, and a long form leaning over my chair and:

'Excuse me for troublin' yer; I'm always troublin' yer; but there's that there poor woman . . . '

And I wish I could immortalise him!

The character Mitchell appears in many of Lawson's western stories. He is portrayed as a philosophical thinker and reasoner, 'self-assertive and diplomatic'. He appears to be reasonably well educated and there is little bush slang in his language, providing a contrast to the rough, ill-spoken shearers.

As was often the case, events and locations were often stored away in Lawson's mind, to be brought out later, changed and rearranged. With time, the characteristics of the people he met merged and blended until they became entities of their own, such as Jack Mitchell. The idea for the series was probably conceived from 'Mitchell — A Character Sketch', which was published in the *Bulletin* on 15 April 1893, while Lawson was still living in Bourke.

It is probable that the character of Mitchell was largely based on Lawson's mate Jim Gordon. In his 'Letter re Henry Lawson's Fictional Characters', Lawson states that 'Mitchell was just Mitchell, and I don't know where he is now. There were many other Mitchells, both before and since. In fact there is one living here [Leeton] now.' And in 'By the Banks of the Murrumbidgee' he reveals 'There used to be two young fellers knockin' about Bourke and west-o'-Bourke named Joe Swallow and Jack Mitchell in those old days', thus identifying himself as Joe Swallow (a pseudonym he often used) and Jim Gordon as Jack Mitchell.

In Lawson's stories, Mitchell is always portrayed as a deep thinker, analytical, able to understand an opposing view though he didn't necessarily agree with it. In 'Mitchell Doesn't Believe in the Sack', which was published in the *Bulletin* in 1893, Mitchell has devised, by way of reason, a logical way to avoid 'getting the sack'.

MITCHELL DOESN'T BELIEVE IN THE SACK

'If ever I do get a job again,' said Mitchell, 'I'll stick to it while there's a hand's turn of work to do, and put a few pounds together. I won't be the fool I always was. If I'd had sense a couple of years ago, I wouldn't be tramping through this damned sand and mulga now. I'll get a job on a station, or at some toff's house, knocking about the stables and garden, and I'll make up my mind to settle down to graft for four or five years.'

'But supposing you git the sack?' said his mate.

'I won't take it. Only for taking the sack I wouldn't be hard up to-day. The boss might come round and say:

'"I won't want you after this week, Mitchell. I haven't got any more work for you to do. Come up and see me at the office presently."

'So I'll go up and get my money; but I'll be pottering round as usual on Monday, and come up to the kitchen for my breakfast. Some time in the day the boss'll be knocking round and see me.

'"Why, Mitchell," he'll say, "I thought you was gone."

'"I didn't say I was going," I'll say. "Who told you that — or what made you think so?"

'"I thought I told you on Saturday that I wouldn't want you any more," he'll say, a bit short. "I haven't got enough work to keep a man going; I told you that; I thought you understood. *Didn't I give you the sack on Saturday?*"

"'It's no use,' I'll say, "that sort of thing's played out. I've been had too often that way; I've been sacked once too often. Taking the sack's been the cause of all my trouble; I don't believe in it. If I'd never taken the sack I'd have been a rich man today; it might be all very well for horses, but it doesn't suit me; it doesn't hurt you, but it hurts me. I made up my mind that when I got a place to suit me, I'd stick in it. I'm comfortable here and satisfied, and you've had no cause to find fault with me. It's no use you trying to sack me, because I won't take it. I've been there before, and you might as well try to catch an old bird with chaff."

"'Well, I won't pay you, and you'd better be off," he'll say, trying not to grin.

"'Never mind the money", I'll say, "the bit of tucker won't cost you anything, and I'll find something to do round the house till you have some more work. I won't ask you for anything, and, surely to God I'll find enough to do to pay for my grub!"

'So I'll potter round and take things easy and call up at the kitchen as usual at meal times, and by-and-by the boss'll think to himself: "Well, if I've got to feed this chap I might as well get some work out of him."

'So he'll find me something regular to do — a bit of fencing, or carpentering, or painting, or something, and then I'll begin to call up for my stuff again, as usual.'

Mitchell's power of persuasive debate is also shown in another story of Lawson's which has all the earmarkings of having had its origins in Bourke. 'Lord Douglas' was probably written as late as 1901, while Lawson was living in London, and appeared in the 1902 edition of *Children of the Bush*.

In Lawson's story, Lord Douglas was the licensee of the Imperial Hotel, a two-storeyed building which was patronised by pastoralists and civil servants. This was most probably a literary disguise for the large two-storeyed Post Office Hotel in Oxley Street which was taken over in about 1892 by Paddy Fitzgerald. This hotel was home to pastoralists, overseers and jackaroos while visiting Bourke. Harry (the Breaker) Morant is said to have been a one-time guest there while on a visit from one of the border sheep stations where he worked for several years as a horse breaker. Lawson could also have been referring to the other two-storeyed hotel named the Caledonia, which was situated not far from his own cottage in Mitchell Street. It was said to have been a favourite watering-hole of the pastoralists, though not of the unionists.

It is difficult to pinpoint the real character upon whom the sketch was based. It is possible that Lord Douglas was Joseph Donohue, who at that time was the licensee of the Gladstone Hotel, which was situated on the corner of Richard and Mitchell Streets. The hotel, a single-storey building, was de-licensed in the early part of the century; later it became a boarding house and operated as such until the post World War II years. Lawson often passed this hotel on his daily walks through that part of town, and no doubt stopped there to have a drink at some time.

According to local legend, Joseph Donohue was an unusual character. During the heat wave of 1896–97, it was said that he abandoned his wife and children in Bourke, availed himself of the local rail service and headed for the relative coolness of Sydney's foreshores.

Probably the character Lord Douglas was based on a medley of local Bourke characters and, as there was no pub named the Imperial in Bourke at any time, the hotel perhaps was a varied mish-mash of impressions of the local pastoralist-patronised hotels.

LORD DOUGLAS

'They hold him true, who's true to one,
However false he be—'
'The Rouseabout of Rouseabouts'

The Imperial Hotel was rather an unfortunate name for an outback town pub, for outback is the stronghold of Australian democracy; it was the outback vote and influence that brought about 'One Man

One Vote', 'Payment of Members', and most of the democratic legislation of late years, and from outback came the overwhelming vote in favour of Australian as against Imperial federation.

The name Royal Hotel is as familiar as that of the Railway Hotel, and passes unnoticed and ungrowled at, even by Bush republicans. The Royal Hotel at Bourke was kept by an Irishman, one O'Donohoo, who was Union to the backbone, loudly in favour of 'Australia for the Australians', and, of course, against even the democratic New South Wales Government of the time. He went round town all one St Patrick's morning with a bunch of green ribbon fastened to his coat tail with a large fish hook, and wasn't aware of the fact till he sat down on the point of it. But that's got nothing to do with it.

The Imperial Hotel at Bourke was unpopular from the first. It was said that the very existence of the house was the result of a swindle. It had been built with money borrowed on certain allotments in the centre of town and on the understanding that it should be built on the mortgaged land, whereas it was erected on a free allotment. Which fact was discovered, greatly to its surprise, by the building society when it came to foreclose on the allotments some years later. While the building was being erected the Bourke people understood, in a vague way, that it was to be a convent (perhaps the building society thought so, too) and when certain ornaments in brick and cement in the shape of a bishop's mitre were placed over the corners of the walls the question seemed decided. But when the place was finished a bar was fitted up, and up went the sign, to the disgust of the other publicans, who didn't know a licence had been taken out — for licensing didn't go by local option in those days. It was rumoured that the place belonged to, and the whole business was engineered by, a priest. And priests are men of the world.

The Imperial Hotel was patronised by the Pastoralists, the civil servants, the bank manager and clerks — all the scrub aristocracy; it was the headquarters of the *Pastoralists' Union* in Bourke; a barracks for blacklegs brought up from Sydney to take the place of Union shearers on strike; and the new Governor, on his inevitable visit to Bourke, was banqueted at the Imperial Hotel. The editor of the local 'Capitalistic rag' stayed there; the Pastoralists' member was elected mostly by dark ways and means devised at the Imperial Hotel, and one of its managers had stood as a dummy candidate to split the Labour vote; the management of the hotel was his reward. In short, it was there that most of the plots were hatched to circumvent Freedom, and put away or deliver into the clutches of law and order certain sons of Light and Liberty who believed in converting blacklegs into jellies by force of fists when bribes, gentle persuasion and pure Australian language failed to convert them to clean Unionism. The Imperial Hotel was called the 'Squatters' Club', the 'Scabbery', and other and more expressive names.

The hotel became still more unpopular after Percy Douglas had managed it for a while. He was an avowed enemy of Labour Unionists. He employed Chinese cooks, and that in the height of the anti-Chinese agitation in Australia, and he was known to have kindly feelings towards the Afghans who, with their camels, were running white carriers off the roads. If an excited Unionist called a man a 'blackleg' or 'scab' in the Imperial bar he was run out — sometimes with great difficulty, and occasionally as far as the lock-up.

Percy Douglas was a fine-looking man, 'wid a chest on him an' well hung — a fine fee-*gure* of a man', as O'Donohoo pronounced it. He was tall and erect, he dressed well, wore small side whiskers, had an eagle nose, and looked like an aristocrat. Like many of his type, who start sometimes as billiard-markers and suddenly become hotel managers in Australia, nothing was known of his past. Jack Mitchell reckoned, by the way he treated his *employés* and spoke to workmen, that he was the educated son of an English farmer — gone wrong and sent out to Australia. Someone called him 'Lord Douglas', and the nickname caught on.

He made himself well hated. He got One-eyed Bogan 'three months' hard' for taking a bottle of whisky off the Imperial bar counter because he (Bogan) was drunk and thirsty and had knocked down his cheque, and because there was no one minding the bar at the moment.

Lord Douglas dismissed the barmaid, and, as she was leaving, he had her boxes searched and gave her in charge for stealing certain articles belonging to the hotel. The chaps subscribed to defend the case, and subsequently put a few pounds together for the girl. She proved her gratitude by bringing a charge of a baby against one of the chaps — but that was only one of the little ways of the world, as Mitchell said. She joined a Chinese camp later on.

Lord Douglas employed a carpenter to do some work about the hotel, and because the carpenter left before the job was finished Lord Douglas locked his tools in an outhouse and refused to give them up; and when the carpenter, with the spirit of an Australian workman, broke the padlock and removed the tool-chest, the landlord gave him in charge for breaking and entering. The chaps defended the case and won it, and hated Lord Douglas as much as if he were their elder brother. Mitchell was the only one to put in a good word for him.

'I've been puzzling it out,' said Mitchell, as he sat nursing his best leg in the Union Office, 'and, as far as I can see, it all amounts to this — We're all mistaken in Lord Douglas. We don't know the man. He's all right. We don't understand him. He's really a sensitive, good-hearted man who's been shoved a bit off the track by the world. It's the world's fault — he's not to blame. You see, when he was a youngster he was the most good-natured kid in the school; he was always soft, and, consequently, he was always being imposed upon, and bullied, and knocked about. Whenever he got a penny to buy lollies he'd count 'em out carefully and divide 'em round amongst his schoolmates and brothers and sisters. He was the only one that worked at home, and consequently they all hated him. His father respected him; but didn't love him, because he wasn't a younger son, and wasn't bringing his father's grey hairs down in sorrow to the grave. If it was in Australia, probably Lord Douglas was an elder son and had to do all the hard graft, and teach himself at night, and sleep in a bark skillion while his younger brothers benefited — they were born in the new brick house and went to boarding schools. His mother had a contempt for him because he wasn't a black sheep and a prodigal, and, when the old man died, the rest of the family got all the stuff and Lord Douglas was kicked out because they could do without him now. And the family hated him like poison ever afterwards (especially his mother), and spread lies about him — because they had treated him shamefully and because his mouth was shut — they knew he wouldn't speak. Then probably he went in for Democracy and worked for Freedom, till Freedom trod on him once too often with her hob-nailed boots. Then the chances are, in the end, he was ruined by a girl or woman, and driven, against his will, to take refuge in pure individualism. He's all right, only we don't appreciate him. He's only fighting against his old ideals — his old self that comes up sometimes — and that's what makes him sweat his barmaids and servants, and hate us, and run us in; and perhaps when he cuts up extra rough it's because his conscience kicks him when he thinks of the damned soft fool he used to be. He's all right — take my word for it. It's all a mask. Why, he might be one of the kindest-hearted men in Bourke underneath.'

Tom Hall rubbed his head and blinked, as if he was worried by an idea that there might be some facts in Mitchell's theories.

'You're allers findin' excuses for blacklegs an' scabs, Mitchell,' said Barcoo-Rot, who took Mitchell seriously (and who would have taken a laughing jackass seriously). 'Why, you'd find a white spot on a squatter. I wouldn't be surprised if you blacklegged yourself in the end.'

This was an unpardonable insult, from a Union point of view, and the chaps half-unconsciously made room on the floor for Barcoo-Rot to fall after Jack Mitchell hit him. But Mitchell took the insult philosophically.

'Well, Barcoo-Rot,' he said, nursing the other leg, 'for the matter of that, I did find a white spot on a squatter once. He lent me a quid when I was hard up. There's white spots on the blackest characters if you only drop prejudice and look close enough. I suppose even Jack-the-Ripper's character was speckled. Why, I can even see spots on your character, sometimes, Barcoo-Rot. I've known white spots to spread on chaps' characters until they were little short of saints. Sometimes I even fancy I can feel my own wings sprouting. And as for turning blackleg — well, I suppose I've got a bit of the crawler in my composition (most of us have), and a man never knows what might happen to his principles.'

'Well,' said Barcoo-Rot, 'I beg your pardon — ain't that enough?'

'No,' said Mitchell, 'you ought to wear a three-bushel bag and ashes for three months, and drink water; but since the police would send you to an asylum if you did that, I think the best thing we can do is go out and have a drink.'

Lord Douglas married an Australian girl somewhere, somehow, and brought her to Bourke, and there were two little girls — regular little fairies. She was a gentle, kind-hearted little woman, but she didn't seem to improve him much, save that he was very good to her.

'It's mostly that way,' commented Mitchell. 'When a boss gets married and has children he thinks he's got a greater right to grind his fellow men and rob their wives and children. I'd never work for a boss with a big family — it's hard enough to keep a single boss nowdays in this country.'

After one stormy election, at the end of a long and bitter shearing strike, One-eyed Bogan, his trusty enemy, Barcoo-Rot, and one or two other enthusiastic reformers were charged with rioting, and got from one to three months' hard. And they had only smashed three windows of the Imperial Hotel and chased the Chinese cook into the river.

'I used to have some hopes for Democracy,' commented Mitchell, 'but I've got none now. How can you expect Liberty, Equality or Fraternity — how can you expect Freedom and Universal

Brotherhood and Equal Rights in a country where Sons of Light get three months' hard for breaking windows and bashing a Chinaman? It almost makes me long to sail away in a gallant barque.'

There were other cases in connection with the rotten-egging of Capitalistic candidates on the Imperial Hotel balcony, and it was partly on the evidence of Douglas and his friends that certain respectable Labour Leaders got heavy terms of imprisonment for rioting and 'sedition' and 'inciting', in connection with organised attacks on blacklegs and their escorts.

Retribution, if it was retribution, came suddenly and in a most unexpected manner to Lord Douglas.

It seems he employed a second carpenter for six months to repair and make certain additions to the hotel, and put him off under various pretences until he owed him a hundred pounds or thereabout. At last, immediately after an exciting interview with Lord Douglas, the carpenter died suddenly of heart disease. The widow, a strong-minded Bushwoman, put a bailiff in the hotel on very short notice — and against the advice of her lawyer, who thought the case hopeless — and the Lord Douglas bubble promptly burst. He had somehow come to be regarded as the proprietor of the hotel, but now the real proprietors or proprietor — he was still said to be a priest — turned Douglas out and put in a new manager. The old servants were paid after some trouble. The local storekeepers and one or two firms in Sydney, who had large accounts against the Imperial Hotel (and had trusted it, mainly because it was patronised by Capitalism and Fat), were never paid.

Lord Douglas cleared out to Sydney, leaving his wife and children, for the present, with her brother, a hay-and-corn storekeeper, who also had a large and hopeless account against the hotel; and when the brother went broke and left the district she rented a two-roomed cottage and took in dressmaking.

Dressmaking didn't pay so well in the Bush as it did in the old diggings' days when sewing machines were scarce and the possession of one meant an independent living to any girl — when diggers paid ten shillings for a strip of 'flannen' doubled over and sewn together, with holes for arms and legs, and called a shirt. Mrs Douglas had a hard time, with her two little girls, who were still better and more prettily dressed than any other children in Bourke. One grocer still called on her for orders and pretended to be satisfied to wait 'till Mr Douglas came back', and when she would no longer order what he considered sufficient provisions for her and the children, and commenced buying sugar, etc., by the pound, for cash, he one day sent a box of groceries round to her. He pretended it was a mistake.

'However,' he said, 'I'd be very much obliged if you could use 'em, Mrs Douglas. I'm overstocked now; haven't got room for another tin of sardines in the shop. Don't you worry about bills, Mrs Douglas; I can wait till Douglas comes home. I did well enough out of the Imperial Hotel when your husband had it, and a pounds' worth o' groceries won't hurt me now. I'm only too glad to get rid of some of the stock.'

She cried a little, thought of the children, and kept the groceries.

'I suppose I'll be sold up soon meself if things don't git brighter,' said the grocer to a friend, 'so it doesn't matter much.'

The same with Foley the butcher, who had a brogue with a sort of drawling groan in it, and was a cynic of the Mitchell school.

'You see,' he said, 'she's as proud as the devil, but when I send round a bit o' rawst, or porrk, or the undercut o' the blade-bawn, she thinks o' the little gur-r-ls before she thinks o' sendin' it back to me. That's where I've got the pull on her.'

The Giraffe borrowed a horse and tip-dray one day at the beginning of winter and cut a load of firewood in the Bush, and next morning, at daylight, Mrs Douglas was nearly startled out of her life by a crash at the end of the cottage, which made her think that the chimney had fallen in, or a tree fallen on the house; and when she slipped on a wrapper and looked out, she saw a load of short-cut wood by the chimney, and caught a glimpse of the back view of the Giraffe, who stood in the dray with his legs wide apart and was

289

disappearing into the edge of the scrub; and soon the rapid clock-clock-clock of the wheels died away in the west, as if he were making for West Australia.

The next we heard of Lord Douglas he had got two years' hard for embezzlement in connection with some canvassing he had taken up. Mrs Douglas fell ill — a touch of brain-fever — and one of the labourers' wives took care of the children while two others took turns in nursing. While she was recovering, Bob Brothers sent round the hat, and, after a conclave in the Union office — as mysterious as any meeting ever called with the object of downing bloated Capitalism — it was discovered that one of the chaps — who didn't wish his name to be mentioned — had borrowed just twenty-five pounds from Lord Douglas in the old days and now wished to return it to Mrs Douglas. So the thing was managed, and if she had any suspicions she kept them to herself. She started a little fancy goods shop and got along fairly comfortable.

Douglas, by the way, was, publicly, supposed, for her sake and because of the little girls, to be away in West Australia on the goldfields.

Time passes without much notice outback, and one hot day, when the sun hung behind the fierce sandstorms from the north-west as dully lurid as he ever showed in a London fog, Lord Douglas got out of the train that had just finished its five-hundred-miles' run, and not seeing a new-chum porter, who started forward by force of habit to take his bag, he walked stiffly off the platform and down the main street towards his wife's cottage.

He was very gaunt, and his eyes, to those who passed him closely, seemed to have a furtive, haunted expression. He had let his beard grow, and it had grown grey.

It was within a few days of Christmas — the same Christmas that we lost the pretty girl in the Salvation Army. As a rule the big shearing sheds within a fortnight of Bourke cut out in time for the shearers to reach the town and have their Christmas dinners and sprees — and for some of them to be locked up over Christmas day — within sound of a church-going bell. Most of the chaps gathered in the Shearers' Union Office on New Year's Eve and discussed Douglas amongst other things.

'I vote we kick the cow out of town!' snarled One-eyed Bogan viciously.

'We can't do that,' said Bob Brothers (the Giraffe), speaking more promptly than usual. 'There's his wife and youngsters to consider, yer know.'

'He something well deserted his wife,' snarled Bogan, 'an' now he comes crawlin' back to her to keep him.'

'Well,' said Mitchell, mildly, 'but we ain't all got as much against him as you have, Bogan.'

'He made a crimson gaol-bird of me!' snapped Bogan.

'Well,' said Mitchell, 'that didn't hurt you much, anyway; it rather improved your character if anything. Besides, he made a gaol-bird of himself afterwards, so you ought to have a fellow-feeling — a feathered-feeling, so to speak. Now you needn't be offended, Bogan, we're all gaol-birds at heart, only we haven't all got the pluck.'

'I'm in favour of blanky well tarrin' and featherin' him and kickin' him out of the town!' shouted Bogan. 'It would be a good turn to his wife, too; she'd be well rid of the —'

'Perhaps she's fond of him,' suggested Mitchell; 'I've known such cases before. I saw them sitting together on the verandah last night when they thought no one was looking.'

'He deserted her,' said One-eyed Bogan, in a climbing-down tone, 'and left her to starve.'

'Perhaps the police were to blame for that,' said Mitchell. 'You know you deserted all your old mates once for three months, Bogan, and it wasn't your fault ,'

'He seems to be a crimson pet of yours, Jack Mitchell,' said Bogan, firing up.

'Ah, well, all I know,' said Mitchell, standing up and stretching himself wearily, 'all I know is that he looked like a gentleman once,

291

and treated us like gentlemen, and cheated us like gentlemen, and ran some of us in like a gentleman, and, as far as I can see, served his time like a gentleman and come back to face us and live himself down like a man. I always had a sneaking regard for a gentleman.'

'Why, Mitchell, I'm beginning to think you are a gentleman yourself,' said Jack Boreham.

'Well,' said Mitchell, 'I used to have a suspicion once that I had a drop of blue blood in me somewhere, and it worried me a lot; but I asked my old mother about it one day, and she scalded me — God bless her! — and father chased me with a stockwhip, so I gave up making enquiries.'

'You'll join the bloomin' Capitalists next,' sneered One-eyed Bogan.

'I wish I could,' said Mitchell. 'I'd take a trip to Paris and see for myself whether the Frenchwomen are as bad as they're made out to be, or go to Japan. But what are we going to do about Douglas?'

'Kick the skunk out of town, or boycott him!' said one or two. 'He ought to be tarred and feathered and hanged.'

'Couldn't do worse than hang him,' commented Jack Boreham cheerfully.

'Oh yes, we could,' said Mitchell, sitting down, resting his elbows on his knees, and marking his points with one finger on the other. 'For instance, we might boil him slow in tar. We might skin him alive. We might put him in a cage and poke him with sticks, with his wife and children in another cage to look on and enjoy the fun.'

The chaps, who had been sitting quietly listening to Mitchell, and grinning, suddenly became serious and shifted their positions uneasily.

'But I can tell you what would hurt his feelings more than anything else we could do,' said Mitchell.

'Well, what is it, Jack?' said Tom Hall, rather impatiently.

'Send round the hat and take up a collection for him,' said Mitchell, 'enough to let him get away with his wife and children and start life again in some less respectable town than Bourke. You needn't grin, I'm serious about it.'

There was a thoughtful pause, and one or two scratched their heads.

'His wife seems pretty sick,' Mitchell went on in a reflective tone. 'I passed the place this morning and saw him scrubbing out the floor. He's been doing a bit of house painting for old Heegard today. I suppose he learnt it in gaol. I saw him at work and touched my hat to him.'

'What!' cried Tom Hall, affecting to shrink from Mitchell in horror.

'Yes,' said Mitchell, 'I'm not sure that I didn't take my hat off. Now I know it's not Bush religion for a man to touch his hat, except at a funeral, or a strange roof or woman sometimes; but when I meet a braver man than myself I salute him. I've only met two in my life.'

'And who were they, Jack?' asked Jack Boreham.

'One,' said Mitchell, 'one is Douglas, and the other — well, the other was the man I used to be. But that's got nothing to do with it.'

'But perhaps Douglas thought you were crowing over him when you took your hat off to him — sneerin' at him, like, Mitchell,' reflected Jack Boreham.

'No, Jake,' said Mitchell, growing serious suddenly. 'There are ways of doing things that another man understands.'

They all thought for a while.

'Well,' said Tom Hall, 'supposing we do take up a collection for him, he'd be too damned proud to take it.'

'But that's where we've got the pull on him,' said Mitchell, brightening up. 'I heard Dr Morgan say that Mrs Douglas wouldn't live if she wasn't sent away to a cooler place, and Douglas knows it; and, besides, one of the little girls is sick. We've got him in a corner and he'll have to take the stuff. Besides, two years in gaol takes a lot of the pride out of a man.'

'Well, I'm damned if I'll give a sprat to help the man who tried his best to crush the Unions!' said One-eyed Bogan.

'Damned if I will either!' said Barcoo-Rot.

'Now, look here, One-eyed Bogan,' said Mitchell, 'I don't like to harp on old things, for I know they bore you, but when you returned to public life that time no one talked of kicking you out of town. In fact I heard that the chaps put a few pounds together to help you get away for a while till you got over your modesty.'

No one spoke.

'I passed Douglas's place on my way here from my camp to-night,' Mitchell went on musingly, 'and I saw him walking up and down in the yard with his sick child in his arms. You remember that little girl, Bogan? I saw her run and pick up your hat and give it to you one day when you were trying to put it on with your feet. You remember, Bogan? The shock nearly sobered you.'

There was a very awkward pause. The position had become too psychological altogether and had to be ended somehow. The awkward silence had to be broken, and Bogan broke it. He turned up Bob Brothers' hat, which was lying on the table, and 'chucked in' a 'quid', qualifying the hat and the quid, and disguising his feelings with the national oath of the land.

'We've had enough of this gory, maudlin, sentimental tommy-rot,' he said. 'Here, Barcoo, stump up or I'll belt it out of your hide. I'll — I'll take yer to pieces!'

But Douglas didn't leave the town. He sent his wife and children to Sydney until the heat wave was past, built a new room onto the cottage, and started a book and newspaper shop, and a poultry farm in the back paddock, and flourished.

They called him Mr Douglas for a while, then Douglas, then Percy Douglas, and now he is well-known as Old Daddy Douglas, and the *Sydney Worker, Truth* and *Bulletin* and other democratic rags are on sale at his shop. He is big with schemes for locking the Darling River, and he gets his drink at O'Donohoo's. He is scarcely yet regarded as a straight-out democrat. He was a gentleman once, Mitchell said, and the old blood was not to be trusted. But, last elections, Douglas worked quietly for Unionism, and gave the leaders certain hints, and put them up to various electioneering dodges which enabled them to return, in the face of Monopoly, a Labour member who is as likely to go straight as long as any other Labour member.

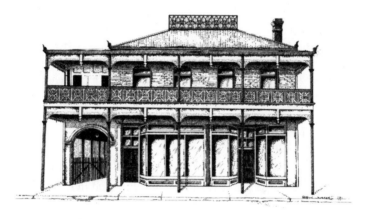

Old Historic Building, Mitchell Street — Bourke, NSW

CHAPTER 16

Back to the City

> *I am back from up the country, up the country where I*
>   *went*
> *Seeking for the Southern poets' land whereon to pitch*
>   *my tent;*
> *I have shattered many idols out along the dusty track,*
> *Burnt a lot of fancy verses — and I'm glad that I am*
>   *back.*[80]

The original manuscript for Lawson's poem 'All Unyun Men' was dated Bourke, June 1893,[81] suggesting that Lawson was still residing in the town in the early part of that month. By this time he was heartily sick of life in the west and desperate to return to the city. A lack of funds resulted in an unusual and innovative means of escape. Jim Gordon elaborated:

> It was then that Lawson met his Peter Anderson & Co. That firm secured him a drover's pass, with sheep travelling by rail to Homebush, or was it Flemington? And so we parted, not to meet again for over a quarter of a century, and then it was too late to do much, for we were both older than our years. Although we often planned and planned and talked of another trip together, it never

came off. Circumstances did not permit. After all, perhaps, it was just as well, for I know that at least one of us would have been very, very disappointed.[82]

Lawson confirmed Gordon"s account of his return to the city when he wrote: 'then came back to Sydney in charge of five trucks of cattle. Bourke people will understand that dodge.'[83]

In the early 1890s, the business of John Anderson & Co. operated from one of the small corrugated iron buildings in Mitchell Street owned by Cobb & Co., near Lawson's cottage and close to the Carriers' Arms Hotel. An advertisement in the *Western Herald* on 22 September 1892 describes Anderson as being a stock, station, forwarding, insurance and general commission agent. At some stage he was also the agent for Cobb & Co. in Bourke.

Broke and desperate, it was to Anderson's Mitchell Street office that Lawson applied for, and was subsequently granted, a free rail pass to the city, taking advantage of the railway regulation that every five carriages of livestock had to be accompanied by a drover. The pass was not obtained easily. 'We had haunted local influences at Comanavadrink for two long, anxious, heart-breaking weeks ere we got the pass; and we had put up with all the indignities, the humiliation in short, had suffered all that poor devils suffer whilst besieging Local Influence. We only thought of escaping from the bush.' [84]

Lawson later proclaimed his gratitude to Anderson by penning 'Peter Anderson & Co.', which was published in the *Bulletin* on 17 August 1895.

PETER ANDERSON AND CO.

He had offices in Sydney, not so many years ago,
And his shingle bore the legend 'Peter Anderson and
    Co.',
But his real name was Careless, as the fellows
    understood —
And his relatives decided that he wasn't any good.

'Twas their gentle tongues that blasted any 'character'
    he had —
He was fond of beer and leisure — and the Co. was
    just as bad.
It was limited in number to a unit, was the Co. —
'Twas a bosom chum of Peter, and his Christian name
    was Joe.

'Tis a class of men belonging to these soul-forsaken
    years:
Third rate canvassers, collectors, journalists and
    auctioneers.
They are never very shabby, they are never very
    spruce —
Going cheerfully and carelessly and smoothly to the
    deuce.
Some are wanderers by profession, 'turning up' and
    gone as soon,
Travelling second-class, or steerage (when it's cheap
    they go saloon);
Free from 'ists' and 'isms', troubled little by belief or
    doubt —
Lazy, purposeless, and useless — knocking round and
    hanging out.

They will take what they can get, and they will give
    what they can give,
God alone knows how they manage — God alone
    knows how they live!
They are nearly always hard-up, but are cheerful all
    the while —
Men whose energy and trousers wear out sooner than
    their smile!
They, no doubt, like us, are haunted by the boresome
    'if' or 'might',

But their ghosts are ghosts of daylight — they are men
   who live at night!

Peter met you with the comic smile of one who knows
   you well,
And is mightily glad to see you, and has got a joke to
   tell;
He could laugh when all was gloomy, he could grin
   when all was blue,
Sing a comic song and act it, and appreciate it, too.
Only cynical in cases where his own self was the jest,
And the humour of his good yarns made atonement for
   the rest.
Seldom serious — doing business just as 'twere a
   friendly game —
Cards or billiard — nothing graver. And the Co. was
   much the same.

They tried everything and nothing 'twixt the shovel and
   the press,
And were more or less successful in their ventures —
   mostly less.
Once they ran a country paper till the plant was seized
   for debt,
And the local sinners chuckle over dingy copies yet.

They'd been through it all and knew it in the land of
   Bills and Jims —
Using Peter's own expression, they had been in
   'various swims'.
Now and then they'd take an office, as they called it
   — make a dash
Into business life as 'agents' — something not
   requiring cash.

(*You can always furnish cheaply, when your cash or
    credit fails,*
*With a packing case, a hammer, and a pound of two-
    inch nails —*
*And, maybe, a drop of varnish and sienna, too, for
    tints,*
*And a scrap or two of oilcloth, and a yard or two of
    chintz.*)
They would pull themselves together, pay a week's rent
    in advance,
But it never lasted longer than a month by any chance.

The office was their haven, for they lived there when
    hard-up —
A 'daily' for a table cloth — a jam tin for a cup;
And if the landlord's bailiff happened round in times
    like these
And seize the office fittings — well, there wasn't much
    to seize.
They would leave him in possession. But at other times
    they shot
The moon, and took an office where the landlord knew
    them not.
And when morning brought the bailiff there'd be
    nothing to be seen
Save a piece of bevelled cedar where the tenant's plate
    had been;
There would be no sign of Peter — there would be no
    sign of Joe —
But another portal boasted 'Peter Anderson and Co.'

And when times were locomotive, billiard-rooms and
    private bars —
Spicy parties at the café — long cab-drives beneath the
    stars;

Private picnics down the Harbour — shady campings-
    outs, you know,
No one would have dreamed 'twas Peter — no one
    would have thought 'twas Joe!
Free-and-easies in their 'diggings', when the funds
    began to fail,
Bosom chums, cigars, tobacco, and a case of English
    ale —
Gloriously drunk and happy, till they heard the
    roosters crow —
And the landlady and neighbours made complaints
    about the Co.
But that life! it might be likened to a reckless drinking-
    song,
For it can't go on forever, and it never lasted long.

Debt-collecting ruined Peter — people talked him
    round too oft,
For his heart was soft as butter (and the Co.'s was just
    as soft);
He would cheer the haggard missus, and he'd tell her
    not to fret,
And he'd ask the worried debtor round with him to
    have a wet;
He would ask him round the corner, and it seemed to
    him and her,
After each of Peter's visits, things were brighter than
    they were.
But, of course it wasn't business — only Peter's
    careless way;
And perhaps it pays in heaven, but on earth it doesn't
    pay.
They got harder up than ever, and, to make it worse,
    the Co.

Went more often round the corner than was good for
    him to go.

'I might live,' he said to Peter, 'but I haven't got the
    nerve —
I am going, Peter, going — going, going — no
    reserve.
Eat and drink and love they tell us, for tomorrow we
    may die,
Buy experience — and we bought it — we're
    experienced, you and I.'
Then, with a weary movement of his hand across his
    brow —
'The death of such philosophy's the death I'm dying
    now.
Pull yourself together, Peter; 'tis the dying wish of Joe
That the business world shall honour Peter Anderson
    and Co.

'When you feel your life is sinking in a dull and useless
    course,
And begin to find in drinking keener pleasure and
    remorse —
When you feel the love of leisure on your careless
    heart take holt,
Break away from friends and pleasure, though it gives
    your heart a jolt.
Shun the poison breath of cities — billiard rooms and
    private bars,
Go where you can breathe God's air and see the
    grandeur of the stars!
Find again and follow up the old ambitions that you
    had —
See if you can raise a drink, old man, I'm feelin'
    mighty bad —

Hot and sweetened, nip o' butter — squeeze o' lemon,
    Pete,' he sighed.
And, while Peter went to fetch it, Joseph went to sleep
    and died
With a smile — anticipation, maybe, of the peace to
    come,
Or a joke to try on Peter — or, perhaps it was the
    rum.

Peter staggered, gripped the table, swerved as some old
    drunkard swerves;
At a gulp he drank the toddy, just to brace his
    shattered nerves.
It was awful, if you like. But then he hadn't time to
    think —
All is nothing! Nothing matters! Fill your glasses —
    dead man's drink.

Yet, to show his heart was not of human decency
    bereft,
Peter paid the undertaker. He got drunk on what was
    left;
Then he shed some tears, half-maudlin, on the grave
    where lay the Co.,
And he drifted to a township where the city failures go.
Where, though haunted by the man he was, the wreck
    he yet might be,
Or the man he might have been, or by each spectre of
    the three,
And the dying words of Joseph, ringing through his
    own despair,
Peter 'pulled himself together', and he started business
    there.

But his life was very lonely, and his heart was very
 sad,
And no help to reformation was the company he
 had —
Men who might have been, who had been, but who
 were not in the swim —
'Twas a town of wrecks and failures — they
 appreciated him.
They would ask him who the Co. was — that queer
 company he kept —
And he'd always answer vaguely — he would say his
 partner slept;
That he had a 'sleeping partner' — jesting while his
 spirit broke —
And they grinned above their glasses, for they took it
 for a joke.

He would shout while he had money, he would joke
 while he had breath —
No one seemed to care, or notice, how he drank
 himself to death;
Till at last there came a morning when his smile was
 seen no more —
He was gone from out the office, and his shingle from
 the door;
And a boundary rider jogging out across the
 neighbouring run
Was attracted by a something that was blazing in the
 sun;
And he found that it was Peter, lying peacefully at
 rest,
With a bottle close beside him and the shingle on his
 breast.

Well, they analysed the liquor, and it would appear
  that he
Qualified his drink with something good for setting
  spirits free.
Though 'twas plainly self-destruction — ' 'twas his
  own affair,' they said;
And the jury viewed him sadly, and they found — that
  he was dead.

Finally, the drover's pass was issued, courtesy of Anderson & Co. Lawson himself was elated to be leaving town. Although no record remains to tell of the date, it was during a time of local rain, and he penned his sketch 'In a Wet Season' to commemorate his departure. It was published in the *Bulletin* on 2 December 1893.

It was raining — 'general rain'.

The train left Bourke, and then there began the long, long agony of scrub and wire fence, with here and there a natural clearing, which seemed even more dismal than the funereal 'timber' itself. The only thing which might seem in keeping with one of these soddened flats would be the ghost of a funeral — a city funeral with plain hearse and string of cabs — going very slowly across from the scrub on one side to the scrub on the other. Sky like a wet, grey blanket; plains like dead seas, save for the tufts of coarse grass sticking up out of the water; scrub indescribably dismal — everything damp, dark, and unspeakably dreary.

Somewhere along here we saw a swagman's camp — a square of calico stretched across a horizontal stick, some rags steaming on another stick in front of a fire, and two billies to the leeward of the blaze. We knew by instinct that there was a piece of beef in the larger one. Small, hopeless-looking man standing with his back to the fire, with his hands behind him, watching the train; also, a damp, sorry-looking dingo warming itself and shivering by the fire. The train had held up for a while. We saw two or three similar camps further on, forming a temporary suburb of Byrock . . .

The rain had eased. At Byrock the railway platform was crowded with men who 'looked cheerfully and patiently dismal' and wore 'old overcoats and damp, soft felt hats; one trooper in a waterproof'. They had come to farewell friends en route to the city. Lawson was 'glad when the bell rang' to signal their departure. He settled back in his seat and read to pass the time. After a while he closed his book and turned his attention back to the wet scenery, seeing a 'hawker's turn-out which was too sorrowful for description'. The train slowed as it passed a teamsters' camp. There, three or four wagons were 'covered with tarpaulins which hung down in the mud all round and suggested death'. A tall, thin man wearing a shabby coat 'and a damp felt hat' strode along the road past the camp. A cattle-dog crept stealthily out from under a nearby wagon and nipped the man smartly on the heel.

... We remember stopping — for an age it seemed — at half-a-dozen straggling shanties on a flat of mud and water. There was a rotten weatherboard pub, with a low, dripping verandah, and three wretchedly forlorn horses hanging, in the rain, to a post outside. We saw no more, but we knew that there were several apologies for men hanging about the rickety bar inside — or round the parlour fire. Streams of cold, clay-coloured water ran in all directions, cutting fresh gutters, and raising a yeasty froth whenever the water fell a few inches. As we left, we saw a big man in an overcoat riding across a culvert; the tails of the coat spread over the horse's rump, and almost hid it. In fancy still we saw him — hanging up his weary, hungry, little horse in the rain, and swaggering into the bar; and we almost heard someone say, in a drawling tone: "'Ello, Tom! 'Ow are yer poppin' up?"

The train stopped (for about a year) within a mile of the next station. Trucking-yards in the foreground, like any other trucking-yards along the line; they looked drearier than usual, because the rain had darkened the posts and rails. Small plain beyond, covered with water and tufts of grass. The inevitable, God-forgotten 'timber', black in the distance; dull, grey sky and misty rain all over. A small dark-looking flock of sheep was crawling slowly in across the flat from the unknown, with three men on horseback zigzagging

306

patiently behind. The horses just moved — that was all. One man wore an oilskin, one an old tweed overcoat, and the third had a three-bushel bag over his head and shoulders.

Had we returned an hour later, we should have seen the sheep huddled together in a corner of the yards, and the three horses hanging up outside the local shanty.

The town of Nyngan did not impress Lawson. Here the train was delayed for several hours while the five trucks of cattle were unhitched and shunted away to be later taken on to the city by a 'goods' train. John Anderson had given him a 'note of introduction' to be delivered to the cattle-agent at Nyngan. However the agent was absent, leaving his office in charge of a labourer and a clerk, whom Lawson chose to ignore. Later, when he re-boarded the train, Lawson amused himself by reading the note, which read: 'Dear Old Man — Please send this beggar on; and I hope that he'll be landed safely at Orange — or — or wherever the cattle go. — Yours, —'

. . . After Nyngan the bush grew darker and drearier, and the plains more like ghastly oceans; and here and there the 'dominant note of Australian scenery' was accentuated, as it were, by naked, white, ring-barked trees standing in the water and haunting the ghostly surroundings.

We spent that night in a passenger compartment of a van which had originally been attached to old No. 1 engine. There was only one damp cushion in the whole concern. We lent that to a lady who travelled for a few hours in the other half of the next compartment. The seats were about nine inches wide and sloped in at a sharp angle to the bare match-board wall, with a bead on the outer edge; and the cracks having become well caulked with the grease and dirt of generations, they held several gallons of water each. We scuttled one, rolled ourselves in a rug, and tried to sleep; but all night long, overcoated and comfortered bushmen would get in, let down all the windows, and then get out again at the next station. Then we would wake up frozen and shut the windows.

We dozed off again, and woke at daylight, and recognised the ridgy gum-country between Dubbo and Orange. It didn't look any drearier than the country further west — because it couldn't. There is scarcely a part of the country out west which looks less inviting or more horrible than any other part.

The drover's pass, which had been issued in the name of John Smith, entitled Lawson to return to Bourke by 'ordinary passenger-train within two days' at no cost. Lawson had no intention of availing himself of the offer and gave the pass away to an 'unemployed in Orange, who wanted to go out back'. By this stage the rain had cleared, a good omen for his return to the city, and they 'had sunlight for Orange, Bathurst, the Blue Mountains, and Sydney. They deserve it; also as much rain as they need.'

CHAPTER 17

Afterwards

Blacksoil plains were grey soil, grey soil in the drought.
Fifteen years away, and five hundred miles out;
Swag and bag and billy carried all our care
Before we were married, and I wish that I were
there.[85]

In commenting on Lawson's trip to Bourke and his subsequent return to Sydney, A. G. Stephens of the *Bulletin* recorded some years later: 'He endured all kinds of variegated misery, till he set his broken boots (again) on Sydney pavement with 'Never again!' But he could feel and he could see and he could write what he saw, and he wrote the truth.'

The publication of three new radical socialist poems in Sydney in June also marked Lawson's return to the city about this time. With his bush experiences still uppermost in his mind, the remainder of 1893 saw the publication of more Bourke-inspired pieces. These included 'A Love Story'[86], 'Hungerford', 'Knocked Up', 'Ladies in the Shed', 'Lake Eliza', 'Louth, on the Darling', 'Outback', 'Says You', 'Tally Town', 'The Great Flood of '90', 'The Great Grey Plain', 'The Western Stars', and 'Some Popular Australian Mistakes'.

On his return to Sydney, Lawson worked as an unpaid editor for the *Worker*, believing that he would be offered the job full-time. However, the position never eventuated and, disappointed, he sailed for New Zealand on 18 November, the same day that 'Some Popular Australian Mistakes' was published in the *Bulletin*. He wrote 'The Emigration to New Zealand', which was published in William Willis's *Truth*.

> I'm off to make enquiries as to when the next boat
>   sails:
> I'm sick of all these colonies, but most of New South
>   Wales,
> An' if you meet a friend of mine who wants to find my
>   track,
> Say you, 'he's gone to Maoriland, and isn't coming
>   back.'

Lawson was not only tired of the bush, he was fed up with the whole country.

As an alternative to Paraguay, and a little less dry in the bar-room department, some of Lawson's Bourke mates had also left for New Zealand, where work was reported to be plentiful and conditions better. One such man was Bob Brothers, Lawson's 'Giraffe' in 'Send Round the Hat'. In December, Lawson wrote to Aunt Emma from Wellington: 'Bob Brothers got back to Sydney [from Wellington] about the time I left. Got a letter to say his baby and wife were ill. Baby dead and buried when he got back ... Meet old chums at every corner. Lot of Bourke people on the boat yesterday ...'

The following year Lawson's mother, Louisa, printed 1000 copies of *Short Stories in Prose and Verse* on behalf of her son. Amongst the contents were 'Rats', 'A Bushman's Funeral' (later to become 'The Union Buries Its Dead'), and 'Macquarie's Mate', subtitled 'A Darling River Sketch'. Despite some criticism of the book in literary circles, not only for the choice of cover and printing, but for the arrangement of the contents, the publication brought together the best of Lawson's work to that date, and from then on his reputation as a short story writer grew.

Lawson's months in the bush had only served to reinforce his views on the over-stated, romantic concept of the outback. In 'Australian Bards and Bush Reviewers', which was published in the *Worker* on 18 August 1894, he berated the poets who still painted the Australian bush in glowing colours.

AUSTRALIAN BARDS AND BUSH REVIEWERS

While you use your best endeavour to immortalise in
    verse
The gambling and the drink which are your country's
    greatest curse,
While you glorify the bully and take the spieler's part —
You're a clever southern writer, scarce inferior to Bret
    Harte.

And you sing of waving grasses when the plains are
    dry as bricks,
And discover shining rivers where there's only mud
    and sticks;
If you picture 'mighty forests' where the mulga spoils
    the view —
You're superior to Kendall, and ahead of Gordon too.

If you swear there's not a country like the land that
    gave you birth,
And its sons are just the noblest and most glorious
    chaps on earth;
If in every girl a Venus your poetic eye discerns,
You are gracefully referred to as the 'young Australian
    Burns'.

But if you should find that bushmen — spite of all the
    poets say —

Are just common brother-sinners, and you're quite as
   good as they —
You're a drunkard, and a liar, and a cynic, and a
   sneak,
Your grammar's simply awful and your intellect is
   weak.

Lured by the promise of a job on a new daily edition of the *Worker*, appropriately named the *Daily Worker*, Lawson returned to Sydney in July 1894, only to find that the newspaper had already ceased production, after only one month.

During that same year the Amalgamated Shearers' Union and the General Labourers' Union merged to form the Australian Workers' Union. The country was experiencing severe financial problems, especially within the wool-growing industry. The Pastoralists' Union demanded lower rates of pay for shearers. The wages dispute was rekindled and in a short time groups of striking shearers again set up large camps, including along the Darling. The three eastern states and South Australia were the worst affected.

By this time, Lawson was the 'provincial editor' with the weekly *Worker*, reporting union news. He picked up his pen and wrote, defending the shearers and their principles. 'Beautiful Maoriland' (subtitled 'Love and the Union') was published in that same newspaper on 25 August 1894. The poem tells of a penniless, homesick New Zealand union shearer (who had 'stuck to the union, hard and fast') who was offered a 'vacant stand' in a blackleg shed, but adhered to his principles and refused the job.

BEAUTIFUL MAORILAND

A shearer came to a blackleg shed, when most of the
   sheds were full;
He'd tramped and tramped till his hope was dead, and
   never got hands in wool.

He'd stuck to the Union, hard and fast, with no one to
    understand
How his heart had longed, as the weeks dragged past,
    for his love and his Maoriland.

'Fern and tussock and flax; range and river and sea.
A strain on my heart that will never relax — a
    heart that will never be free.
Oh, why should I break my heart?' he sighs; 'Will
    the Union break thro' me?
She draws me back with her great brown eyes,
    over the leagues of sea.
Beautiful Maoriland! Glorious Maoriland!
Oh, my heart for my darling waits, down yonder in
    Maoriland!'

'Go in and sign,' said the boss once more, 'for we
    can't wait here all day.'
The shearer turn'd to the office door, and again he
    turn'd away.
His spirit shrank from the dreadful track, and here was
    a 'vacant stand' —
The chance of a cheque that would take him back to
    his home in Maoriland.

'You've nothing to fear,' said the boss again, 'for the
    law protects you now.'
The shearer turn'd with a twinge of pain, and wearily
    wiped his brow;
His ears grew dull, and his eyes grew dim, as he gazed
    on the burning sand,
And thought of his darling who watched for him, at
    home in his Maoriland.

'Sign yer name there,' said the mulga clerk; 'write yer
    name there,' he said.
The shearer read and his brow grew dark as the
    shameful clause he read.
The squatters' agreement before him spread — the pen
    in his trembling hand —
A few short weeks in the shearing shed — then home
    to his Maoriland.

Then never a train too swift could run, nor a ship
    could sail too fast,
When the shed cut out and the cheque was won, and
    he followed his heart at last.
He stooped to sign, when it seemed to him that a cold
    breath touched his hand,
And a sweet, clear voice he knew called 'Jim!' from
    the past and Maoriland.

As you'd drop a snake, so he dropped the pen, and a
    short, sharp breath he drew,
Oh was it a spirit that whispered then: 'Be true to your
    mates; be true!'?
He shouldered his swag, and he faced the track — the
    heat, and the flies, and sand —
To die perhaps in the hell, out back, for the honour of
    Maoriland.

He followed the light of the Union star — his love was
    a thing apart,
But a heavier load than his swag, by far, was the load
    on the shearer's heart;
And long ere the season had passed away his heart was
    a 'vacant stand',
He learned that his darling had died that day in his
    dreary Maoriland.

'Fern and tussock and flax; range and river and sea.
A strain on my heart that will not relax — a heart
    that will never be free.
Promises fair in the future rise; what are they all to
    me?
She haunts me still with her great brown eyes,
    over the leagues of sea.
Beautiful Maoriland! Dreary Maoriland!
Oh! my heart! for my heart lies dead in desolate
    Maoriland.'

Though Lawson's earlier sympathies appeared to be with the shearers and the unionists, for some reason he suddenly ceased to be as moved by their plight. In a series of scathing articles, reminiscent of the 1892 Lawson–Paterson duel of verse, he turned his attention instead to the city versus bush attitude, unions and shearers. 'Get rid of the idea that the shearers are the only wronged men on earth and the squatters the only tyrants,' he chastised in 'A Word in Season', which was written around 1894 and later published in the *Worker*.

A WORD IN SEASON

The shearers have fought a good fight and gained real victories, of which not the least is that which they have in many cases gained over themselves. But these successes, together with the prominence — the great advertisement — which the strike has given them, are very likely to do harm in an unpicketed direction. A word in season will do no harm anyway.

Let a certain class of shearers remember that there are millions of workers in the world who are nearly as good as the bushmen, and yet do not know a ram from a ewe, and are not particularly troubled on account of their ignorance in that direction either.

Remember that the world, or even Australia, might worry along if there wasn't a sign of a sheep on earth.

Get rid of the idea that nothing but — and jackeroos come out of the cities.

Get rid of the idea that the shearers are the only wronged men on earth and the squatters the only tyrants.

Remember that the hardship of bush life at its worst is not a circumstance compared with what thousands of poor women in cities have to go through.

Remember that there are bitter struggles and grander battles fought by the poor of the cities than ever in the country.

Remember that the fathers, the heroes of modern Liberty, fought and threw away their lives on barricades in the streets of cities.

Remember that if every bushman and townsman in Australia made one determined stand for Right and Justice they could not succeed without the capital.

Remember that there are thousands of men in the city who are very nearly as good and true as you are; try to learn more about their lives; try to strengthen the bond of sympathy between town and bush; do not show your ignorance of the world by your contemptuous treatment of the jackeroo or new-chum; do not expect him to know as much about bush life as you do; remember that if you went into city society you might look just as foolish as he does on a horse for the first time — only that you wouldn't be reminded of it so often and brutally as you remind him. Gain a wider knowledge of your 'fellow workman'.

Remember that this is written to a certain class of bushmen.

These ideas were expanded in 'The City and the Bush', published in the *Worker* on 8 December 1894. The article was directed to 'a certain class of Australian Bushmen', stating that the 'average townsman knows little more about the bush than ... the average bushman's knowledge of city life'. In an attempt to strengthen the 'bond of sympathy between the bush workers and those in the cities', Lawson took a swipe at the treatment of new-chum jackaroos by experienced bushmen, and 'bush-union egotism and clannishness'.

THE CITY AND THE BUSH

There should, in the interests of true Democracy, be a strong bond of sympathy between the bush workers and those in the cities of Australia — and there isn't. There is little or no real sympathy between them, because they do not understand — or, rather, misunderstand — each other, and this is the result of ignorance of the circumstances surrounding each other's lives — of the lives themselves in many cases. They don't know — they don't understand; that's what's the matter with Australia — and with the world today. The different classes ought to know more of each other's lives.

The average townsman knows little more about the bush than the English know of Australia, and the same might be said with regard to the average bushman's knowledge of city life. Bill or Jim takes a run down to the city for a spree — to have a knock round and see some life; the 'life' he sees is mostly a false side of city life, set up especially for the benefit of those who have more money than city experience, or who plunge into drink and dissipation whenever they can so as to forget their troubles for a while — to find oblivion from the hell which devilish greed has made on earth to-day. This life lasts just as long as your cheque or cash does.

Bill (or Jim) goes back up country with false or mutilated ideas of life in the city, and he sows those ideas amongst his youthful or less-travelled mates, said ideas being strengthened by comparison with the notions of other mates who have had similar adventures.

Mind, we are not speaking of the city bushman who has been all round. He, by the way, could, if he liked, greatly help in the bringing of the bush and city workers closer together.

Many bushmen think the 'towny' mean with his money, not considering — perhaps not knowing — that he is haunted by the spectre of the eighteen bob a week which he has to pay for board and lodgings. If he doesn't pay it he is turned out to join the unemployed and sleep in the Domain; and camping out in the city is very

317

different from camping out in the bush. In the city it is called 'vagrancy', and you are in constant danger of being run in and getting a month hard, like a criminal, for not being able to get a job. In the bush you go to a shed or station and ask for some tucker as a matter of course. But to go to a back gate in the city and do the same thing is a crime, and a policeman would run you in like a pickpocket the first time he caught you at it.

Then, again, it doesn't matter if you are in rags on the track; it doesn't attract notice — it seems all right and natural; but if you are a man of spirit, and are used to better days, you need a stout heart to go out and hold your head up in rags and poverty and face the world in the city, where at any moment you might meet someone you know, and who knew you when you were better off. You can't take up your swag and walk straight away from it all. Some will ask, 'Why not?' Well, why doesn't the bushman walk into the city when he's hard up on the track? Eh?

When a jackaroo goes out back into a shearing shed he is mostly treated according to the time-honoured bush fashion of treating new-chums, and then if he returns to the city prejudiced against the shearers and bush life — well, it is their own fault. I could never see any sense or reason in the treatment which the Australian new-chum receives and has always been subjected to at the hands of a certain class of Australian bushmen. He had been the butt of bush 'humour' ever since there was a sheep station in Australia; his 'blunders' and 'adventures' have been the themes of columns and columns of bosh written by Australian funny writers, we can't call them humorists; and the alleged bush artist has never been far behind in this respect. And why? It cannot be because of that priggish idea — held by a certain class of Unionists — that everything in the shape of a man that comes out of the city is a blackleg, for it was even so in the days when nearly every bushman had been a new-chum himself once. It cannot be because a certain class of bushmen expect the jackaroo to know as much about bush work and life as they do — only rank idiots would expect that much of him. Is it because they have a lurking, aggravating idea that he might be equal or superior to them in some respects — that, if he does not show it, he thinks it? Anyway, the majority of the shearers and labourers out back regard the 'new-chum jackaroo' — and, indeed, townspeople in general — with contempt, and take no pains to hide it; while, on the other hand, most city men think of the bushmen with respect, and treat them so.

In one shed where we worked — and supposed to be a good Union shed too — a young man from the city was guyed and mocked daily, and finally became the 'laughing stock' of the shed, because he looked intellectual — or 'soft', if you like it better — cleaned his teeth regularly, combed his hair before meals, sounded the 'g' in words that end in 'ing', and didn't put an oath before every other noun and adjective he used. And no one in that shed seemed to know enough of the world to see that it was just as square and natural for him to do those things as it was for his tormentors not to. They didn't understand him, because they knew nothing of the conditions under which he had lived. *He* studied and understood them, and is a good democrat still.

And let me state that to hear the same old senseless oaths over and over again used before every other word, all day long in the shed — it gets monotonous; it sounds childish.

Speaking of the treatment of the new-chum, it is pretty much the same all over the world — with the new boy in an English school, with the raw recruit at the barracks, with the 'tender-foot' in America, and the new boy, the tender-foot, the raw recruit and the new-chum, when they get hardened, mostly treat others as they themselves have been treated. This is a cowardly custom, because the victim is generally unable to defend himself. It does no good; it only brutalises men. I can see nothing in it but ignorant brutality. It might be said that such a course of treatment is necessary to 'make a man' of a green-hand — or, as bushmen say, to take the 'trimmings off of him'. But, judging by results, God help such 'manliness'! I'd prefer a man with the 'trimmings' left on.

Before this goes on I wish to deny that I am inkslinging abuse at the bushmen, as some of my critics kindly (and ignorantly) stated in the *Worker*. I am simply trying to point out what many intelligent Unionists believe to be glaring faults, and, consequently, very weak places in Unionism; and I'm doing this in the interests of what I believe to be a wider and truer Democracy than many of my fellow workmen seem able to realise or willing to listen to — unwilling, because of widespread bush-union egotism and clannishness.

It is a mistake to think that city workers are less democratic than bushmen. They are equally so — perhaps more so — only they have less time to pitch about it.

It is a mistake to think the hardships of the bush can be compared with those of the city. What of the poor city women — widows and the wives of loafing or drunken husbands — who have to keep their children and pay the rent on ten shillings or fifteen shillings per week? What of the women who have to work twelve or thirteen hours a day for from 2s. 6d. to five shillings per day — and do a strong man's work at that? What of the girls in sweating dens at five shillings per week? But the list would be endless. I could take a bushman through the back streets of Sydney and show him scenes at every step that would hurt his heart, and make him wish he had a million pounds to give away, and so mitigate the awful misery he would see.

A shearing shed and a pound a hundred is not the end of all things.

And, lastly — though, of course, I run the risk of being laughed at — it is a mistake to come down to the city and swagger through the streets in the dirty, worn-out clothes you wear about the hut, when there is no necessity for it. It is only false democratic egotism, and an insult to the customs of the city. You are pretty touchy about the customs of the shed. What would you think of, and how would you treat, a jackaroo who came into the hut with a stand-up collar and the rest of 'em on? Eh? Wouldn't it be as fair, or otherwise, for the jackaroo at home to sneer at your clothes as for you to sneer at his rig? But he doesn't. As I heard a bush union secretary say the other day, 'Sydney people don't take much stock in clothes, I'll say that to their credit; a bushy can walk round all day in a shirt and pair of dirty moles without anyone seeming to take any notice.'

'The Cant and Dirt of Labour Literature' was published in the *Worker* on 6 October 1894. Here Lawson turned his wrath on the unions, ridiculing the 'ignorant, cowardly, and brutal' use of the word 'scab'.

THE CANT AND DIRT OF LABOUR LITERATURE
[excerpt]

It is a great pity that the word 'scab' ever dirtied the pages of a workman's newspaper. It is a filthy term in its present meaning — objectionable every way you look at it. It should never be used by one man in reference to another, no matter how bad the other may be. It is a cowardly word, because it is mostly used behind a man's back; few men, except bullies who have the brute strength to back them, would call a man so to his face. If it is used face to face, it is only in the heat of a drunken row, the prelude to a fight, or in cases where the other man is physically weaker. It is a low, ignorant word, and only appeals to ignorance and brutality. It does no good — you can't convert a man by using that word behind his back; and if you do use it so, then he's as good a man as you are. It is a low, filthy, evil-working, ignorant, cowardly, and brutal term, and belongs to the slang of the brainless, apish larrikins and the drunken prostitutes of the city slums. A man only uses it when he hasn't got the brains to say something clean and cutting. You will often find that the bushman who doesn't swear or mix dirt with his language can cut sharper with his tongue when he likes than the men who do.

The word free labourer is unsuitable because it conveys a false impression — one might as well say 'independent'. No labourer is 'free', anyway. Let us use 'non-Unionist' until, at least, a better word turns up . . .

There are four words which will be fondly remembered by us when we are old men, and when the A.W.U. will only remember with shame that so many of its members were foolish and ignorant enough to use and admire such words as 'scab', and 'Skitely Wing'.* These four words — 'chum', 'jolly', 'mate' and 'sweetheart' — will never die.

* Whitely King was the chairman of the Pastoralists' Union.

In the same article, Lawson went on to take a swipe at 'mateship' and bush brotherhood, a concept he had often dwelt on in his writings. He attacked the word, announcing that it existed only as a myth.

. . . That egotistic word 'mateship' — which was born of New Australian imagination, and gushed about to a sickening extent — implied a state of things which never existed any more than the glorious old unionism which was going to bear us on to freedom on one wave. The one was altogether too glorious, and the other too angelistic to exist amongst mortals. We must look at the nasty side of truth as well as the other, the conceited side. When our ideal 'mateship' is realised, the monopolists will not be able to hold the land from us.

It seemed that Lawson's disillusionment with mateship was only temporary, or confined solely to the bush fraternity. In 1895, he went on to write the poem 'To An Old Mate', which was later published in *In the Days When the World Was Wide*. Though he may have had several collective 'mates' in mind when he wrote the words, the references to 'the jovial nights of December the solemn first days of the year, long tramps through the clearings and timber, short partings on platform and pier' may have been a nostalgic glance back at the time he and Gordon spent trekking out to Hungerford after the Christmas of 1892.

In 1895, too, Lawson farewelled his Bourke friend Billy Wood and his family as they left for William Lane's settlement in Cosme, Paraguay. Before he departed, Wood spent

> a couple of nights with Henry, and we farewelled each other. After I had been living over here [Paraguay] about four years, I wrote, inviting him to try and make the trip and spend a few months with us, but, unfortunately, it didn't come about, most likely the getting together of the necessary cash was the obstacle. Had Lawson got here, he would have been able to get together plenty of data for some capital yarns.[87]

Some time during that year, John Le Gay Brereton, a friend of Lawson's, wrote suggesting that Lawson, 'go to Angus and Robertson's and see what terms you can get there for a book. I know they made Banjo a good offer and are going to publish a volume for him. Ask for Robertson . . . he told me the other night he'd like to see you about it.'[88] The bookselling firm of Angus and Robertson had been established nine years earlier, when George Robertson purchased a half share in David Angus's bookshop at 110½ Market Street in Sydney. The enterprising pair of Scots soon extended their business to include a publishing company, presided over by Robertson.

By 1895, the company had already established itself as a publishing house, and Banjo Paterson's first book, *The Man From Snowy River and Other Verses*, was still in the production process when George Robertson struck an agreement with Lawson to publish one volume of verse, and one of prose. The profits were to be divided equally between author and publisher. Before the release of the book, however, Lawson, penniless as usual, sold the copyright to Robertson for £54, fourteen pounds of which he had already received. The volume of poetry, *In the Days When the World was Wide and Other Verses*, was published on 14 February 1896, marking the beginning of a long association between Lawson and Angus and Robertson. The book included many of Lawson's 'Bourke-based' poems, including 'Out Back' and 'Knocked Up'. A. G. Stephens, of *Bulletin* fame, was critical of the arrangement of the contents of the book, stating that 'the haphazardous mixture jolts the mind like an unexpected top step.'[89]

Lawson, however, had other things on his mind. Several weeks after the release of the book, he married Bertha Bredt, and the newly-married couple left for Western Australia, where he worked as a painter and penned several stories which he sold to the *West Australian*. His volume of short stories, *While the Billy Boils*, was published in August and by September all copies had been sold and the book was being reprinted.

Lawson seemed disinclined to settle anywhere. The couple's return to Sydney was followed by a twelve-month stint in New Zealand, where Lawson wrote and worked for a time as a school teacher. Their first child was born there, a son whom they named Joseph Henry, though he was mostly known as 'Jim'.

Lawson wrote steadily, his writing interspersed with regular bouts of drinking. Despite his moderate success, he was disillusioned with the Australian press and thought longingly of England. 'My advice to any young Australian writer ... would be to go steerage, stow away, swim, and seek London, Yankeeland or Timbucktoo', he wrote, 'rather than stay in Australia till his genius turned to gall, or beer.'[90] Meanwhile, Angus and Robertson were preparing proofs for another two Lawson volumes of prose, *On the Track* and *By the Sliprails*, and another volume of verse, *Verses Popular and Humorous*. These books were all released to the reading public in 1900. In February that year, a daughter was born, whom they called Bertha, after her mother. Several months later the family set sail for England aboard the *Damascus*.

While in England, Lawson published three more books: *The Country I Come From* and *Joe Wilson and His Mates* in 1901, followed by *Children of the Bush* in 1902. By that year, illness, lack of money and the failing state of the Lawsons' marriage brought them back to Australia. Apart for the first few weeks after their arrival in Sydney, Lawson and Bertha took separate accommodation, and later obtained a judicial divorce.

Always broke, Lawson failed to provide for his children and Bertha was forced to find work. Between 1905 and 1910, the poet was regularly gaoled for drunkenness and failure to pay maintenance, and spent a considerable amount of time in mental hospitals. The bitterness of the couple's separation emerged in several poems, such as 'The Separated Woman' and 'Divorced'. Angus and Robertson brought out two new volumes in 1907: *Send Round the Hat* and *The Romance of the Swag*. Most of the contents, however, were not new, but merely a re-issue of *Children of the Bush* as two separate titles.

Lawson continued to write over the next few years, his life plagued with periods of alcoholism and ill-health, and mood swings where he alternated between bouts of deep depression and periods of high elation. Relief finally came in 1916 when he was offered the position of publicity officer for the Water Conservation and Irrigation Commission in Leeton. The town was known as a 'dry' area, meaning that no grog could be bought locally. The nearest alcohol was located at Narrandera, twenty miles (32 km) away.

The proposal included the use of a small cottage, rent free. Lawson accepted the job and made the break from city life, moving into the 'little place on a two-acre block, with an orchard, and gum saplings growing along the back fence.'

It was here in Leeton that Lawson and Jim Gordon renewed their acquaintance after a separation of many years. In the *Lawsonian* in September 1979, Harry Pearce briefly explained the course of Jim Gordon's life, after he and Lawson had parted company in Bourke in 1893.

> Jim then spent twenty years roaming around western New South Wales, and for some time went bullock-driving, and later became manager of two stations, Gundabooka of three hundred thousand acres; and Curranyalpa of one hundred thousand acres. In 1902 he got married to go to the latter station, 100 miles S.W. from Bourke on the Darling River. Then he went droving for some years, then boundary-riding on Walgut [sic, Walgett] Station. Finally, with three horses in a trap with his wife and two children in 1912 he drove to Leeton where he took up what he called 'a bit of a farm' . . . Finally, he was appointed an Inspector for the Irrigation Commission until

he retired . . . he first began to write 'doggrel' when he was about twenty-one years old . . . Jim . . . said he was more of a 'thinker' than a speaker, and said that on his long inspecting drives the opportunities gave him time to think about many things and write. Here we see the character of 'Mitchell' clearly illustrated.

Jim Gordon had married Celia McEntyre in Bourke in 1902, and the two children who accompanied them to Leeton in 1912 with 'three horses in a trap' were Margaret and Frank. Eventually Jim had made somewhat of a name for himself as a poet, writing and living under the pseudonym of 'Jim Grahame'. Apparently it was by this new name that Jim now preferred to be known, which came as a surprise to Lawson.

Jim Grahame, hearing of his old mate's arrival in town, wrote to Lawson, suggesting a meeting. Jim, not knowing 'how the applause of all Australia and other parts of the world might have affected him' was understandably nervous, but he was happy to receive the following reply:

Pine Avenue, Leeton,
(Damn the date)

Dear Mr Grahame,
I was delighted to get your note. I've had two other such already,
and both from farms — one from Mr McCausland, I have written
to him also. We all seem to be here — there's Alec (Leslie) McGill,
the brewer of soft tack: he's another old Bourke mate. I go up for a
chat nearly every evening. I am just camping here, and my affairs
are all mucked up just now. I'm working like hell to get 'em
straight, and waiting to see what the department is going to do with
me. Drop in any day and we'll 'get acquaint' again and arrange for
a long chat either here or at your place, and I'll tell you the fates of
the characters mentioned in your note, as far as I know.

Yours sincerely,
Henry Lawson

Jim Grahame took up the story:

> That evening I walked up the street in the hope of meeting him, and saw him coming down the hill, his broad-leafed hat turned up at the back, and a small parcel under his arm. Of course I knew him at once. I do not think anyone would fail to recognise Lawson after once seeing him. But what surprised me was that he knew me when we were yet ten yards apart. What a hearty, silent handshake we had! And great peering into faces, and looking up and down. Then he insisted I must go with him to his bungalow. I went, and soon we were all good friends . . . '[91]

The pair talked long into the night, reminiscing over old times and reliving their trekking days in Bourke. Lawson was 'full of bright hopes' for the future.

Henry Lawson was accepted unquestioningly into the Grahame family and he spent a considerable amount of time at Jim's and Celia's home. His attachment to the household is evident from several pieces written during this period. One of these, 'Bonnie of our Area', is a touching tongue-in-cheek portrayal of Jim Grahame's youngest daughter who was 'two years and nine months old'. It was published in the *Bulletin*.

> 'Jim Gordon owns a ten-acre block a couple of miles from the Lawson homestead, and when the poet is not there helping him gather pumpkins or plough, Jim is sitting over his mate's fire, telling yarns, planning stories and discussing a play yet to be written, which is to make them . . . famous. Jim, who has been almost everything from stockman to commercial traveller during his wanderings out west, is something of a poet himself, and writes verses in his spare time. He is tall and rather delicate-looking, with a typical Scottish face that reminds one of Robert Louis Stevenson. He and Lawson were mates twenty-five years ago in Bourke and they are both busy now renewing a friendship broken by that interval of years . . . '[92]

It was not until Lawson penned 'By the Banks of the Murrumbidgee' in 1916 that he finally publicly acknowledged the presence of Jim Gordon, now Grahame, in Bourke during 1892–93.

> My mate, James Grahame, ex-farm boy, ex-cocky's slave, ex-stationhand, shearer, drover, station storekeeper, city bushman, hawker, battler, commercial traveller; ex-almost anything you can think of in Australia, and now settler and road maintenance man on the Yanco Irrigation Area . . . We first met in Bourke some twenty-five years ago, and thus we share two pasts, so as to speak; but we were very young men then, those pasts are boys' pasts; and being but recently re-mated we haven't got to speak of those pasts yet. There's a certain shyness about the matter, if you understand, which may or may not deepen as those two twenty-five-year pasts are cleared up. They'll *have* to be cleared up first, and it is mainly for that reason we have come out into the gnarledest, wildest, weirdest, oldest bush in Australia, to 'camp on the river' for a night or two under the pretence of fishing.
>
> Our faces and voices have already grown re-familiar to each other, and we seem to have changed not at all. Not to each other. I am getting into the habit of calling him Jim and he of calling me Harry, and we are both getting out of the habit of calling each other by names we went by in the strenuous old Union days of Ninety-one [*sic*] and Ninety-two.

Lawson's position in Leeton was terminated in September 1918 but, unlike their parting in Bourke years earlier, the pair kept in regular contact. In March 1920, Lawson again contacted his mate Jim, giving his address as care of a local storekeeper in Coolac, New South Wales, near Gundagai.

> *Dear Old Jim,*
> *. . . I've been sentenced to six months' bush again, and shanghaied here, but I'm satisfied with my fate. No need to describe the place —*
> *you'll know. . . . hold out for prices between the Bulletin and Smith's*

*Weekly (rogues both) — you'll think out a way to manage them
either by letter or word of mouth. Ask (or demand) to know what
their rates of payment are, and how much per word you are getting,
and work one against the other. Send your best to Bully; requesting
them to return 'rejects' promptly. Then send rejects to Smith's
Weekly — they'll jump at 'em . . . And above all, save all your
clippings and original copies with a view to submitting them to A & R
or someone for book publication . . . your stuff is all good, some
splendid . . . But then you had all the experience and I next to none
— except for six months in Bourke and beyond in '90–'92 . . .
from your old mate,
Uncle Harry.*

Jim Grahame continued to live in Leeton for many years and eventually two books of his poems were released: *Call of the Bush*, published by the Bread and Cheese Club in Melbourne in 1940, and *Under Wide Skies*, published in 1947 by the Citizens of Leeton.

During the 1930s Jim Grahame's nephew, Bruce Turnbull, visited the Gordon household in Leeton. Bruce, now a grazier from the Brewarrina district near Bourke, recalled seeing a hat and coat that had previously belonged to Henry Lawson (probably left behind on some social visit) hanging in a room. Apparently Grahame, out of some sense of nostalgia, had kept the coat and hat long after Lawson's death as some personal memento to remind him of their friendship. Jim Grahame later wrote of that coat in *Under Wide Skies*.

THE POET'S COAT

*I've brought it out from the lumber-room,
Where it hung on a rusty hook;
Its folds are frayed and dusty and stiff
As the leaves of an ancient book.
It has been a treasure for ten long years,
Shoddy and cheap and mean;
'Twas bought when the poet's purse was light*

And the poet's years were lean.

The cuffs are ragged, the collar grimed;
The elbows are threadbare worn;
The pockets hang with their mouths agape,
With the edges tattered and torn.
Its colour is known as pepper-and-salt,
A ready-made kind of sac,
And cut to a style that's out of date
With a little slit at the back.

One lone black button hangs by a thread —
'Twas often he buttoned it tight
To cover rents in a worn out shirt
When the wind blew cold in the night.
My mind goes back to a dull grey day
(He'd plenty of them in the past),
And he was a sick and broken man —
It was then that he wore it last.

To the gaping pockets I slip my hand
(It was seldom they yielded cash);
A small bone stud and a broken nib
Lie buried in dust and ash.
In the left-hand breast, and folded neat,
There's a bill for a load of wood.
Ah me, though he paid us all in kind
He'd have paid in cash if he could!

I will hang it back on its rusty hook
In the dust of the lumber room,
Away from the clutch of a careless hand
And the restless sweep of the broom.
And thither I'll still repair at times

330

When I'm tired of men and their ways,
And dream awhile by my old mate's coat
That he wore in the olden days.

Jim's friendship with Henry Lawson had endured the test of time and distance. They met again several times in Sydney before Lawson's death, drawn together by some invisible bond: the sharing of hardships and dreams. Jim Gordon died in 1949 at the age of seventy-five.

Just prior to his own death, on Saturday 2 September 1922, Lawson took up residence in a small cottage in the Sydney suburb of Abbotsford. On hearing of the poet's passing, Edwin Brady later wrote:

> The chapter had closed. I was a long way off. Not much to do. Nothing much to say. What is there to say anyway? Express it in State and federal funeral and a belated statue? That is the accustomed way. For myself I sent what wires I had to send, then solemnly poured full libation, faced square to the setting sun, alone, and drank safe passage Westward to the soul of Henry Lawson, one of Australia's best.[93]

Jim Grahame wrote the following verses which were published in the *Bulletin* a fortnight later, knowing well that Lawson would have appreciated the sincerity and simplicity of them. The poem later appeared in *Under Wide Skies*.

THE BUSH MOURNS

The drover out by Cooper's Creek,
The shepherd camped beside the fold,
The ragged deadbeat of the street
Have lived the yarns that Lawson told.
The miners in the golden west,
The wool-king's dame with jewels hung,
The soldiers at the battle front
Have sung the songs that Lawson sung.

When mulga wire and horseback mail
The word had brought that he was dead;
Our pipes went out, our tones were hushed;
And then the news was sent ahead.
From south to north and through the west,
From home to home, the word was flashed;
And many a rumpled sleeve was wet
Where tears of lonely men had splashed.

To us, the men of hill and plain,
The people that he called his own,
When sharp and clear the message came,
'Twas like a knife-thrust to the bone.
He loved the bush and loved it well;
And one of us that he'd called 'Mate'
Remembered things he'd left undone —
And now — the end — and it's too late!

The sky is dark and dull the sun,
The world itself seems cold and grey;
And rough and rugged is the track,
And long and dreary is the way.
Where sliprail takes the place of gate
And fences lie beneath the sand
Proud men are they out there today
To claim they once held Lawson's hand.

After being given a State funeral the following Monday, Henry Lawson's body was laid to rest in Waverley cemetery which overlooks the ocean. A member of Angus and Robertson's editorial staff, W. E. FitzHenry, summed up the general feeling of that day when he wrote:

> When the soft afternoon light turned into the haze of dusk that
> Monday; and the roar of increased street traffic mingled with the
> rumble of the big printing presses, a few of us at the *Bulletin* thought

of the to-morrow. To-morrow, Henry would travel the long, winding road to a cemetery by the sea . . . Whilst trouble and affliction would be buried with him, his indomitable straightforwardness and lovable laughter would always be rooted deep in the hearts of his countrymen.[94]

Epilogue

I warp my life on pavement stones
That drag me ever down,
A paltry slave to little things,
By custom chained to town.
I've lost the strength to strike alone,
The heart to do and dare —
When swag and will were still my own
I'd tramp to God-knows-where.[95]

Though he often maligned the outback in his writing, Lawson never forgot his days in Bourke and beyond in 1892–93. He came to regard the bush as the great leveller of society, and the scenery, the inhabitants, the mateship, and the special and unique brand of outback humour he found there provided the basis for much of his writing for many years after his departure from the 'metropolis of the great scrubs'.

His later stories, such as 'Send Round the Hat' and 'That Pretty Girl in the Army', written years afterwards in England, were coloured with a tinge of pathos, and a layer of farcical bush humour, as though Lawson was allowing himself a nostalgic glimpse of the outback, a reflection and reconsideration on past impressions and opinions. In hindsight he wrote:

But every dream and every track — and there were
    many that I knew,
All lead on, or they lead back, to Bourke in Ninety-
    one and two.
And could I roll the summers back, or bring the dead
    time here again,
Or from the grave or world-wide track recall to Bourke
    the vanished men,
With mind content I'd go to sleep, and leave those
    mates to judge me true,
And leave my name to Bourke to keep — the Bourke
    of Ninety-one and two.[96]

Finally, no longer did Lawson regard himself as a Stranger on the Darling.

BIBLIOGRAPHY

General references on Henry Lawson and his work
Cronin, Leonard (ed.), *A Camp-Fire Yarn*, Lansdowne Press, 1984
Cronin, Leonard (ed.), *A Fantasy of Man*, Lansdowne Press, 1984
Kiernann, Brian, *The Essential Henry Lawson*, Currey O'Neil, 1982
Lawson, Bertha and Le Gay Brereton, John, *Henry Lawson by his Mates*, Angus & Robertson, 1931
Matthews, Brian, *The Receding Wave*, Melbourne University Press, 1972
Matthews, Brian, *Louisa*, Penguin, 1987
Prout, D., *Henry Lawson: The Grey Dreamer*, Rigby, 1963
Roderick, Colin, *Henry Lawson — A Life*, Angus & Robertson, 1991
Roderick, Colin, *Henry Lawson: The Master Story-teller*, Angus & Robertson, 1984
Roderick, Colin, *The Real Henry Lawson*, Rigby, 1982
Roderick, Colin (ed.), *Henry Lawson Criticism 1894–1971*, Angus & Robertson, 1972
Roderick, Colin (ed.), *Henry Lawson Letters 1890–1922*, Angus & Robertson, 1970
Stone, W. (ed.), *The World of Henry Lawson*, Hamlyn, 1974

Published books by Henry Lawson
Children of the Bush, Methuen & Co., 1902; Angus & Robertson, 1907
For Australia and Other Poems, Standard Publishing Co., 1913
In the Days When the World Was Wide, Angus & Robertson, 1896
Joe Wilson and His Mates, Blackwood, 1901; Angus & Robertson, 1902
My Army O My Army!, Angus & Robertson, 1915
On the Track, Angus & Robertson, 1900
On the Track and Over the Sliprails, Angus & Robertson, 1900
Over the Sliprails, Angus & Robertson, 1900
Selected Poems, Angus & Robertson, 1918
Send Round the Hat, Angus & Robertson, 1907
Short Stories in Prose and Verse, Louisa Lawson, 1894
The Country I Come From, Blackwood, 1901
The Rising of the Court and Other Sketches, Angus & Robertson, 1910
The Romance of the Swag, Angus & Robertson, 1907
The Skyline Rider and Other Verses, Lockley, 1910
Triangles of Life, Standard Publishing Co., 1913
Verses Popular and Humorous, Angus & Robertson, 1900
When I Was King and Other Verses, Angus & Robertson, 1905
While the Billy Boils, Angus & Robertson, 1896

Newspapers & Magazines
Aussie, 15 December 1926
Bulletin, 25 November 1893, 2 December 1893, 14 December 1893, 18 December 1893, 26 February 1897, 21 January 1899, 19 February, 1899, 22 January 1925, 19 February 1925, 22 February 1925
Freeman's Journal 1890
Geo, Volume IX No. 1
Sydney Morning Herald, 20 February 1939
Sydney Morning Herald 'Good Weekend', 24 January 1984
Sunday Mail Magazine, 21 June 1992
The Lawsonian, No. 219, September 1979
The Worker, 26 August 1893, 2 December 1893, 1 June 1938
Town and Country Journal 1888
Truth 16 April 1893*Western Herald*, 28 September 1892–29 October 1892
Windsor and Richmond Gazette, 9 October 1931, 24 September 1926

General
Barker, A.W., *Dear Robertson*, Angus and Robertson, 1982
Grahame, Jim, *Call of the Bush*, The Bread and Cheese Club, 1940
Grahame, Jim, *Under Wide Skies*, Citizens of Leeton, 1947
Nairn, B. & Serle, G. (ed.), *Australian Dictionary of Biography 1891–1939*, Melbourne University Press, 1986
Stone, Walter (ed.), *The Best of Banjo Paterson*, Paul Hamlyn, 1977
Wilding, Michael, *The Paraguayan Experiment*, Penguin, 1984

General books on Bourke and region
Centenary of Fords Bridge (1890–1990)
Centenary of Hungerford (1875–1975)
Centenary of Tilpa Post Office (1880–1980)
History of Bourke, vols I to XII, Bourke Historical Society
Barnett, W. H., *Written Memoirs of Bourke (of the 1890s)* (unpublished)
Barton, A. R., *Upper Darling River Navigation* (unpublished)
Bean, C. E. W., *On the Wool Track*, Scribner & Sons, 1947
Mudie, Ian, *River Boats*, Rigby, 1961

Oral information (interviews) on Bourke
Joseph Barry, Harry Bell, Roy Dunk, Jim Moses, Les Ryan, W. H. Barnett

Oral information on Henry Lawson
Wilkie W. Davis (poet and grazier, Bourke), Phil Downs (Sydney)

INDEX

A

'Across the Warrego' 165
Aborigines 124, 162
Afghans 161, 166, 265–67
Amalgamated Shearers' Union 14, 30, 42, 44, 50–79, 234, 312
'An Answer to Various Bards' 5
Anderson, John & Co. 295, 307
Anderson, 'Scotty' 233
Andrews, Arthur 45, 79, 233
Andrews, John 45, 49, 85
Angus & Robertson 322–24, 332
Archibald, J. F. 3, 7, 10, 12, 14, 16, 100, 102, 114
Australian Workers' Union 48, 50, 58, 312

B

Barnett, W. H. 235
Barringun 38, 217
Barton, Edmund vi, ix, 57
bicycles 167
Bijou Theatre 32
Bloxham, Horace K. 78
Boreham, Jack (Jake) 49, 233, 237, 247, 260, 290–93
bores x, 2, 158, 190, 196, 218
Bourke
  banks 40, 282
  bond stores 99
  communications 41
  Eight Hour Day 76
  health and hygiene 41
  hospital 28, 98
  hotels 20, 22, 32, 36, 42, 74, 94, 98, 106, 234, 282
  Labour League 20, 58
  punt 38, 46, 112, 168, 178
  river boats 32
  social life 30–31, 74, 232
  transport 31, 45, 165
  wool production 30–34, 45–47, 146, 168

'Bourke Bridge, The' 104, 178
Bournes, W. J. 190–92
Brady, Edwin J. x, 6, 10–14, 68, 89, 120–122
Braithwaite, Watson (Watty) 72, 79, 94, 232–36
Bredt, Bertha 324
Brewarrina 24, 32–34, 46, 52, 55, 328
Bridge Hotel 38
Brindingabba Bore 225
Brookes, Emma (Aunt) 7–10, 18–24, 68, 78, 212–15, 225–26, 230–32, 310
Brothers, Bob 49, 51, 237, 239, 243, 247, 255, 258, 310
Bulletin, the 2, 4, 5, 7, 10–17, 20–24, 62, 101–105, 131–41, 195, 199, 204–31
bullock teams 4, 31, 39, 127, 166
Burke and Wills 221
'Bush Mourns, The' 330
Byrock 19, 35, 305

C

Caledonian Hotel 32, 234
camels 20, 50, 169, 266, 284
carriers' committee 79
Carriers' Union 45, 53, 169
Carriers' Arms Hotel 32, 72, 74, 119, 222, 233–40, 255, 265–67, 276, 278, 297
Central Australian and Bourke Telegraph 7, 57, 68, 80, 85
Central Australian Hotel 108
Chapman, Philip, 24, 57, 68, 74, 80, 85, 96
'Clancy of the Overflow' 4
coach services 31
Coachbuilders' Union 43
Cobb & Co. 32, 34, 45, 79, 165, 166, 234, 236, 299
Costello, John 199
Currie brothers 51, 83, 85
Cuttaburra Creek 190, 198

D

Darling River 7, 8, 20, 21, 24, 25, 30,
32, 35, 37, 38, 45, 46, 57, 68, 74, 80,
96, 97, 102, 116, 121, 129, 158, 169,
178, 240, 294, 310, 325
Davis, Ebenezer 229
Davis, William (Wilkie) 230
Davis, William Walter 52, 73, 74, 190,
226
De Guinney, Ernest x, 146, 176
Doughty brothers 234
Doughty's Horse Bazaar 236
drought 25, 27, 29, 34, 42, 66, 67, 75,
78, 126–28, 158, 166, 169, 195, 199,
240, 273, 309
Dunlop Station 45, 114
Durack, Patrick 199

E

Enngonia 96, 234

F

Fitzgerald's Post Office Hotel 32
FitzHenry, W. E. 9, 332
flood 20, 24, 25, 30, 34, 36, 39, 40, 41,
101, 161, 196, 219, 220, 235, 264,
309
Florence Annie 33
Fords Bridge 119
Fort Bourke Station 53, 68, 113

G

General Labourers' Union viii, 45, 50,
53, 79, 102, 103, 108, 172, 312
Gibbs, Jimmy 120, 121, 122
Gladstone Hotel 85, 282
Golden Stairs Hotel 234
Goonery 158, 159, 162, 166
Gordon, James William (Jim) 99, 103,
113, 115, 116, 118, 122, 133, 157,
162, 164, 170, 176, 280, 296, 325,
327, 331
Grahame, Jim (pseudonym) 326, 329,
331
Great Western Hotel viii, 20, 101
Gumbalie Hotel 117, 162

H

Hall, Christine 172
Hall, Thomas Hicks 45, 51, 85, 102,
172, 174–76, 259
Hawley, John viii, 9, 80, 89, 101, 102,
235
Heseler, Edward Otto 101
Howe, James Peter 52, 53, 74
Hungerford vii, ix, 2, 8, 39, 55, 158,
163, 168, 170–78, 190–95, 201–203,
213–23, 232, 250, 253, 259, 309,
322
Hungerford, Thomas (Sir) 221
Hurdis, Tommy 51

I

'In Defence of the Bush' 5–6

J

James, Jimmy 132, 133, 139
'Jimmy Gibbs — the Shearer' 120–22
Joe Swallow (pseudonym) 74–78, 98,
280

K

Kelly's Camp Bore 164, 181
Kenmere Bore 225
Kerribree Station 52, 226
Kerribree Creek 190, 226
Kulkyne Creek 116

L

Labour Party 47, 51, 71, 265
Lake Eliza 15, 177, 190–95, 198, 225,
309
Lake Eliza Hotel 190
Lane, William 4, 14, 175, 323
Langwell, Hugh 51–56, 68, 74, 89
Lawson, Henry
short stories, sketches, miscellaneous
'A Bush Funeral' (see 'The Union
Buries Its Dead') ix, 106
'Australian Rivers: On the Darling'
35–38
'Baldy Thompson' 52, 215, 226,
227, 228–29

'Bush Terms' 126
'By the Banks of the
  Murrumbidgee' 104, 280, 328
'Cant and Dirt of Labour
  Literature, The' 320
'City and the Bush, The' vii, 11,
  316, 317–21
'Carriers' 167, 168–69
'Crawlalong' 40
'Darling River, The' (see 'Australian
  Rivers') 24–25
'Enter Mitchell' 204–206, 184
'Ghosts of Many Christmases, The'
  173
'Great Flood of '90, the' 40–41, 309
'Hungerford' vii, 218–21
'In a Dry Season' viii, 17, 102, 167
'In a Wet Season' 305, 172
'It Was Awful' 61, 62–63
'Ladies in the Shed' 140, 309
'Letter re Henry Lawson's Fictional
  Characters' 279
'Lord Douglas' 157, 281, 282–95
'Louth, on the Darling' 126–28
'Love Story, A' 309
'Mitchell: A Character Sketch' 233,
  279
'Mitchell Doesn't Believe in the
  Sack' 233, 280–81
'On the Edge of a Plain' 233
'Pursuing Literature in Australia' 8
'Rats' ix, 233, 310
'Romance of the Swag, The'
  206–212, 325
'Rough Shed, A' 137, 149–156
'Send Round the Hat' vii, 51, 101,
  232, 260–79, 310, 325, 334
'Sketch of Mateship, A' 118–120
'Some Popular Australian Mistakes'
  123–126, 309, 310
'Stragglers' ix, 184–200, 234
'That Pretty Girl in the Army' 51,
  142, 233, 239, 247–258, 259,
  334
'That Swag' (see 'Enter Mitchell')
  204

'That's What it Was' 164, 165
'Union Buries Its Dead, The' vii–ix,
  15, 105–12, 310
'Word in Season, A' 51, 315–16
Verse
'All Unyun Men' vii, ix, 43, 47–49,
  296
'Australian Bards and Bush
  Reviewers' 311–12
'Ballad of the Rouseabout, The'
  142–46
'Beautiful Maoriland' 312–15
'Booth's Drum' 238
'Borderland' (see 'Up the Country')
  5
'Boss Over the Board, The' 132,
  137–140
'Boss's Boots, The' 132, 133–37
'Bourke' 8, 9, 26–30
'Cambaroora Star, The' 4, 12
'City Bushman, The' (see 'In
  Answer to Banjo and Otherwise')
  6
'Delegates: 1 Then, The' 63–66
'Donald Macdonell' 59–61, 74
'Great Grey Plain, The' 159–161,
  309
'Greenhand Rouseabout, The'
  146–49
'Grog-an'-Grumble Steeplechase' 6
'Have You Heard' viii, 89, 93–94
'Heart of the Swag, The' vii, 9,
  203–204
'House of Fossils, The' 4, 85
'In Answer to Banjo and
  Otherwise' 6, 22
'Knocked Up' 199–201, 309, 323
'Lake Eliza' 15, 179, 190–94, 309
'Lissington Verdict, The' vii, 96–97
'Martin Farrell' 54–56
'More Echoes from the Old
  Museum' 4, 85
'Old Labour and the Echo' viii,
  94–96
'Our Members Present and Future'
  viii, 69–73, 79, 80, 114, 226

'Out Back' 195, 196–98, 323
'Paroo River, The' 223–25
'Peter Anderson & Co.' 297–305
'Poet by Telegraph, The' viii, 85–88
'Poet on the Central, The' vii, viii,
    80–85, 114
'Says You' 180–81, 309
'Song of the Darling River, The'
    24–25
'Stranger on the Darling, A' iii, viii,
    8, 75, 76–78, 79
'Stranger's Friend, The' 51
'Swagman and His Mate, The'
    182–84
'Sweeney' 20
'Tally Town' 75, 309
'Up the Country' 5
'Wales the First' 4, 85
'Wander-light, the' 9
'Western Stars, the' 198, 309
'What Huey Didn't Do' viii, 89–92
'When the Army Prays For Watty'
    viii, ix, 235, 236–38
'When the Ladies Come to the
    Shearing Shed' 140–42
'Years After the War in Australia'
    131–32
Lennon, John (Jack) 20, 74, 85, 101
Lindsay's Brewing Company 32
Louth 33, 38, 40, 45, 126–29, 170

M
Macdonell, Donald 51, 53, 57, 59, 74,
    173, 233, 239, 260
McCaughey, Samuel 53, 114, 115
McCaughey, John 132
Meehan, Jack 51
Merrick, John (Jack) 142, 239, 250
Millen, Edward Davis 24
Millen, W. K. 24
Murphy's Exchange Hotel 159

N
New Australia Co-operative Settlement
    Association 14, 175
North Bourke viii, 38, 39, 47, 105,
    106, 170, 178, 180
Norton, John 4, 13, 85
Nyngan 19, 35, 307

O
O'Brien, Mick 51, 233
Occidental Hotel 39
Overland Hotel 39

P
Parker, Arthur viii, ix, 16, 102–105,
    115, 163, 172, 174, 175, 178
Paroo River vi, 2, 54, 58, 122, 203, 223
Pastoralists' Union 14, 32, 46, 47
Paterson, A. B. (Banjo) 4, 5, 6, 7, 13,
    21, 22, 78, 85, 323
'Poet's Coat, the' 329–31
Pride of Erin Hotel 324
Public Watering Places 158, 169

R
Robertson, George 333
Royal Hotel 218, 253, 283

S
Salmon Ford Hotel 181
Salvation Army 30, 235, 236, 238–40,
    244–47, 254, 269
seasonal conditions 170
Shakespeare Hotel 45, 234, 235
Smoko (pseudonym) 80–93, 96
'Somebody's Victim' 215, 216–17
Spence, William G. 45
Stanley, Ben 45
Stephens, A. G. 3–6, 17, 122, 309, 323
Sutherland's Lake 164, 181, 229
swag 17–19, 46, 55, 105–106, 112,
    121–27, 142–44, 164–67, 186–89,
    193–98, 202–12, 214, 216, 225, 227,
    232, 314, 318, 334
Sydney Trades and Labour Council 11

T
Tally (pseudonym) 73, 74, 80, 88, 89,
    92, 94–97, 99
Teamsters' Union 47, 235

Thargomindah 214, 215
Thompson, Teddy 51, 172, 173, 260, 263
Thylungra Station 199
Toorale Station 113, 114
Towers Drug Company 31
Travellers' Rest Hotel 159
Travelling Stock Routes 158
Truth newspaper 52, 74

U
unions 9, 32, 43, 44, 45, 47, 50, 53, 58, 61, 67, 68, 79, 163, 169, 227, 269, 293, 315, 321

W
Waddell, Thomas 52, 53, 67, 74, 114
Wade, Abdul 163
Walgett 35, 40, 57, 325
Waroo Springs 199
Warrego River ix, 158, 159, 161, 162, 163, 181, 190, 226
Warrego Inn 234
Western Herald and Darling River Advocate 7, 8, 57, 68, 80, 97
White, Thomas x, 51, 83, 85
Wilcannia 33
Willis, William Nicholas 4, 52, 74, 93
Wilson, Charles 22, 31
Wood, William (Billy) x, 9, 50, 51, 53–54, 68, 79, 80, 85, 107, 146, 172, 173, 176, 177, 233, 236, 239, 259, 260, 322
Worker, the ix, x, 4, 51, 54, 60, 61, 126, 140, 164, 167, 179, 215, 226, 310, 311, 312, 315, 316, 320, 321

Y
Yantabulla 56, 192, 193, 198, 225
Youngerina Bore 190, 225

INDEX OF FIRST LINES OF VERSE

A rouseabout of rouseabouts, from any land — or none 142
A shearer came to a blackleg shed, when most of the sheds were full 312
A shearer tramped from Borderland 75
Bourke in the early nineties 59
Call this hot? I beg your pardon, Hot! — you don't know what it means 146
Did you hear in last September how a certain 'Labour' member 93
From north to south throughout the year 182
He had offices in Sydney, not so many years ago 297
I heard old Labour call across 94
I'm lyin' on the barren ground that's baked and cracked with drought 199
I spent a year in Junee 63
It was a week from Christmas-time 223
I've followed all my tracks and ways, from old bark school to Leicester Square
    26
Just before the last elections, and the chaps were fighting well 54
Oh, the cheek of poetasters! Oh, the self conceit of men! 86
Oh, the track through the scrub groweth ever more dreary 203
On my blankets I was lyin' 198
Out West, where the stars are brightest 159
'The ladies are coming,' the super says 140
The old year went, and the new returned, in the withering weeks of drought
    195
The sand was heavy on our feet 190
The shearers squint along the pens, they squint along the 'shoots' 133
The skies are brass and the plains are bare 24
There was joy along the Darling when the labour war begun 69
There's a poet on the Central, and his verses are sublime 80
They say thirteen at Lissington 96
'Twas a big shed on the Darlin' 47
'What's Huey done for Labour?' 89
When a fellow strikes the Darling, after coming from the East 76
When he's over a rough and unpopular shed 137
When the heavy sand is yielding backward from your blistered feet 180
When the kindly hours of darkness, save for light of moon and star 236
While you use your best endeavour to immortalise in verse 311

INDEX OF VERSE TITLES

All Unyun Men 47
Australian Bards and Bush Reviewers 311
Ballad of the Rouseabout, The 142
Beautiful Maoriland 312
Boss Over the Board, The 137
Boss's Boots, The 133
Bourke 26
Delegates: 1 Then, The 63
Donald Macdonell 59
Great Grey Plain, The 159
Greenhand Rouseabout, The 146
Have You Heard 93
Heart of the Swag, The 203
Knocked Up 199
Lake Eliza 190
Lissington Verdict, The 96
Martin Farrell 54
Old Labour and the Echo 94
Our Members Present and Future 69
Out Back 195
Paroo River, The 223
Peter Anderson and Co. 297
Poet by Telegraph, The 86
Poet on the Central, The 80
Says You 180
Song of the Darling River, The 24
Stranger on the Darling, A 76
Swagman and His Mate, The 182
Tally Town 75
Western Stars, The 198
What Huey Didn't Do 89
When the Army Prays for Watty 236
When the Ladies Come to the Shearing Shed 140

INDEX OF PROSE TITLES

Australian Rivers: On the Darling No. 1 (The Darling River) 35
Baldy Thompson 227
Bush Funeral, A (The Union Buries Its Dead) 108
Bush Terms 126
Carriers (The Lost Soul's Hotel) 168
City and the Bush, The 317
Crawlalong 222
Darling River (Australian Rivers:) 35
Enter Mitchell 204
Great Flood of '90, the 40
Hungerford 218
It Was Awful 62
Lord Douglas 282
Lost Souls' Hotel, The (Carriers) 168
Louth, on the Darling 126
Mitchell Doesn't Believe in the Sack 280
Romance of the Swag, The 207
Rough Shed, A 149
Send Round the Hat 260
Sketch of Mateship, A 118
Some Popular Australian Mistakes 123
Stragglers 184
That Pretty Girl in the Army 239
That's What it Was 165
Union Buries Its Dead, The (A Bush Funeral) 108
Word in Season, A 315

ENDNOTES

1 Henry Lawson, 'Pursuing Literature in Australia', *Bulletin*, 19 February 1899.

2 Henry Lawson, 'Over the Ranges and Into the West', *Freeman's Journal*, 1890.

3 E. J. Brady, 'Henry Lawson', *Bulletin*, 22 January 1925.

4 A. B. Paterson, 'Clancy of the Overflow', *Bulletin*, 1889.

5 *supra* n3.

6 Henry Lawson, 'Sweeney', *Bulletin*, 16 December, 1893.

7 Henry Lawson, 'That Pretty Girl in the Army', in *Children of the Bush*, Methuen & Co., 1902; Angus & Robertson, 1902.

8 Henry Lawson, 'The Darling River', first published as 'Australian Rivers: On the Darling No.1', *Worker*, 26 August 1893.

9 *ibid.*

10 Henry Lawson, 'The Stranger's Friend', in *Verses Popular and Humorous*, Angus & Robertson, 1900.

11 Harry Smith, 'Memories of Old Bourke', *Worker*, 1 June 1938.

12 The original manuscript for the poem 'All Unyun Men' is dated June 1893, Bourke. It was eventually published in the *Worker*.

13 *supra* n11.

14 William Wood, 'Bourke: A Letter From Paraguay', in Bertha Lawson and John Le Gay Brereton, *Henry Lawson by His Mates*, Angus & Robertson, 1931.

15 *ibid.*

16 *ibid.*

17 *ibid.*, p. 34.

18 Henry Lawson, 'Our Leaders Present and Future', *Western Herald*, 28 September 1892.

19 Henry Lawson, 'A Stranger on the Darling', *Western Herald*, 1 October 1892.

20 Letter by John Hawley, *Sydney Morning Herald*, 20 February 1939.

21 William Wood, *op.cit.*, p. 35.

22 *supra* n20.

23 Henry Lawson, 'By the Banks of the Murrumbidgee', *Bulletin*, 1916.

24 Harry Pearce, 'Jim Grahame', *Lawsonian*, No. 219 September 1979.

25 Jim Grahame, 'Amongst My Own People', in Lawson and Le Gay Brereton, *op.cit.*, p. 212.

26 Reminiscences by Jim Gordon published in Colin Roderick, *Henry Lawson — A Life*, Angus & Robertson, 1991, p. 92.

27 *supra* n25.

28 *ibid.*

29 *supra* n26.

30 Arthur Parker, 'Beginnings', in Lawson and Le Gay Brereton, *op.cit.*, p. 17.

31 Henry Lawson, 'The Union Buries Its Dead' (originally 'The Bushman's Funeral'), *Truth*, 16 April 1893.

32 Letter written by William Wood, *Windsor and Richmond Gazette*, 9 October 1931.

33 Henry Lawson, 'Some Popular Australian Mistakes', *Bulletin*, 18 November 1892.

34 Colin Roderick, *op.cit.*, p. 93.

35 *supra* n25.

36 *ibid*.

37 Jim Grahame, 'Henry Lawson on the Track', *Bulletin*, 19 February 1925.

38 *supra* n34.

39 *ibid*.

40 *supra* n7.

41 *supra* n37.

42 *History of Bourke*, Volume IX, Bourke Historical Society, p. 200.

43 E. J. Brady, 'Mallacoota Days', in Lawson and Le Gay Brereton, *op.cit.*, pp. 135–6.

44 Jim Grahame, 'Amongst My Own People', p. 211.

45 Henry Lawson, 'The Bush and the Ideal', *Bulletin*, 26 February, 1897.

46 Henry Lawson, 'Out on the Roofs of Hell', *Bulletin*, 1898.

47 *supra* n25.

48 Henry Lawson, 'Shearers' Song', *Town and Country Journal*, 1888.

49 Jim Grahame, 'Amongst My Own People', pp 212–213.

50 *supra* n37.

51 *ibid*.

52 Jim Grahame, *Under Wide Skies*, Citizens of Leeton, 1947.

53 Henry Lawson, 'Louth, on the Darling', *Worker*, 1893.

54 *supra* n45.

55 *supra* n37.

56 *ibid*.

57 Henry Lawson, 'The Ghosts of Many Christmases', in *Children of the Bush*.

58 Billy Wood, 'Reminiscences of Henry Lawson', *Windsor and Richmond Gazette*, 24 September 1926.

59 *ibid*.

60 *supra* n7.

61 *supra* n45.

62 Henry Lawson, 'The Ballad of the Rouseabout', in *Verses Popular and Humorous*.

63 *supra* n58.

64 *supra* n32.

65 *supra* n45.

66 Henry Lawson, 'The Romance of the Swag', in *Children of the Bush*.

67 *supra* n37.

68 Henry Lawson, 'Hungerford', *Bulletin*, 14 December 1893.

69 *supra* n5.

70 *supra* n7.

71 *supra* n32.

72 *supra* n7.

73 Henry Lawson, 'Send Round the Hat', in *Children of the Bush*.

74 *supra* n7.

75 John Hawley, 'Henry Lawson', *Sydney Morning Herald*, 20 February 1939.

76 *supra* n21.

77 *supra* n73.

78 Henry Lawson, 'Letter re Henry Lawson's Fictional Characters', *Sunday Times*, in Leonard Cronin, *A Camp-Fire Yarn*, Lansdowne Press, 1984.

79 *supra* n21.

80 Henry Lawson, 'Up the Country' (originally published as 'Borderland', 9 July 1892, *Bulletin*) in *In the Days When the World Was Wide*, Angus & Robertson, 1896.

81 Colin Roderick, *op.cit.*, p. 97.

82 *supra* n37.

83 Henry Lawson, 'Pursuing Literature in Australia', *Bulletin*, 21 January 1899.

84 Henry Lawson, 'In a Wet Season', *Bulletin*, 2 December 1893.

85 Henry Lawson, 'Before We Were Married', in *For Australia and Other Poems*, Stamdard Publishing Co., 1913.

86 Henry Lawson, 'A Love Story', *Bulletin*, 25 November 1893.

87 *supra* n58.

88 A. W. Barker, *Dear Robertson*, Angus & Robertson, 1982, p. 12.

89 *ibid.*

90 *supra* n83.

91 Jim Grahame, 'Amongst My Own People', pp. 216–17.

92 Isabelle Ramsay, 'Poet and Peasant', in Lawson and Le Gay Brereton, *op.cit.*, pp. 206–7.

93 Letter from Edwin Brady, *Bulletin*, 22 January 1925.

94 W. E. FitzHenry, 'Afterwards', in Lawson and Le Gay Brereton, *op.cit.*, pp. 304–5.

95 Henry Lawson, 'A Voice From the City', written and first published in 1903 and later included in *When I Was King and Other Verses*, Angus & Robertson, 1905.

96 Henry Lawson, 'Bourke', written in 1902 and published in *When I Was King and Other Verses*.

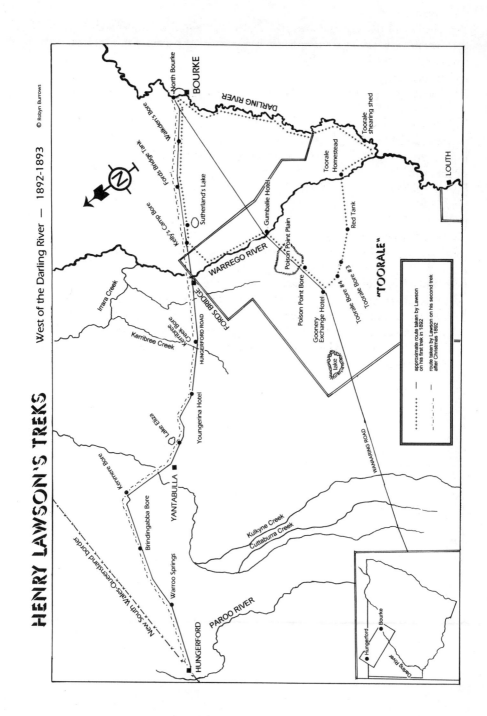

HENRY LAWSON'S TREKS

West of the Darling River — 1892-1893

© Robyn Burrows

approximate route taken by Lawson on his first trek in 1892

route taken by Lawson on his second trek after Christmas 1892

BOURKE

North Bourke

DARLING RIVER

LOUTH

Toorale shearing shed

Toorale Homestead

Red Tank

Gumbalie Hotel

Poison Point Plain

Poison Point Bore

Goonery Exchange Hotel

Toorale Bore #3

Toorale Bore #4

"TOORALE"

WARREGO RIVER

Sutherland's Lake

Walker's Bore

Ford's Bridge Tank

Kelly's Camp Bore

Irrara Creek

Kerribree Creek

Kerribree Creek Bore

FORD'S BRIDGE

HUNGERFORD ROAD

Youngerina Hotel

Lake Eliza

Kerrmree Bore

Brindingabba Bore

YANTABULLA

Warroo Springs

PAROO RIVER

Kulkyne Creek

Cuttaburra Creek

WANARING ROAD

Lake

New South Wales Queensland border

HUNGERFORD

Hungerford

Bourke

Darling River

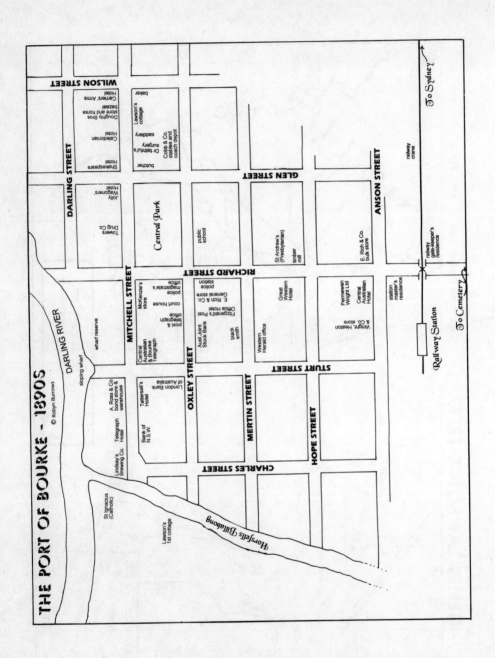

THE PORT OF BOURKE - 1890s

© Robyn Burrows

DARLING RIVER

Horsfall's Billabong

St Ignacius (Catholic)

Lawson's 1st cottage

sloping wharf

wharf reserve

Lindsay's Brewing Co.

Telegraph Hotel

A. Ross & Co. bond store & warehouse

Bank of N.S.W.

London Bank of Australia

Tattersall's Hotel

CHARLES STREET

OXLEY STREET

MERTIN STREET

HOPE STREET

Central Australian & Bourke Telegraph

post & telegraph office

court house

police station

magistrate's office

McKenzie's store

Aust Joint Stock Bank

black smith

E. Rich & Co. General store

Fitzgerald's Post Office Hotel

Western Herald office

Great Western Hotel

Wright, Heaton & Co. store

Parmewan Wright Ltd

Central Australian Hotel

MITCHELL STREET

STURT STREET

RICHARD STREET

Towers Drug Co.

Jolly Wagoners' Hotel

Central Park

public school

St Andrew's (Presbyterian)

timber mill

E. Rich & Co. bulk store

DARLING STREET

GLEN STREET

ANSON STREET

Shakespeare Hotel

Caledonian Hotel

Doughty Bros store and horse bazaar

Carrier's Arms Hotel

butcher

Dr Faithful's surgery

saddlery

Lawson's cottage

Cobb & Co. stables and coach depot

baker

WILSON STREET

To Sydney

railway crane

railway gate-keeper's residence

station master's residence

Railway Station

To Cemetery